IN SAIL AND STEAM

CAPTAIN V. L. MAKING

IN SAIL AND STEAM

BEHIND THE SCENES
OF THE MERCHANT SERVICE
1902—1927

BY

CAPT. VICTOR LESLIE MAKING
EXTRA-MASTER
LATE LIEUTENANT, R.N.R.

LONDON
SIDGWICK & JACKSON LTD.

First published 1937

Printed in Great Britain by
Billing and Sons Ltd., Guildford and Esher

TO

P'TITE

CONTENTS

CONTENTS

LIST OF ILLUSTRATIONS

PLATES

IN THE TEXT

SKETCH-MAPS

PROLOGUE TO YOU-WHO-LIVE-ASHORE

DURING the years that I was in command of the S.S. *Pennland*, Red Star Line, the innumerable questions asked me by passengers impressed upon me that, even in these prosaic days of oil-fuel and internal-combustion engines, people ashore are still keenly interested in ships and the sea-life, particularly in sailing-ships, which apparently have lost none of the glamour of romance that has always surrounded them.

On Christmas Eve, 1934, my story-telling days at sea were brought to an untimely end. We docked in Antwerp, our homeport, that afternoon, and after wishing us a Merry Christmas the company's officials informed us that most of the officers were to be discharged at once, as the ships were being laid up to be sold.

For some time the fear of being "stranded on the beach" was allayed by the news that a British syndicate was trying to buy them and would retain us in the positions we then held. Eventually, however, for reasons that gave rise to questions in Parliament and to comments in the Press, it was prevented from doing so, and the Red Star Line was taken over by the Bernstein Line of Hamburg. On February 20th, 1935, those of us who still remained on board watched the British Ensign hauled down and a German flag run up in its place; and a few minutes later we walked down the gangway, involuntary recruits for the army of unemployed.

What made matters worse was that the prospects of finding employment in another company were not very bright. One of the officers, a man of about 40 years of age, married, with one child, who for some years had been First Officer of a 16,000-ton Red Star liner, was eventually obliged to take a job as quartermaster. Another, an older man with a family, who had served as First Officer on the 27,000-ton S.S. *Belgenland*, was unable to get another ship and finally found work in a London office. After a while he had to give that up on account of his health.

In my case, the handing over of the ship to my German successor was almost coincidental with the death of my father, which brought to light a box full of old letters. Among them were all those I had written to my parents during five years that I was apprentice and Third Mate on a sailing-ship, after leaving home in 1902 at the age of 15. There were also many later ones, written from all sorts and conditions of ships, ranging from a Dreadnought battleship to a 2,000-ton cargo boat and a 30-ton drift-net fisherman. One of my ships had been lost at sea by fire. We abandoned her, were some days in the boats, and then spent a Robinson-Crusoe existence on the uninhabited island of St. Paul. A diary that I kept of it was in the box.

As I looked through these letters I realised that I possessed not only answers to all the questions ever asked by passengers, but also the material for a sea-yarn that might be equally interesting and amusing to people ashore generally. It might even prove instructive, for although the British have always been so essentially a sea-faring race, it is extraordinary to a seaman how few books dealing with the subject do so accurately and comprehensively. There seemed to be the opportunity to depict, with the help of those letters, the life as lived by myself, without the exaggeration that is so liable to creep in after an interval of years, provided I were able to convert my marline-spike into a pen—no easy task.

Being " on the beach " myself, with nothing to occupy

my time, I decided to attempt it, and I finally succeeded in weaving that raw material into the "yarn" which follows. Now I venture to submit it to You-Who-Live-Ashore, hoping that it may give you some idea both of the life and training of us ordinary men as we pass upon the sea "on our Lawful Occasions" and of the conditions under which we have to do our "business in great waters"—a business no less vital to the life of Britain and of the Dominions overseas than that of the Royal Navy.

That, however, is the end of the story. I will hark back to the beginning by using as a stepping-stone a question that was frequently asked me by those passengers: "Why did you go to sea?"

Strictly speaking, I did not go to sea at all, because my whole life has been spent by, in, or on it. I was born within a mile of it. For years much of my play-time was divided between the Downs and the Beach. Lying on the former, watching the ships pass up and down Channel, my rather imaginative mind conjured up scenes of romance and adventure surpassing anything that a life at sea has produced. The fishermen, most of them old sailors, let me sail their boats, and they told me stories of ships on which they had sailed and of countries they had seen—magnets that slowly but surely drew me seawards.

To that pull must be added my intense reaction to all the sea stories that came the way of the average boy. It is hardly surprising, therefore, that at the age of 14, when my father first broached the subject of my future, there came the spontaneous and inevitable reply: "I'm going to sea!"

To him it meant my career and livelihood; to me, merely that I should enlarge my playground and make a business of my pleasure.

He was then faced with the problem of finding some

way of sending me to sea. About that time *The Cruise of the Cachalot* was circulating round the family, and he had the inspiration to write to the author, Mr. Frank T. Bullen. He received in reply a letter full of helpful advice which enabled him to apprentice me to a Liverpool firm of shipowners, and my indentures were signed shortly after my fifteenth birthday.

Within two months I received orders to join the ship *Aristomene* in Cardiff, where she was to load a cargo of coal for Monte Video; and on the appointed day, accompanied by my father, I left home in my first uniform—a pocket-edition " robust and brass-bound man."

V. L. M.

PART I

" When the robust and brass-bound man commissioned first for sea
His fragile raft, Poseidon laughed, and, ' Mariner,' said he,
' Behold a Law immutable I lay on thee and thine,
That never shall ye act or tell a falsehood at my shrine.'

* * * * *

" In dromond and in catafract—wet, wakeful, windward-eyed—
He kept Poseidon's Law intact (his ship and freight beside)
But, once discharged the dromond's hold, the bireme beached once
 more,
Splendaciously mendacious rolled the brass-bound man ashore."

       RUDYARD KIPLING : *Poseidon's Law.*

" THE BOY MAKING "

CHAPTER I

MY DEBUT

" Praise the sea, but keep on land."—GEORGE HERBERT.

To those of you who have imagined sailing-ships to be
surrounded by the glamour of romance mentioned in the
Prologue, this first chapter will come as a disillusion. In
my mind, my début at the age of 15 on the *Aristomene*,
a three-masted, full-rigged ship of 1,662 tons, is closely
associated with blistered hands, an aching back, and
clouds of coal-dust.

There were, of course, innumerable emotions, impressions, and reactions, but they were so confused that it
would have been difficult even at the time to describe
them. During the intervening years so much water has
flowed under the bridge—and past the many bridges on
which I have kept watch—that now it is impossible. My
memories of those early days resemble one of the old
silent movies, of which parts of the film are missing and
much of the remainder is out of focus.

My arrival on board, however, is still quite distinct.
After climbing up a steep ladder my father and I, complete with sea-chest, were standing on deck near the mainmast, looking round and wondering where to go and what
to do next.

"I wonder where your cabin is, old chap," he said.

"Oh! That will be near the Captain's and officers',"
I replied confidently.

A moment later we heard a voice behind us. "I'll
show you the way to the half-deck," it said.

We turned round. A boy of about my own age in a
suit of blue dungarees was standing there.

3

"Good afternoon, sir," he said to my father. "I'm one of the apprentices. We live aft."

We followed "Beaky," as he afterwards became known to us, to the after end of the main deck where a ladder on each side led up to the poop. Behind the starboard one was an iron door opening into a small room.

"This is the half-deck, where we live," Beaky said to me.

I eagerly peered in, and a picture of it was registered indelibly on my mind. My, or rather our, cabin was disillusion No. 1. It was about 14 feet by 8 feet, and was the home of four other boys and myself. On my right was a bulkhead, or wall, on which were two upper and two lower bunks. Facing me was another upper and lower "pew," and a few rough shelves on which were tin plates, pannikins, jars, and bottles. The third "wall," on my left, was the bare iron of the ship's side. In it were two portholes, and a small table was secured to it with hinges. Immediately on the left of the door were six wooden pegs on which were hanging oilskins and sou'westers. A piece of dirty canvas was spread over the wooden deck, and the sea-chests were stowed round in front of the lower bunks, serving the triple purpose of wardrobe, chair, and step to upper bunk.

"Not very big," remarked my father. "How many of you live here?"

"Oh! Only five," replied Beaky. "There are six bunks, but we're a man short this voyage."

Two other apprentices, who before long learned to answer to the names of Paddy and Mac, were there when we entered. We four boys were first voyagers, though Beaky was our senior. He had served two years on the training ship *Conway* which counted as a year at sea. The fifth, who had already made a voyage in the ship, was at home on leave and rejoined shortly before we sailed.

After they had helped me drag my sea-chest into the half-deck they showed my father and myself round the ship.

Probably some of you who read this have visited a modern "luxury liner." With its expanse of promenade and sports decks and its spacious public rooms, it is as unlike its windjammer predecessor as you are unlike the *Homo Heidelbergensis*. I will therefore digress for a few moments to give a brief description of the *Aristomene*, she being typical of the forbears of the "Stateliest Ship in Being."

At the stern was a raised deck, called the poop. On it were the wheel, compass binnacle, a capstan, and a sky-light and companion to the Captain's and officers' quarters, which, like the half-deck, were underneath the poop. There was also down there a space—the sail-locker, as it was called—and a small dining saloon in which was a hatch to the lazarette, where ropes and pro-visions were stored.

The weather, or windward, side of the poop was sacro-sanct ground to the Captain, or, if he were below, the Mate on watch. If an absent-minded, dungaree-clad, first-voyage apprentice strolled up the ladder on that side, he was invariably met with an expression such as one sees in a certain "Bateman" sketch, he being in the place of, and feeling like, the "Damnèd Spot."

There was a similar raised deck forward, the forecastle head, where the anchors were secured at sea. Here one had a "close-up" of the figurehead, though, after years of battering round the Horn, and innumerable coats of paint, blistered by tropical suns, it probably bore no resemblance to, and was hardly a flattering replica of, the original.

Underneath the forecastle head was an open space. A small hatch in the centre of it gave access to the forepeak, in which paints, oils, and tar were stored. On one side of it were several lockers, full of old junk, and on the other a pigsty in which two pigs were usually accommodated. It is perhaps not generally known on shore that when a pig was killed at sea it was held down in the scupper with its snout pointing towards the stern. That was supposed to bring a fair wind!

In case any of you find a difficulty in "swallowing that yarn," I will add that I have had to hang on to a hind leg of several of them while the cook "conned them dead-on" and the steward stood by with the knife. I have seen a live cat thrown overboard for the same reason, to give another example of the superstitions of those men.

The sanitary arrangement for all the men and the apprentices was constructed at one end of the pigsty. It was very primitive—and, being right in the eyes of her, very awkward when the ship was diving into a head sea.

Between the poop and the forecastle head was the main deck. On each side of it was a bulwark, about 4 feet high, and a scupper, or gutter, from which water drained overboard through holes cut in the side.

On this deck, between the forecastle head and the fore-mast, were the fore hatch and the windlass. The latter was a back-breaking contraption for heaving up the anchor. It had a long lever on each side that was worked up and down like an old-fashioned fire pump.

In the picture of the ship can be seen an oblong erection on the deck, abaft the foremast. This was known as the " Midship House." It contained two large rooms, called fo'c'sles, for the port and starboard watches; a smaller one for the boatswain, carpenter and sailmaker; and the galley. The latter extended right across it and had a door on each side.

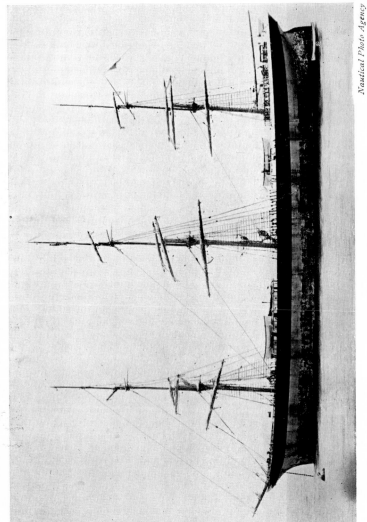

THE "ARISTOMENE"

Sometimes during bad weather, when the cook, or "doctor," as we usually called him, was busily engaged in trying to "boil water without burning it," a heavy sea rolled over the bulwark and burst in his weather door. His shouts and curses and the clanging of his pots and pans as he and they were swept out through the lee door on to the deck were an S.O.S. to the rest of us. We splashed along in the water and dragged him into one of the fo'c'sles. That always happened in high latitudes and correspondingly low temperatures, and no tea, coffee, or warm food could be had until he was reinstated and reorganised. His expressions of annoyance, therefore, were echoed on all sides of the midship house.

A space of 2 feet divided this "house" from the main hatch, which was a meeting-place for the men. During the dog-watches in "flying-fish weather" they sat round it, cutting up their tobacco, patching their clothes, and exchanging highly coloured reminiscences of other ships on which they had sailed and of record passages they had made that gave evidence of considerable creative talent.

Round the foot of the mainmast was a heavy teak-wood rail, called the "fife-rail," in which were fitted numerous belaying-pins. These resemble wooden or iron truncheons, about 14 inches long and an inch thick.

Between the mainmast and the "skids" was a clear space of deck on which was a capstan. This was chiefly used to hoist the heavier yards when sails were being set.

The "skids" was a light platform, about 7 feet above the deck. A boat was carried on each side of it, and a hen-coop had been fitted underneath. The eggs were for the use of the Captain and Mates only, but sometimes in the still watches of the night uneasy rustlings and sleepily indignant clucks indicated that an apprentice would have one to mix with his breakfast coffee.

The after hatch, close to the poop, was the apprentices' school. During hot evenings in the tropics, while the men swopped lies on the main hatch and the Captain paced up and down in solitary state the sacrosanct weather side of the poop, the Mates and apprentices sat there, the former telling the latter among other things what they had had to do when they first went to sea.

As the steady trade wind drove the ship southward towards "Mother Carey" they could look from there over the starboard bulwark and watch the sun dip below the horizon; and in the growing darkness the only sounds, other than the men's voices and the creaking of the yards, was the ship's bell, struck every half-hour, and the cry from the look-out man on the forecastle head: "All's well!"

When we had seen round the ship my father had supper with us in the half-deck. The meal consisted of a kind of stew that Beaky called "lobscouse," hard tack (ship's biscuits), and what was alleged to be tea. The biscuits, very hard round ones, called Liverpool Pantiles, defeated him. Following the example of the others, we broke them into small pieces by banging them on the edge of the table, and then my teeth, like theirs, were able to do the rest. His were not, and he had to soak his pieces in his tin pannikin of milkless tea.

At half-past five the following morning we were awakened by the voice of the night-watchman.

"Rise and shine! Come on, show a leg!" he shouted at the door.

I sat up with a start, rubbed my eyes and looked round, wondering for a moment where I was. The other boys proceeded to show their legs by putting them over the edge of their bunks and sliding down on to the sea-chests. While I was making my first attempt at the acrobatic and contortive feat of descending from an upper bunk Beaky said, "Better hurry up. It's your turn to get the coffee this morning!"

"Where from?" I asked.

"The galley, of course," he replied. "Here you are, take this tin. Don't forget to tell the cook there are five of us now."

I pulled on my stiff new suit of dungarees, and, having after a struggle settled my sheath-knife in its right place, hurried along the deck to the galley.

"I've come for the apprentices' coffee," I told the cook, an undersized, wizened old man, with a grey straggly beard and bald head. "There are five of us now."

"Five!" he exclaimed. "Nobody told me. 'Oo's the noo boy?"

"I am," I replied. "I came yesterday."

"'Ow do I know 'ow many to cook for if nobody don't tell me?" he growled, filling the tin can from an enormous black iron pot that smelt of anything but coffee.

"I don't know, I'm sure," I answered rather timidly —he did not seem an easy man to get on with.

"You!" he grunted scornfully, looking me up and down. "'Course *you* don't know. D'yuh know what to do wi' the key o' the ke'lson?"

"—Er—no. I haven't learned that yet," I admitted.

"Yuh gotta lot to learn yet, me lad. 'Ere y'are. 'Ere's yer cawfee. Yuh never drunk stuff like that at 'ome!"

I carried the "stuff" back to the half-deck, having experienced disillusion No. 2. That tin can of "cawfee," my uncomfortable dungarees, and the conversation with the cook did not create the impression that I should be looked upon as one of the "young gentlemen," like Peter Simple and other of my heroes.

2

At 6 o'clock we were drinking the last drops and eating a biscuit. Four bells were struck, and a man appeared at the door. He was dressed in a blue serge patrol-suit and a cheese-cutter cap. Except for a lack of neatness in his appearance, he bore a close resemblance to Captain Kettle as he would be at the age of about sixty. The little red beard was streaked with grey, but the pugilistic glint in his eyes equalled that of his prototype. He fixed them on me.

" Who're you?" he barked.

" I'm the new apprentice," I replied.

" I know that. What's yer name?"

" Making," I answered.

His eyes wandered slowly up and down me, taking in every detail. He emitted a loud " Humph!" and then, having grunted the words " Turn to!" disappeared.

" Who's that?" I asked.

" The Mate, of course," answered Paddy. " You'd better stand up and say ' sir ' when you speak to him. Come on."

I followed him out, and we began a day's work that lasted until 6 p.m., there being a break of forty-five minutes for breakfast and an hour for dinner.

My father was on board again that morning. He spent most of it on the after hatch, talking to the Mate and watching us drag sacks of flour and barrels of sugar along the deck to the lazarette. In the evening I went ashore with him—and with blisters on my hands and a man-sized ache in my boy-sized back.

There is now a break in the continuity of my memories which brings me to the latter part of our stay, when the ship was loading coal. My recollections of the last few days are of nothing but coal-dust and discomfort—of coal-dust all over the ship and in the half-deck, on our food and in our coffee and tea, we and our clothes black with

it; of being called out in the night to shift the ship under
the coal-tip and having to handle ropes that were buried
in it; of the utter hopelessness of trying to clean ourselves—four boys in that room, 14 feet by 8 feet, a film
of coal-dust over everything and one bucket to wash in.
One night while running along the deck and tripping over
ropes and heaps of coal I was definitely given to understand my status: one o' them bloody boys!

However, as truck after truck was hoisted up the
coal-tip and emptied down the chute into the hold, the
ship slowly but surely settled to her "marks"; and the
last few feet of this "mental movie" show myself, a
chimney-sweep rather than a robust and brass-bound
man, sitting on my sea-chest and, by the light of an oil
lantern, writing my last letter home before sailing.

CHAPTER II

FIRST PASSAGE

" The magic of the sea."—LONGFELLOW.

WHEN Vasco Nuñez de Balboa and his conquistadores
stood on the hills at Panama and looked at the Pacific
Ocean they must have felt as I did when for the first time
I gazed over a ship's bulwark at the Atlantic.

On second thoughts, though, our sensations would not
be quite the same. They merely looked at their ocean.
I was on mine, and it was causing a queasiness that they
would not experience and which made me feel anything
but a conquistador. Nevertheless it was the sea; and, in
my case as in theirs, dreams had come true.

"Come on, young feller-me-lad! Wake up!" said a
gruff voice behind me.

I awoke from my day-dream with a start and came
back to earth, or rather to sea-level, where the watch on
deck was sand-and-canvassing.

The present-day spoilt housewife, who starts her
spring-cleaning with the necessary vim and vigour supplied in tins and packets by her grocer, may be interested
to know something about the sailing-ship cleanser:
"sand-and-canvas." It is simplicity itself. Take one
piece of canvas (about 6 inches square), one bucket of
sand and one bucket of sea-water. Place a little sand on
the wet canvas, add plenty of windjammer vim (*i.e.*,
elbow grease), and rub your dirty paint or woodwork
until an omnipresent and all-seeing Mate decides they are
clean. We were then using that method to scrub coal-
dust off white paint on the iron bulwarks. Being a

novitiate in those rites, I was merely a sort of Gunga Din, carrying buckets of water along the deck to the men.

I must ask those of you who are beginning to lose all hope of finding any glamour of romance around the *Aristomene* to bear patiently with me a little longer. After the aching back and the dust of the "black diamonds" in Cardiff I had to go through another unromantic period: mal-de-mer! It was short-lived, and apparently I was fortunate, for according to the letter I wrote: "All the other chaps were sick. I felt jolly ill."

I think it was my awe of the Mate rather than my good fortune that prevented me from going beyond the "feeling" stage. I was closer under his eye than the other chaps. Every time I felt an urge to drop my bucket and rush to the lee rail I noticed him gazing at me with an expression that echoed Mr. Punch's advice to those about to marry. I therefore swallowed hard and didn't.

Before long the inner man had adjusted himself to those changing conditions and was busily engaged in the task of digesting Liverpool Pantiles and "salt horse." Neither was it very long before I began to realise that there were other things in the life than aching backs and sea-sickness. During this first passage when everything was new to me there were some wonderful moments. I experienced the thrill that every boy must feel when for the first time he sees a school of flying-fish leave the water, sparkle in the tropical sunshine for a few seconds and then splash back, only to reappear almost immediately, followed by blue-and-gold dolphins that leap out of the water after them; or when he first succeeds in climbing to the royal yard. Almost at the masthead, between not the devil but heaven and the deep blue sea, he clings on tightly and gazes down at his world below. It seems so far away that even hard-case Mates appear small and harmless. And last, but not least, when he is told to

" tail on to the end of a rope " and hears his first chantey. After the second verse he is able to " lay back on it " and join in the chorus with all hands:

" Spend my money on Sally Brown."

In addition to those pleasurable moments there were others, of course, when I was in a state bordering on bewilderment. Everything in that new life was unlike anything I had ever known before. I had literally been transplanted to another world. There was as great a contrast between the people I had to live with on the ship and those at home as between their natural elements—the sea and the land. It not only required time to understand their ways, but even to speak their language.

For a while the Captain, a huge man who " lived alone like a little God in Heaven," inspired me with the most profound awe with his fore-topsail-yard-ahoy voice, bushy-black whiskers, wooden stump in lieu of left forearm, and ferocious black eyes that saw through the most cast-iron alibi. Later on, however, when he had pulled to pieces one of mine and reduced me to a state of fear and trembling, I happened to notice something resembling a grin on his face as he remarked: " Young feller-me-lad, you won't go to hell without an excuse!"

That grin taught me that even little gods who are compelled by circumstances to live aloof from their fellow-men are but human, not divine.

As for the crew, there was a world of difference between the men as you would have seen them ashore in those days, rolling around drunk and throwing away their pay-days, and as I came to know them and like them at sea. Half-frightened of them, I watched them come on board in Cardiff, a dirty, motley, drunken crowd, cursing and fighting. In other chapters I hope to be able to show you what they were like in their natural environment, the

"Great Waters." Drunken swabs as they doubtless were ashore, unless one has some knowledge of that, it is not fair to pass judgment on them.

To give a detailed description of the passages between all the ports visited by a sailing-ship during five years would soon become tedious reading, there was so much similarity between them. For that reason the first part of this book, dealing with sail, is not a connected story. I have merely endeavoured to give you a few impressions of the conditions under which I lived and of the types and characters of the men with whom I worked and associated during those impressionable years.

My first passage, however, when I began to know and to understand my new companions and to adapt myself to the life, was such an important step for me that I will quote most of the letter I wrote home from Monte Video, my first port, at the age of 15. It not only describes the voyage from Cardiff to Monte Video better than I can, but also some of my earliest reactions to my strange associates and environment:

"We sailed on the Friday at 3.30 p.m. We were to leave at one o'clock on Thursday night, but had not finished loading. All the men came on board drunk except one or two. They always do, and the apprentices have to sail the ship. As we were leaving, the cook, who had gone ashore in the morning and got drunk, fell overboard between the ship and the wharf. How he escaped I don't know. A rope was lowered, and the Third Mate and two sober men went down and pulled him up. He was nearly killed three ways: drowning, breaking his head against the wharf, and being crushed between the wharf and the ship, which was moving. He only hurt his shoulder a bit.

"We picked watches at eight o'clock. I am in the port, or Mate's, watch, under him and the Third Mate.

At two o'clock on Saturday morning the tug left us at
Lundy Isle, and both watches had to turn out to set sail.
We had a strong head wind so had to tack, and were two
or three days getting out of the Bristol Channel.

"Next day it was fairly rough and all the other chaps
were sick. I felt jolly ill, but did not sick at all. None
of us have been bad since, so the fishes have not been fed
much. We were clearing up decks all day.

"On Sunday we did no work except tack every four
hours. We passed a steamer from Cork, called the
Avocet.

"Next day we hauled up and lashed the anchors and
did odd jobs. I had to clean out the pigsty. We passed
a homeward-bound Norwegian ship and signalled her.
She wanted to know the longitude, so we told her. It
was 11° 25′ west.

"That was a pleasant night. In our watch on deck a
tremendous storm of rain came on, the wind freshened,
and we had to take in some sail. We could not leave the
deck to put on oilskins, and were messing about for two
hours or more, soaked to the skin. It cleared up when we
went below. That is the time to hear the men's language
—and the officers', too.

"It was lovely and fine next day, so we set sail again.
I had to stow coal for the galley all day. That morning
while washing down the deck the Mate was swearing at
us for not going up aloft to help the men. We had always
been told not to go up for a month or two. In Cardiff
the Mate himself had told us that, and we were only
about a week out. He said that when he first went to sea
he had to go up the first night, and that we had no guts
in us, no ambition; so I thought we would see about guts.

"The very next day the mainsail carried away (slit
down the middle), and we had to unbend it and bend on
a new one. When the men went up aloft to make it fast I

was nearly the first one up. The same day we were caught in a squall and had to take in sail, so I went up with the rest. During the squall we saw a young whale or shark.

"On Sunday the steward promised to make us a plum-duff, as he had some raisins that the rats had got at and were no good. We thought we were in for a good feed. Dinner came, and so did the duff. Oh, Lor'! The cook had boiled it in salt water, straight from the sea. Still, we put nearly a week's ration of sugar with it and it tasted good enough to eat. We did no work, as it was a Sunday, and I caught a cold, but it soon went away.

"For two days we were sand-and-canvasing the bulwarks and forecastle head. The next four days we overhauled blocks—that is, taking a block to pieces, oiling it, black-leading it, painting it, and fixing it up again. We did every block in the ship. One of them fell on Paddy's head and cut it badly. It bled a lot, and I had to keep his watch at night.

"On Sunday I scrubbed out the half-deck (our place), and we saw the first flying-fish. They are about the same size as a herring, and on a large one the wings are 12 to 14 inches across, nearly as long as the fish. Those wings are on the shoulder. Closer to the tail is a smaller sort of fin. The tail is very wide. That night one flew on board and one of the other apprentices caught it. None have come on board in my watch yet. The first one I get I am going to stuff and bring home with the wings and tail spread out like you do butterflies.

"Next day we had a narrow go. I was in the lazarette with the Captain, Third Mate, and another apprentice, sizing some ropes, when the bottom of the lamp fell out between the ropes and the bulkhead, and all the oil blazed up. The Third Mate got some water and we put it out, but my heart jumped into my mouth.

"A few nights ago the Mate was on to me because I could not steer. He said: 'If you can't steer before you cross the Line, you are slow, very slow, —— slow!' (The dash is unmentionable.)

"I asked him if I could go to the wheel, and I went that night for the first time. I could steer some time before we crossed the Line, and go every night now when the Captain is not there. The Mate was only stuffing about being slow. We are not supposed to take the wheel. Still, we shan't have to learn later on.

"The men caught two fish, called 'bonito,' and gave us some to eat. I made arrangements with one of them to change my sugar for his marmalade. *This day we crossed the Equator.* Every day we see schools of flying-fish. Fifty or so at a time fly out of the water for a hundred yards or more. I had to scrub out the Mate's cabin. We passed a three-masted, full-rigged ship, called the *Illara*, and signalled her for more than an hour.

"I forgot to say that we have concerts in the half-deck two or three times a week. We each sing a solo and all join in the chorus: 'Dolly Grey,' 'Honeysuckle and the Bee,' etc. Every Sunday evening we sing hymns, Ancient and Modern, from seven to eight. The Third Mate and Steward join us. Last Sunday the Second Mate came in, and as he is a boozer, we struck up the Sankey and Moody 'Temperance boys and girls are we.' He retired to the ante-chamber.

"The men tell me I am in the Mate's good books. Still, he swears at me, though he is better to me than to the others. He gave me some bread and butter once. I am getting on well with navigation, do half or three-quarters of an hour each day. The Third Mate asked me if I did any, and I said 'yes,' so in our watch on deck at night he explains things to me. The other day he called me into his cabin and told me a lot. He gave me an exercise book and ink and told me to go to him whenever I wanted to. He is strict about my keeping it neat. I can do most of second mate's exams.

" We passed a three-masted barque, a homeward-bounder—lucky bounder, excuse that. I had to scrub out the Mate's cabin. My little toe swelled up. I could not get a boot on and could hardly walk. The cook gave me a little hot water at night and I bathed it. It was better next day.

" That Sunday we did no work and had a treat. We had plum-duff for dinner, and the Captain gave us a tin of greengages for tea. I worked out the latitude for the Third Mate. It was 22° South, longitude 38° West. I also worked out the distance to Monte Video—1,220 miles.

" While taking in sail that night I caught a good-sized flying-fish, and on Monday in my watch below I cut it open, took out its inside, and put it in a cask of salt beef for a week to preserve it. Then I shall take it out, fill it with oakum, stick the cut together, spread out its wings and varnish it, and it will be just as it was when alive. I shall bring it home. One of the men is making me an exact model of a full-rigged ship, with every rope, block, and fitting. I am going to bring that home.

" That day we had hard work, unbending all the sails off the yards and lowering them down on deck, and then sending others up and bending them on. As you are running up and down the rigging all the time, you get pretty tired. Still, I like that all right, as it teaches you what to do and gives you experience up aloft. We had to do that because there is one set of sails for fine weather in the tropics and another for bad weather.

" I had a row with the sailmaker, an Italian, a cocky little bounder. He swore at me because I would not stop on deck and help him. I told him my place was up aloft with the men and I should go there—I came to sea to be a sailor, not to stick on deck all the time. He asked me what I could do up aloft. I said I helped the men. He said I was no good up aloft, so I asked him if he thought he was the only good man in the ship. He said: ' If you have any —— cheek, I will —— well make it worse for you.'

" I said: ' Oh! ' and he did not say any more.

" There was a heavy swell and the ship rolled tremendously on Monday and Tuesday. The bulwarks nearly went under at each roll. Sometimes they did quite. I had to lash my sea-chest, as it started to waltz round the deck. We had a fine breeze. It took us 180 miles in a day. The next day also, but she rolled worse than ever.

" I have not got tired of the sea yet and have no intention of leaving it. What I don't like is being sworn at so much, although the officers don't mean it. They don't know they do it, so it counts for nothing. The others say you soon get used to being sworn at, but I have not got used to it yet. Still, I am being helped by the Third Mate and the Mate is all right to me, so I am quite contented. The men said they were going to shave us when we crossed the Line, but they did not.

" I forgot to say that I am bringing home the tail of the first bonito I saw and ate. I tried to preserve the head, but soon malodorous effluvia pervaded the half-deck, and the other apprentices made me ' consign it to the deep,' as Sarah used to say.

" We are nearly there now. For two days we sand-and-canvased the poop, and were in latitude 32° South and longitude 48° West. Then we got the anchors over the side, but it began to blow, and before night was blowing a gale. It was very cold because the wind was south and came from Cape Horn. Next day, Sunday, it blew even worse and we were hove-to under lower topsails and two staysails. Some water came into the half-deck, so we were nice and comfortable. I thought of you, going to church and having hot roast beef, bread, vegetables, and hot pudding. The wind and sea went down again at midnight, so we set sail.

"We had another little blow on Tuesday, but nothing much. We saw Cape hens, Cape pigeons, and Mother Carey's chickens. One of the men caught a Cape pigeon. He killed it and kept its skin. To catch them you tie a bent pin on to a line and stick a bit of pork on it. They swallow pin and all and you haul them in.

"On Thursday a pilot boat came alongside and offered to pilot us in for £21. The skipper offered £5. That was no go and the pilot went off. The same day another came alongside, and as he and the skipper came to terms, he boarded us.

"On Friday we sighted land north of Monte Video. At daybreak next day we could just see it. From Friday at 4 p.m. until Saturday at 9 p.m. we only had two hours' sleep. We were tacking, anchoring, getting up anchor, clewing up sails, and unbending them. We were dead-beat when we arrived off Monte Video at 8 p.m. We have to keep two hours' anchor watch every night.

"I must now close this edition. I cannot say anything about Monte Video yet, as I have not seen it. We shall not be allowed ashore, as there are no docks and we are anchored out, but I will let you know all I can about it. I have seen the natives, called 'Dagos.' They are about the most treacherous, evil-looking scoundrels I ever saw.

"I forgot to say that the Mate sometimes brings me the latitude and longitude and makes me work out the course and distance.

"I must now clap a stopper on my jaw-tackle!"

CHAPTER III

FOOD

" So shout, boys : ' Hooray ! ' I tell you for a fact :
  There's nothing done in a lime-juice ship contrary to the Act ;
  So what's the use of growling when you know you get your whack
  Of lime-juice and vinegar according to the Act?''

THE above "Eloquence of Truth" is the grace we used
to sing in the half-deck at dinner-time when the biscuits
contained an exceptionally large number of weevils and
the "salt horse" exuded a more than usually objection-
able odour.

You may find it hard to believe that one could possibly
eat biscuits that were full of weevils, and salt meat that
literally stank. I admit that now I could not do it myself.
The fact remains, however: given the requisite appetite
and nothing but those biscuits and meat to satisfy it, one
not only can, one does.

I doubt whether the average person ashore, accustomed
to regular and satisfying meals, knows what an appetite
really is. At times he is hungry, but it is not the ravening
hunger of a boy of 15 who, with hardly ever a square
meal, is employed during twelve or more hours a day in
hard manual labour at sea. It is no exaggeration at all
to say that more often than not we came off watch, ate
all there was to eat, and turned into our bunks still
hungry. It is more a craving to feel something solid
inside one than an appetite. A goat, chewing an old boot,
or an ostrich, which, it is alleged, digests nails, would
probably understand what I am trying to explain.

The Liverpool Pantiles, already mentioned, were
usually free from animal life—doubtless they were too

22

hard even for weevils' masticatory organs. In fact, they generally kept in sufficiently good condition for love-sick sailors to paint a picture of the ship on them to take home as keepsakes for their sweethearts and wives. During the long sailing-ship voyages biscuits had also to be bought abroad. These were less hard and easier to eat, but they did not keep so well. After a while it was necessary to split them open and brush off the weevils before eating them.

As for the green, evil-smelling lumps of fat meat, which were kept in casks of brine and dignified with the name of beef and pork, only a fool would try to describe them, as Doctor Johnson would probably say were he writing this.

The food was served out to the crew in accordance with the Board of Trade scale of provisions, the "pound and pint according to the Act," as the men called it. This allowed, among other things, 7 ounces of butter, 7 ounces of marmalade, and 14 ounces of sugar per man, per week —"perhaps," we sometimes added when we thought we were getting short weight. There was also a stated quantity of biscuits, but in our case it was not adhered to and we were given "full and plenty," which, being interpreted, means that we could have as many as we wanted.

The apprentices' food depended on the ship and the company. We were among the unlucky ones and had the same as the men. In future, should you be worried about your vitamins and calories, it may ease your mind to know that, although we had no milk, eggs, fruit, or vegetables of any kind, not excepting potatoes, I still have my health and strength.

Ordinary bread (soft tack) was served out on Sunday, Tuesday, and Thursday, but there was only sufficient of it for one meal. That is why in my first letter I mentioned that the Mate had given me some bread and butter. It was something to write home about!

For breakfast during the cold weather experienced south of latitude 40° we had a watery porridge—no milk in it—called Burgoo, and molasses. Our Sunday joint was a stringy tinned meat that was usually referred to as "Harriet Lane," there being a legend to the effect that the tins contained the earthly remains of a lady of that name. Pea soup was issued three times a week.

With those three exceptions, our breakfasts consisted of biscuits and coffee, and our suppers of biscuits and tea. At dinner-time we sat down to a meal of biscuits and the salt meat I am not fool enough to try to describe.

After being ten days on salt food lime-juice was served out daily to prevent scurvy. Hence the names "Limey," "Lime-juice-ship," or a "Lime-juicer" that were given to British ships.

Occasionally the apprentices, like Lazarus, were given a few crumbs from the rich man's table. In other words, if we were on good terms with the steward, he gave us a bit of hash that was left over from the Captain's and officers' meal; but the quantity was so small that we had a "gentleman's agreement" which allotted it all to the watch below.

During those four irresponsible years only two cares preyed on our minds: "How to get more food" and "How to pass the examination for Second Mate's certificate." I have set them down in what we should have said was the order of their importance.

Various messes were invented to add to our bill of fare. Occasionally at dinner-time we cut off the least repulsive-looking scraps of salt fat, placed them on biscuits that had been soaked in water, and fried them in the galley for supper. The result was a "savoury" we called "slum-gully." It was eventually stopped by the Captain because it was liable to cause boils. As though that mattered!

Anything that lived in the sea and could be caught was

food for us. In fine weather fishing-lines with bits of white rag for bait were always handy on the forecastle head. When fish were seen a man went out on the bowsprit and allowed the rag to dip in and out of the water round the stem. Impulsive and short-sighted dolphin, albacore, and bonito mistook it for their legitimate food, flying-fish, with the result that they were soon en route to the galley to make a meal for us.

A harpoon was kept in the carpenter's shop in readiness for any porpoise that might happen our way. When one was seen showing off its speed by swimming to and fro across our bow, occasionally leaping out of the water, "Chippy" downed tools and hurried forward, brandishing that weapon. The Mate and some of the men on watch ran after him to haul the victim on board, or, if he missed, to explain with the help of lurid sailing-ship adjectives how he should have done it.

During calms in the tropics there was sometimes a shout from the look-out man: "Turtle!"

A boat was immediately put out and rowed cautiously towards it as it lay day-dreaming on the surface, only its shell visible above the water. When within a yard or two a man in the bow speared it with a "grain." A desperate struggle ensued. Slow and cumbersome as they are on land, they move with the rapidity of a fish in the sea. They have very powerful jaws and a sharp claw on each leg. As they usually weighed over seventy pounds, it was no easy task to lift the wounded and kicking, snapping animal over the gunwale into the boat.

Some of them were found to contain as many as a hundred eggs, which gave rise to more culinary efforts. Here is one recipe: "Wrap biscuits in a piece of canvas and hammer them on the deck with an iron belaying-pin until they are powdered. Beat up the turtle's eggs in an empty Harriet Lane tin, pour in the powder, and stir into a thick paste. Add scraps of salt horse to taste and place mixture on galley stove until it appears to be cooked.''

I forget what we called it, but the result might well have been referred to in a song I once heard sung by George Robey: "Solid, Substantial, and Thick!"

Windjammer epicures broke a turtle's egg into their breakfast coffee.

And the moral of this tale is: "Forget all about food fads, pills, and patent medicines. Go out into the fresh air and work. Under- rather than over-nourish the inner man, and he will leave you in peace, and you will live happily ever after.''

CHAPTER IV

FLORIDA TO YOKOHAMA

AFTER discharging the coal in Monte Video, my first port, the ship was sent in ballast to Port Tampa, Florida. There she loaded a cargo of phosphate rock for Yokohama.

Two letters describe the passage of 167 days between these two ports. Being short-handed after leaving Port Tampa, we had to put into Cape Town, and the first one was posted there. The other was sent from Yokohama.

The incidents which occurred during this long run are of such a varied nature, ranging from the tragedy of " Man overboard " to the comedy of " buying a monkey for a few ship's biscuits," that the two letters are an excellent sample of the raw material from which this " yarn " is woven. For that reason I am inserting them here, practically as I wrote them shortly after my sixteenth birthday.

SHIP *Aristomene*,
CAPE TOWN,
May 29th, 1903.

MY DEAREST PARENTS,

I expect you will be very surprised to get a letter from this part of the world, but what with men running away, dying, and falling overboard, we are so short-handed that we had to put into Cape Town for more.

On February 24th we were towed out from the wharf at Port Tampa and anchored a little way out. Just before we left, four men ran away. One was caught, but escaped again. The Skipper, Mate and Second Mate chased him along the dock, captured him once more, and put him into the cabin, with the steward to mount guard over him.

Later he broke down the door, got by the steward, and was escaping for the third time when the Mate managed to catch him and put him in irons (handcuffs).

There was a ladder from the wharf to the ship, and the Skipper, who was coming up it just as the Mate caught the man, got so excited that he let go, lost his balance, and fell overboard with a terrific splash. When he came to the surface he managed to catch hold of the wharf until a boat came, and we hauled him on board.

The next two days we rowed the Skipper ashore each day and waited there for him, doing nothing and talking to people we knew. On the 26th we rowed four new men on board. They were professional hobos, what we call tramps at home, shipped as Able Seamen but knowing nothing about ships.

We were towed out of port the same day, but managed to run aground on a sandbank. There we stuck, the tug unable to move us. Next day three tugs came and pulled together all the afternoon. We did not budge an inch, though they broke three 6-inch and one 8-inch hawsers, a cable-laid rope (about 12 inches), stranded a wire hawser, and carried away two jib guys.

At 10 p.m. a lighter arrived and we discharged 200 tons of cargo to lighten the ship. We got off the following day, and all that night were loading the cargo again. We were towed out to sea in the afternoon. Before the tug cast off the man in irons managed to escape once more and left a note, saying: "Good-bye! I am gone!"

On March 11th it was very hot and we were nearly becalmed. I forgot to say that we had two men laid up with fever. One got over it, but the other died at half-past eleven that night. He was buried immediately. His body was sewn up in canvas, with a lump of iron at the feet to make it sink, and laid on a hatch at the stern, covered with an ensign. While the Skipper read the service the hatch was up-ended and the body slid overboard. The whole ship was fumigated next day, and the wind rose and blew hard all night. We were under three lower topsails.

On the night of the 17th a squall struck us, so the Skipper called all hands on deck. We brought her down to main upper topsail. After the mainsail was clewed up all hands, fifteen men and four boys, were on the main-yard, trying to furl it. It was raining in torrents, and by the time we got up there the bights of the sail were filled with water, so that we could not roll it up on the yard. We lowered it down and clewed it up three times, but each time they filled with water so quickly and were so heavy that at last we had to come down and leave the sail hanging.

It was very hot and we were becalmed on the 19th. The carpenter caught a small dolphin. We unshackled the cables off the anchors and hove them up on deck to chip and tar them. There were 120 fathoms of one and 135 fathoms of the other.

We saw shoals of jelly-fish. Their real name is "Nautilus," but sailors call them "Portuguee Man-o'-War" because you only see them in very smooth water and fine weather. I caught one in a bucket that I lowered over the side. Its body is leg-of-mutton shape, 3 or 4 inches long. On the upper part of it is a kind of fin, also jelly, and triangular in shape, that shows above the water like a small lug-sail. In the sunshine it is all the colours of the rainbow. Sometimes we see hundreds of them to-gether, like fleets of toy sailing-boats with painted shiny sails.

Underneath them, though, are long strings of jelly that sting like billy-ho. I was stung several times, and it didn't half prick and burn.

On the 20th and 21st it was very hot. I scraped all the shovels and oiled them. The next day we shifted twenty tons of cargo from the fore to the after hatch, as the ship would not steer well.

We saw four sperm whales on the 24th. They were blowing just as Bullen says. It looks like steam, actually it is their breath. One jumped right out of the water. They *are* a size. I think if I had to go for them in a boat as whalers do, I should try to have urgent business elsewhere.

We had a gale on the 26th and were under lower topsails. We shipped a lot of water and some came into the half-deck, where we live. It always does in bad weather and wets our dry clothes. Our door leaks. As my bunk is next to the door, I usually get some in that, too. Still, we didn't do any work. We couldn't.

The wind went down a bit next day and we set upper topsails and topgallantsails, but had to furl them again that same night. It rained continually. At last on the 29th we had fine weather and were able to set all sail; but on the night of the 30th the wind increased once more and was blowing hard all the 31st.

At 8 p.m. all hands were on the mainyard, furling the mainsail. We had rolled it up on the yard and were passing the gaskets (thin ropes wound round the sail and the yard to secure the sail). One of the new men, a German, stooped to take the end of the gasket from me under the yard, but he slipped and fell overboard.

We shouted "Man overboard!" and everybody hurried down on deck and mustered aft to see what was going to be done. As we were doing ten knots, with a fairly heavy sea, no attempt was made to save him, so we went up again and furled the sail.

He was the same nationality as the man who died of fever, both Germans and both new men. After the man died of fever one of the other men, a Russian-Finn, swore that he saw his ghost several times walking up and down the break of the poop, outside our place, and said that he had come after his countryman. Nobody believed him, but they were all very scared. Sure enough, the other German fell overboard a few days later.

It was funny that that same evening before he fell overboard he was telling the other men his history, and said: "I don't know what I should do if I fell overboard. I can't swim a stroke."

April 1st, fine weather again and we set all sail. At 4 p.m. the clothes of the men who ran away and fell overboard were sold by auction. I bought nothing.

On the 13th the carpenter caught a porpoise, a monster, and we hauled it on board. It was slate colour, with a triangular hump on the back and a sharp-pointed nose. All round its body was a layer of blubber, an inch thick. The blubber is a hard, white, stringy substance, full of oil. I have got the jaws and teeth as a curio to bring home. We had fresh meat off it for three days. It tastes like a mixture of liver and beef steak, a fine change from "salt junk."

I painted the gig on the 15th. That night we passed three steamers, and had to give way to one of them. By the Rule of the Road at sea, all steamers have to give way to sailing-ships, but I suppose they were not keeping a look-out, so *we* had to get out of the way.

On the 16th I puttied an oil barrel that leaked, and on the 17th and 18th was cleaning a suit of clothes belonging to the Mate with turpentine. That is how apprentices learn seamanship!

I am now up-to-date as I am writing this before we get into port. I may not have much time there. I still do navigation and diary, and like the sea as much as ever except for being sworn at. This may be the only letter I can post from here, so I will tell you what the place is like from Yokohama. The men tell me I am getting fat.

If I get fat in tropical weather when I usually get thin, what shall I be like in cold weather when I generally get fat? We go through the Straits of Sunda.

Farewell. Only another year or so. Heaps of love to you all,

From your loving
SON.

P.S.—May 23rd. Since the 27th April we have done nothing much. We have had bad weather for the last three weeks, shipping water and raining, and have been in sea-boots and oilskins all the time. We had one stiff gale. I looked in the Mate's log-book, and it says: "Fresh gale with terrific squalls, heavy sea running. Ship labouring heavily and shipping much water."

We caught three young sharks one day, about four feet long. They are just as you read of them—white stomachs and they turn on their back to eat the bait. Their mouth stretches half-way round their head. I did not see one smile, but with that mouth it would smile from ear to ear.

I must close now. I hope you are all well. I was never better. Heaps of love to you all,

From your loving
SON AND BROTHER.

P.S.—I hope you can read this. She is rolling heavily. It is as much as I can do to keep off the deck, and the ink pot is promenading round the table.

SHIP Aristomene,
YOKOHAMA,
August 12th, 1903.

MY DEAREST FAMILY,

At last we are about a week's sail from Japan, so I am starting letters. We sighted Table Mountain at daybreak on the 29th, but it was blowing a gale and we were hove-to outside under three lower topsails all day. There was a heavy sea, and we had to wear ship twice—that is, go from one tack to the other by turning round before the sea. When we were broadside on to it the deck was flooded and we were washed about all over the place. That was fine fun; but it was even finer when a sea came into the half-deck, where we live, and flooded that.

In the evening the wind went down, so we sailed in, and then we had a narrow escape. To get into the Bay, we had to go round a point with a lighthouse on it where there was a heavy surf. As there was no pilot on board, the Skipper was not sure of his way and went too close. Suddenly we heard the noise of sea breaking, and then saw the surf close on the bow. The helm was put hard over and the ship came round, just missing it. In another minute we should have been smashed up. We anchored at 11.30 p.m.

We turned out early to have a look at Cape Town. It is situated right at the foot of Table Mountain which runs all round the left side of the Bay. On the right is another mountain, with Cape Town Observatory at the top. At the foot of this are the docks. The anchorage, where we are, is to the left of them.

Next day, the 30th, the doctor came on board and examined us, and the Skipper went ashore for men. Just before dinner a tug arrived alongside with fresh water.

We did no work on Sunday. At 10.30 a.m. four new men came off in a boat. Two of them had never been to sea before, and they had all been at the front (i.e., Boer War). Two of them are Americans. We sailed that afternoon. As we were leaving we passed close to a four-masted ship with her main topgallant yard carried away.

June 1st, shifted fifteen tons of cargo from aft, forward, to make the ship steer better. For three days we did odd jobs, making sennit, etc. On the 5th the wind increased

to a hard gale with terrific squalls. The seas were mountainous and were continually filling the deck. We were
under three lower topsails. On the next day we set all
plain sail, and until the 19th I was cleaning spikes,
shackles, etc., for the mate.

This part of the journey is called: "Running the
Easting down." All vessels bound round the Cape to
Australia or the East Indies, or through the East Indies
as we were, have to go several thousand miles to the east.
They always go down to latitude forty or forty-five south,
as they get good winds there. From Cape Town we went
to latitude forty south, and then ran due east until we
were in longitude eighty or ninety east. Sometimes you
get one continuous gale nearly the whole way. We were
lucky, only had three gales. Sailors say they would rather
go round the Horn than run the easting down. It is very
cold, and the only work you do is sennit and odd jobs.

On the 20th and 21st we had another hard gale, with
constant rain and a very heavy sea. The Mate said the
seas were from 20 to 30 feet high. When one of them falls
on board and comes on top of you, you don't forget it.

On July 5th we passed Java Head at the entrance to the
Straits of Sunda. They are so narrow that we could see
it very well. Java Head is a high hill, covered with a
thick forest. At the foot of it is a white lighthouse on a
square rock, called Friar's Rock. They hoisted the Dutch
flag; we, our ensign.

We passed Anjer Point at the other end of the Straits
on the 6th. There was only a light breeze and we were
going very slowly, so the natives came off to us in dug-out
canoes. They brought bananas, oranges, yams, melons,
and all kinds of tropical fruit. They also had hens, geese,
monkeys, cockatoos, parrots, and everything that sailors
will buy. I bought a monkey, and so did eight others.
I shall try to bring it home. The natives won't take

money—only clothes, etc., and you can nearly make your
own price. Of course they ask a high price, but you can
easily beat them down. One nigger had four cocoa-nuts
and wanted a shirt for them. I offered him a piece of soap
and a box of matches. I got them for a small piece of
soap, one box of matches, and one ship's biscuit. The

MAP 1.—SUMATRA AND JAVA.

biscuits came in handy. They were mad after them and
we got a lot of fruit for them. Most of the natives have
only a cloth round their waist, but a few have shirt and
trousers. All have turbans. One of them was fresh from
the bush and would not look at, or speak to, us. It is an
indignity to them. Their baskets are made of leaves, and

their rope of black hair. I am bringing home a bit of rope to show you. I gave one biscuit for it. They have little wooden anchors in each canoe.

The Skipper bought two or three dozen hens and geese, and as they roam about the deck, there is a fine mess for the *boys* to sweep up after knock-off time. We have fine fun with the monkeys. We tie them all together on the main hatch.

On the 8th we entered Banka Strait. This Strait is very narrow and shallow, so every night we had to take in all sail and anchor. We didn't keep any regular watches there or do any work, but all hands had to keep handy the whole time and come out to work the sails, braces, and anchor. The men call this " Kalashi Watch "—watch on and stop on.

On the 9th we set all sail, but a heavy squall struck us and we had to take it in and drop anchor again. Loosed all sail on the 10th, but as there was no wind, we scrubbed the ship's bottom.

To do that, you have a rope over the bow, leading aft, with a very big, rough sort of mat made fast to it. There is another rope over each side, also fastened to the mat. Several men walk up and down the deck, pulling on these two ropes. In this way the mat is dragged to and fro under the ship's bottom and rubs the barnacles off it.

A Chinese junk came up and anchored close to us. Two negroes were sent to us in a canoe to ask for old shirts, etc. The canoe was propelled by two paddles, both on the same side. The junk was going to Ceylon. She had two lateen sails, and an awning like the roof of a house over the stern. We got clear of the Straits that night.

14th. *My first year is up today.* Three more years and then I hope to walk the poop. We crossed the Line today. On the 23rd the wind increased to a heavy gale and we had to reduce sail to fore and main lower topsails.

This was the heaviest gale we had had and it lasted two days.

We sighted the Philippines on the 27th, but were too far off to distinguish anything. On the 28th we saw Batan Island,* and there we had a terrific gale.

I suppose you know that in the China Sea you get typhoons. These are the same as cyclones, circular storms. If a vessel gets into the centre of one, she cannot live and will founder. This gale was a typhoon, but luckily for us we were in the outside circle. We were hove-to with not one sail set. We only had the weather cloth spread in the mizzen rigging, and the wheel was lashed hard down. You can't imagine the force of the wind. It lasted until the 31st, and then we set sail again.

On the 8th of August we got the anchors over the side and sighted land, part of Japan. Next day we sighted more land and entered the Gulf. On the 10th we could see Yokohama, but the wind dropped.

There was no wind on the morning of the 11th and we had to anchor. After dinner we hove up again, set sail, and got in at half-past three this morning. We were on deck from 4 a.m. on Tuesday until 3.30 a.m. on Wednesday without sleep or rest, pulling ropes, running up aloft, and heaving up the anchor. We were dead beat. We slept from 3.30 a.m. today until 7.30 a.m., except for one hour's anchor watch—three hours' sleep and worked all day today.

I must close now. I will tell you about Yokohama next mail. Heaps of love to you all,

From your loving
SON AND BROTHER.

* Off the north of the Philippine Islands.

CHAPTER V

BAD WEATHER

" Lords of the Bunt and Gasket
And Masters of the Yard,
For whom no land was distant,
To whom no sea was barred."
BASIL LUBBOCK.

IN the foregoing chapters there are words and phrases which probably are only vaguely understood by You-Who-Live-Ashore, although they were in daily use on sailing-ships. Before going any further, therefore, I will explain the meaning of " Bad Weather " which, I suppose, only makes you think of umbrellas and goloshes.

There is, however, far more in it than is dreamed of in that simple shore philosophy, for those two words cover a multitude of others. These range from " hove-to under goose-winged lower topsail " down to the fearsome oaths uttered by the watch below when they are called out on a dark night in a howling gale of wind to " goose-wing " that sail.

In order to simplify this interpretation, I have followed the example of a certain Practical Standard Dictionary of the English language and inserted what it calls a Pictorial Illustration of the yards and sails. To that I add the meanings of the following Foreign Phrases used in Windjammer Speech and Literature:

" Braces " are ropes attached to the ends of the yards (yardarms) by means of which these are pulled round from one side to the other.

" Sheets " are fastened to the " clews," or lower corners, of the sails, to pull these out when they are being set.

38

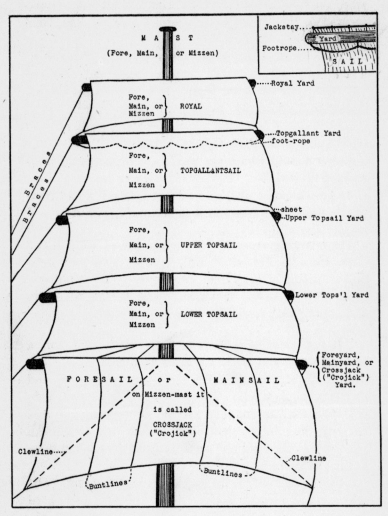

YARDS AND SAILS.

"Clewlines," on the contrary, pull those corners up
when the sails are being furled, while "buntlines," ropes
secured to the "foot," or lower side, of the sail, haul
that up at the same time.

The sail is then said to be "clewed up," and the men,
standing on a "footrope," a wire rope, reach forward
and pull it up on to the yard. It is secured by passing
"gaskets," thin ropes, round both sail and yard.

"Halliards" hoist the upper topsail, topgallant, and
royal yards when those sails are being set.

Lower topsail and lower yards are permanently fixed
and not hoisted.

As a mention of jibs, staysails, or spanker would com-
plicate this description and is unnecessary, I omit it.

The following account of a passage from Cardiff round
Cape Horn to Acapulco* will, I hope, give you some
understanding of what those two words "Bad Weather"
signified to a sailing-ship man. The letter I wrote in
May, 1906, shall begin the story:

"It was pouring with rain when we left Cardiff, a
cheerful start, and we had a head wind that lasted for a
week. We sighted the Irish coast near Waterford, and
the same night saw Waterford light. The Second Mate
mistook it for a fishing light and did not report it. It was
not very clear and suddenly we saw land close to us. All
hands were called out and we tacked and got off, but there
was not much room to spare.

"On the night of the 1st we had an electric storm. The
lightning and thunder were terrific. The wind blew hard
one minute and fell to a dead calm the next, while the
rain came down in torrents. We were taking in a sail
and it got foul of something, so the Second Mate sang out

* The chief Mexican port on the Pacific seaboard.

for a man to go up and clear it. None of them would move and he sent me. While I was up there we had one flash, the finish of the storm, and I won't forget it in a hurry. The whole air seemed in a blaze and the lightning made a noise like wood cracking. I was blinded and clung on like ' grim death to a nigger.' Then the thunder came and I seemed to be in the middle of an explosion. I came down faster than I went up. I thought the cracking noise was one of the masts going.

"On the 10th the Second Mate had a fight with one of the men who had told him to go to—ahem!

"We passed and signalled the lighthouse on Staten Island,* about 145 miles from the Horn, on February 8th. On the 12th we sighted Barnevelt, about 19 miles from it, and on the 15th saw Staten Island again. Head winds had driven us right back there.

"During the first gale we had there was water a foot deep in the half-deck. It was washing to and fro as the ship rolled, and one of the other fellows' sea-chests and my own were filled up. Everything was soaked, and there was no means of drying them, as we could not put them in the galley in that kind of weather. We wrung them out and dried them on us.

"We sighted the Horn on the 17th and passed quite close to it on the 18th. It is a very barren place, only a bare rock. After that head winds took us down to sixty degrees south . . ."

I will now put the letter to one side and carry on with the story myself, to show you what is hidden behind the words " head winds took us down to sixty degrees south."

The weather on the morning of the 18th was fine and dry, though cold, and Cape Horn was passed about 7 a.m. during my watch on deck. At 8 a.m. we went below,

* See sketch-map, p. 58.

4

"scoffed" our burgoo and molasses, and turned in to
sleep until 11.20 a.m. We should then be called to get
our dinner before going on watch again at noon.

Turning in down in those latitudes and under those conditions was far simpler than going to bed at home. As all
our bedding and clothes were wet and we had no stove in
the half-deck either to dry them or to warm ourselves,
we merely removed boots and coat, climbed into our
bunks, and pulled blankets over us. In this way we were
able to keep our wet clothes warm on us, whereas if we
went to bed in the orthodox manner, they were icy-cold
to put on when we turned out. It saved time, too, and in
those days time was sleep, not money. Not only were we
watch and watch (four hours on and four off), but meals
had to be eaten in our watch below, and we were
frequently called out to shorten or set sail.

About ten o'clock, when we were sleeping the sleep of
an apprentice, which is far deeper than that of the just,
the door was flung open.

"All hands on deck!" a voice shouted. "Get a move
on you! You want your oilskins!"

That and the banging of the door awakened us with a
start. Shivering in the cold air, and still half asleep, we
slid over the edge of our bunks on to the sea-chests and
proceeded to "dress up."

Instead of putting on our sea-boot stockings, which
already had holes in them and, like everything else, were
wet and cold, we wrapped paper and burlap (sacking)
round our feet and dragged on our sea-boots. Oilskin
trousers were pulled over these, their legs being lashed
outside them with ropeyarns. Then we climbed into oilskin coats, tied the sleeves round the wrists and wound a
fathom of cord round our waists. This was known as the
"soul and body lashing." It prevented the oilskin coat
from blowing up, and deputised for buttons that had been

wrenched off while leaning over a yard. When our sou'westers were securely fastened on our heads we hurried out on deck. The royals had already been furled, and the three topgallantsails, which were being clewed up, were flapping wildly in a strong north-north-west wind and dense rain.

Before they could be made fast the crossjack had to be taken in—a job for all hands. We hauled, or clewed, it up and climbed to the yard. Standing on the footrope, we reached forward and got hold of a crease in the bellying and flapping canvas. Then, all together, we dragged that on the yard, rested our bodies on it to hold it, and stretched out for more. While the rain beat in our faces and icy-cold rivulets ran down our necks that was repeated again and again. Finally, the whole sail was gathered in and secured on the yard with the gaskets. As we were making fast the last of these a bellow came up to us from the poop: "Make the tuhgansels fast!"

The mizzen was the apprentices' mast. We five boys therefore carried on up to that topgallant yard and secured that sail, while one watch of men furled the fore, and the other the main, topgallantsail.

When we came down from there the wind had already increased to a moderate gale, and the Captain, standing on the weather side of the poop with his wooden arm hooked round a rope, was shouting: "Haul the mains'l up!"

All hands collected amidships at the main clewlines and buntlines, and when the sheet was slacked off began hauling on them. By then the sea was becoming vicious, and as we stood there, pulling on those ropes, heavy spray was whipped over the bulwarks. It mixed with the rain that was driving in our faces and running up our arms and down our necks.

The hardest part of the task of "snugging her down" was beginning. After the three topgallantsails had been

furled the whole crew was required to roll each of the
larger sails on the yard and secure it. The mainsail was
a sample of what was in store for us. When we were all
spread out along the footrope it was some time before
our cold fingers were able to find a bit of canvas they
could grip. Men hammered their fists into it, to try to
make a crease they could hold. When eventually some
of it was pulled on to the yard a violent flap tore it away
from us and we had to begin all over again. After
struggling vainly for about a quarter of an hour the Mate
suddenly appeared in the bunt, or centre of the yard.

" All together now!" he shouted. "Grab a fistful of
it! D'ye want to stop up here all the bloody day?"

We slowly grabbed fistful after fistful, gaining two and
losing one again when it flapped, a battle between cold,
sore fingers and hard, wet canvas. Fingers, of course,
won. They had to! We should "stop there all the
bloody day" until they did.

As we were shinning down the main rigging to the deck
another roar from the Captain met us: " Mizzen upper
taups'l!"

We could see him struggling to lower away those
halliards with his one hand, and both watches ran aft.
While we were manning those buntlines he shouted to the
Mate: " Lower away fore upper taups'l!"

The Mate took an apprentice forward with him, and the
remainder of us dragged our tired legs to the mizzen upper
topsail yard, to begin another battle. Although this sail
was not so big as the mainsail, the fight was almost as
long. The wind was continually increasing, and a big sea
was getting up which, with too much canvas still on her,
was making the ship throw herself about with sharp, jerky
movements that added to our difficulties.

Cape Stiff, as the Horn was sometimes called, was
playing one of its practical jokes on us: after a fine

morning, before the underfed and overworked crew are able to get the huge spread of canvas off the ship, the wind comes away with a bang. One of my windjammer mentors, an elderly Able Seaman, was giving me a lecture on weatherology one day.

"Never trust a woman or the weather off Cape Stiff," he said. "Them's both the same—smiles at yer one minute and scratches yer bloody eyes out the next!"

Before we reached the deck from the mizzen upper top-sail yard the Captain's voice, compared with which the howl of a gale of wind was but a lover's sigh, greeted us with an impersonation of a fog-horn trying to articulate the words: "Geddown out of it! Jump for'ud and make that fore upper taups'l fast!"

We moved as quickly as we could, but the "jump" was leaving us. It was then past noon. For nearly two hours we had been climbing to those yards in heavy leather sea-boots and oilskins, and literally fighting the wildly flapping sails. We were not only wet and bitterly cold, but were also beginning to experience the sickly, sinking feeling inside due to lack of food. Since the previous day's salt-horse-and-biscuit dinner we had only eaten a tea-and-biscuit supper and a watery-burgoo breakfast.

I have no idea how long we were on the fore upper topsail yard. Time after time we managed to drag some of the canvas on to it, only to have it wrenched away from us. By the time it was secured some of the men's knuckles were raw and bleeding.

When we reached the deck again we saw the cook in his oilskins standing by the foresheet. We knew what that meant. Every available man was called out to take in the foresail. Without waiting for an order, we mustered on those clewlines and buntlines. By that time it was not spray alone that was whipped over the bulwarks. "Green

water " occasionally rolled over them and knocked us off
our feet.   While we hauled on those ropes the flaps of the
sail were sufficiently violent to jerk them out of our hands
—an indication of what was in store for us when finally it
was clewed up and we climbed to the yard to " grab
fistfuls " of it.

You who have never had the experience can hardly
realise that task.   Try to imagine that the foresail on the
sketch at the beginning of this chapter is from 80 to 90
feet across and about 40 feet deep, and that it is made
with heavy No. 1 canvas, which is very thick and very
stiff, especially when met.   The foot and clews are hauled
up to the yard and there it hangs, a gale of wind causing
it alternatively to flap violently and to belly out like a
balloon.

On one occasion in winter, when there was snow and
ice on the yards and sails, we had been on the foreyard
in thick snow squalls for nearly an hour, unable even to
catch hold of the canvas.   As usual, all our clothes were
wet.   The temperature was very little above zero Fahrenheit.   Our bodies were miniature icebergs.   The sail *had*
to be secured, and we were getting desperate.   Suddenly
a man clambered off the footrope on to the yard.   Clinging to the topping lift, he stood on that " belly," cursing
it, and stamping his sea-boots on it in an endeavour to
make a crease in it that our frozen fingers could grasp.
He made practically no impression on it!

If you can visualise that balloon, you may have some
idea of our task when, standing on a slippery footrope,
we leaned over the yard and tried to manhandle it.
Meanwhile the ship, that was gaining " jump " with the
rising sea as fast as we were losing it, was rolling heavily
from one side to the other.

When we were mustered on the yard we awaited an
opportunity to grasp a crease in it.   A few eventually

succeeded and struggled to hold it until others could do the same. One could feel the hard, wet canvas rubbing the skin off the knuckles and dragging at the finger-nails. There was a crack like a rifle shot as it flapped and tore itself out of our hands. One man put a finger in his mouth and shouted curses at it—the nail was torn and bleeding.

The Mate, the little sixty-year-old Captain Kettle, was standing in the bunt in his oilskins and sea-boots, clinging to something with one hand and shaking the other fist at us.

"Now! Grab it! God damn it, grab it!" he yelled. "Hold it now! Wait till she rolls back!—Now, in with it!—Hold her again!—*Now's* yer chance! Smother the son of a bitch!"

Eventually, of course, it was "smothered." Somehow or other, no matter how bad the conditions, sails always were. From the sailing-ship dictionary, more perhaps than from any other, the word "can't" had to be deleted. The jobs *had* to be done. If your finger-nail was nearly torn off, nobody would listen to you if you said, "I can't do it!"

"Use the other bloody hand!" would be the advice of the Mate and your shipmates.

It sounded hard at first, but one soon learned that they all practised what they preached. It was their way of teaching a boy that "the ship was more than the crew"; and if he were incapable of learning that lesson, it were better he jumped the ship in the next port and looked for a job ashore. I have met ex-apprentices who had done that. One had risen to be manager of a saw-mill in one of the lumber ports. Others had merely drifted and become beachcombers.

But that is a digression and I will return to the fore-yard. While we were engaged in the struggle there the

Captain had taken the wheel with his one hand and sent the man to lower away the main upper topsail. We could see and hear it flapping as we came down the fore-rigging. Furling it was merely a repetition of what we had been doing for the past four hours, and it expended more of our reserve fund of "jump," deep-sea oaths, and knuckle skin.

That was the last, however. The ship was snug with only the three lower topsails on her. She was headed up as close as possible to the north-north-west wind, and thus was "hove-to under three lower topsails."

It was then past two o'clock. The other watch went below to get their dinner and to sleep until 4 p.m. We had first of all to coil up the ropes clear of the deck, and then some of us were allowed a few minutes to eat ours. We hurriedly swallowed a lump of "salt horse" and a few biscuits, and came out again to relieve the others for them to do likewise.

At 4 p.m. we went below for two hours—the first dog-watch. We took off our sea-boots, wiped the inside of them as dry as possible, and rolled ourselves up in blankets in our bunks to keep warm. At five o'clock a boy from the other watch brought the can of tea, and at 6 p.m., in oilskins, sea-boots, and "soul and body lashings," we went on deck, to spend two hours keeping handy on the poop.

Though she was tumbling about and shipping "green water," the ship was laying quite "comfortably" under the three lower topsails, and there was no more "sail drill." We were able to turn in after eight o'clock and sleep until we were called at 11.45 p.m.

Turning out was the same procedure—lashing our oilskins on us as we stood shivering and more asleep than awake on the sea-chests, while an apprentice from the other watch bailed out water that had leaked in round the

edges of the door. At midnight we returned to the poop.
For four hours we clung to a belaying-pin, buffeted by the
wind, listening to the roar of it aloft and to the crashes of
the seas as they rolled over the bulwarks on to the main
deck, sheets of rain and spray driving over us.

At 4 a.m., dead-tired, hungry, bitterly cold, and
soaked, we crawled into our wet bunks once more, only
to have another joke played on us by " Cape Stiff " About
half-past six I was awakened by a sea splashing over me
and a banging of the door. Blinking water and sleep out
of my eyes and instinctively turning the newly-wet side
of my pillow underneath, I glared over the edge of my
bunk. There was more than a foot of water on the deck,
and an apprentice from the other watch who had mis-
judged the moment to enter and so brought a sea in with
him was lying in it. It was washing over him and over
the sea-chests into the lower bunks, where one boy was
sitting up and wiping his head with a blanket.

There was a chorus of " What the hells?" from us, and
as he struggled to his feet the producer of this *mise-en-
scène* spluttered: " She's caught aback! All hands on
deck! Blowing like hell!"

To be caught aback means a sudden shift of wind that
brings it on the other side of the sails, and in that weather
was a serious matter—that is how " ships have the sticks
taken out of them."

We tumbled out and dragged on our sea-boots and oilskins, the water splashing over our feet as we did so.
The scrunches of the seas falling on the deck were heavier
and more frequent than before, and it was necessary to
stand by the door to await an opportunity to get out.
We heard one. It crashed against the door and gushed in
round the edges. The ship gave a heavy roll, and as the
water ran to the other side we flung open the door and
jumped out on to the poop ladder. Most of the men had

already gathered at the mizzen braces, which were made fast to the "fife-rail," and we floundered along there, knee-deep in water.

A very heavy sea was running. Twice, as we were pulling on the mizzen braces, a mountain of water broke over the bulwark near us. Those close to the fife-rail could hold on to it, but others, who were at the end of the rope, were knocked down like ninepins and swept across the deck. I have one memory of that morning that has never faded during the intervening years. It is that of the apprentice, Paddy, who was one of the unlucky ones at the end of the rope. Sitting stiffly upright in the water, only his head visible above it, his sou'wester askew and an indescribable expression on his face, he drifted across the deck and back again before he could "bring himself up."

"Square yer mainyard, Paddy," shouted one of the men, amidst a chorus of laughs. "Make a fair wind of it!"

In a way it was easier work at the main braces. They were belayed on the bulwark outside the half-deck, and although the seas broke right over us there, we could cling to a rope or a belaying-pin, head into them and keep on our feet.

One of the first lessons a youngster had to learn was that he should never turn his back on a sea. He should face it and head into it, or it would knock him down and almost certainly injure him. Until he was made to realise that, it was a big temptation to turn and run when he saw a wall of water rear up over the bulwark towards him.

When all the yards were round and the ship was safely hove-to on the other tack it was eight o'clock and our watch below was finished. One of us hurried to the galley and brought the coffee and burgoo to the half-deck for breakfast. By the time it arrived it was nearly cold, and in that weather was usually mixed with salt water. Sometimes the boy carrying it was caught by a sea, and then we poor dogs had none. The water was still washing over the sea-chests, and we stood on them while we hurriedly swallowed that meal. In a few minutes we returned on deck to keep the forenoon watch.

During the day in such weather one apprentice remained on the poop to pass along the orders. The rest of the watch kept handy under the forecastle head. Idleness was another word that was deleted from the windjammer dictionary, and they were usually employed in making sennit, or, in other words, doing with ropeyarns what the fair sex did with their hair before the "boyish bob age": plaiting them, using five, seven, or more strands instead of only three.

The ship remained under three lower topsails all that day and night, but in the early hours of the following morning there was less weight in the wind, and when we called the other watch at 7.20 a.m. for their breakfast we had to warn them that they would be "hauled out" a quarter of an hour earlier, to set the main upper topsail.

When they came on deck at 7.45 a.m. the sail was already loosed and the halliards had been taken to the capstan.

"Heave and go, men!" shouted the Mate.

We began to walk it round, but before the pawls had clanked a dozen times a huge "green one" rolled on board in the middle of us and swept most of us into the lee scupper. We picked ourselves up, splashed back, and started again, spitting out a rich mixture of salt water and deep-sea curses. The Mate also had been caught by that one. To all appearances a frail old man, water streaming off his oilskins, he glared over the side and shook his fist.

"Come aboard, ye son of a bitch!" he bellowed at the next sea, and, turning to us, shouted, "One o' ye sing a song! God damn it, ye're worse'n dead men!"

"Wish to Christ we was dead!" one of them growled. "It'd be warm and dry there!"

Then someone began to sing "Shenandoah"; and in spite of the sleep that had been lost, the cold and the misery, the Sailors' Chorus almost drowned the Wind and String Symphony aloft.

In the middle of a verse another sea scattered us, and again we picked ourselves up and collected on the capstan bars. The Mate had dodged that one.

"Walk her round, bullies!" he shouted with a grin. "God damn it, salt water won't hurt ye!"

"Jees! That was a big ——!" remarked the soloist; and after spitting out a mouthful of that harmless fluid he burst into song once more.

Finally there was a roar from the Mate: "High 'nough! Belay-ay-ay!"

We lost more sleep and were washed round the deck a few more times as we got sail on her. By midnight we were under three topgallantsails, foresail and mainsail, shouldering our way through the heavy seas as we made a bit of westing with the southerly wind. It did not last, however, and within thirty hours the wind was back in the north-west and we were again hove-to under three lower topsails.

That spell of "Bad Weather" lasted about a fortnight —a series of north-west gales, veering to the south-west for a while and then backing and beginning anew. There was no chance to dry any clothes, and each gale meant a finger-canvas battle similar to the one I have described.

There was one very bad night, when we were hove-to under *one* lower topsail and had to "goose-wing" that. It incurred a long, hard fight in the darkness and rain.

One half of the sail had to be lashed securely to the yard, leaving only the other half of it set.

At daybreak the seas were literally mountainous. Standing on the poop, one watched them rolling towards the ship at an angle of about 60° from right ahead. As each one neared her the bow sank and she rolled right over and away from it, stabbing it with her bowsprit. The crest could be seen over the foreyard, and sheets of almost solid water that were whipped from it swept over us. The bow began to rise. It was lifted higher and higher until by what sometimes seemed a miracle she reached the summit. As it passed underneath her and roared along level with the bulwarks she rolled the other way and we looked down into a valley of broken water, 50 or 60 feet deep. She almost tumbled into it. Her bowsprit rammed the next one with a crash that made her shudder from stem to stern. Sometimes the crests curled over, and as she rolled through them they fell on the deck with a sickening scrunch, completely filling it.

During those long periods of bad weather one discovered some of the ills to which human windjammer flesh is heir. Sores on knuckles where the skin had been chafed by the canvas would not heal, and remained open until we got north into warmer weather when the hands were not continually wet with salt water. That applied to any cut or sore. Worst of all, though, were "sea-cuts." A "chap" developed in the hard callus of the hands, and was daily enlarged by the pulling on ropes. As they grew larger they became painful, and eventually agonising. During that fortnight one man had them on both hands. On one of them the flesh of the palm opened to the bone and he had to be put off duty.

Fresh water was so scarce that there was never enough to soak the salt out of the skin. A part of our allowance had to be given to the cook for tea, coffee, etc., and as there remained only one quart per day per man for washing and drinking, we five boys each put a little of that into one bucket and all washed in it. At breakfast and supper we saved a little coffee or tea and rinsed our hands in it.

Although at the end of that fortnight we had been driven down to approximately 60° south and were still in about the same longitude as the Horn, that passage would not be considered a particularly bad one. During the winter months, when colder weather and ice up aloft made conditions much worse, ships were sometimes six weeks beating round " Cape Stiff."

Our luck changed there and a fair wind took us up into the Trades, where we could scrub the salt out of our skins and dry our bedding and clothes.

I will now take up the letter again and let it finish the story. Nothing of interest occurred before we crossed the Line, and it picks up the thread there:

" After that we had calms and head winds again. One good thing, we almost live on fish and turtle. This part of the sea simply swarms with fish of every kind, from a whale to a rotifera.

" We caught the first turtle on the 3rd of April, and passed Cocos Island* on the 5th. On the 15th we ran into a tremendous school of fish of all sorts: porpoises, albacore, bonito, dolphin, and turtle. They were jumping out of the water on all sides as far as we could see, and we caught all we could eat. We also got some turtle which we kept alive until we were hard up for fresh food. One of them had eighty eggs in her. They are exactly like ping-pong balls, perfectly round and white, but

* An island between Panama and the Galapagos Islands : not, of course, the better-known Cocos Keeling Island in the Indian Ocean.

with a shell like parchment instead of being hard like a hen's.

"One night I was at the wheel from midnight until 2 a.m. and saw a large fish swimming round the stern. The shark hook is always hanging handy over the rail, so I dropped it into the water and went back to the wheel. In about two minutes something was jerking at the line. I tried to pull it in but could not, so called the Mate. He got some men aft and they hauled up a shark, six feet two inches long. Of course the Mate growled at me for leaving the wheel, but I had the shark (the first one caught this voyage) so did not care. I cut its backbone out next day and am making a walking stick of it to bring home. The following day the men caught another, eleven feet long. It was an ugly-looking brute.

"On the 26th we were becalmed and several turtle were in sight. The Old Man told the Mate to put the gig out and catch some. We swung it out and the Second Mate, five men and myself jumped in and away we went. We caught thirteen and had some good sport. They averaged seventy pounds in weight. We rowed quietly up to them and threw a 'grain' into them. Then we dragged them into the boat. A grain is a thing like a fork, only larger and with more prongs that have barbed ends.

"Most of the turtles have boobies resting on their shells. The booby is a fairly large bird with a long bill. It is either very stupid or very fearless, for when we stopped rowing they came and perched on the oars. One flew bang against my head and cannoned off into the bottom of the boat. They won't get out of the way; the man who had the grain held it up in the way of one, and it flew right on to it and was impaled.

"The turtles are vicious beggars when you get them in the boat. They bite, and kick with their flippers, which have a sharp claw on one side that would give one a nasty cut. We put the head of a dead booby in one's mouth, and it cracked it as easy as winkin'. They are not very good eating—too musky.

"Lately another apprentice and myself have been fishing in our watch on deck for the Skipper's tea and breakfast. We caught four dozen one morning. You bet we take a commission out of it for our own tea.

"On May 5th we caught a turtle that had nearly one hundred eggs in her. We saw a large sword-fish swimming round the stern and chasing the other fish. Two of the men had a fight to relieve the monotony.

"We sighted land on the 15th, and were looking up and down the coast for a fixed light until the 17th. Then a steamboat told us the course. We found that the fixed light had been changed to a flashlight since we left home. There were growls loud and long from the Old Man. We arrived [at Acapulco] at 3 p.m. on the 17th."

CHAPTER VI

THE "WEST COAST"

" Heh ! Walk her round. Break, ah break it out o' that !
Break our starboard bower out, apeak, awash, and clear !
Port—port she casts, with the harbour mud beneath her foot,
And that's the last o' bottom we shall see this year ! "

KIPLING : *Anchor Song.*

OF all the ports visited by a sailing-ship on her " errands over the Great Waters," those situated on the West Coast, as the coast of Chile and Peru was usually called, are probably some of the best-remembered and least-liked. This is due both to the weeks of hard work and monotony connected with them and to the lack of recreation. Being, too, quite unlike seaports with docks and sheltered anchorages such as you who live in England are accustomed to, a description of the life and routine on board during the ship's stay may be interesting.

I will not attempt to describe any of them. My youthful impressions of Antofagasta and Caleta Buena are recorded in Chapter VIII, and I have nothing to add to, or subtract from, them, unless it be to say that, as rain is unknown there, more dreary or depressing places than those little nitrate villages, some of them possessing only one dusty street, can hardly be imagined.

From the point of view of the seaman who wants a sheltered anchorage for his ship, the prospects afloat were no more pleasing. There was no harbour. A ship sailed in to within about a mile from the coast and let go her anchors. Then others were brought off from the shore in a barge, and her stern was moored in such a position that she laid head-on to the swell that rolled in from the Pacific Ocean all the time. There she remained for weeks and

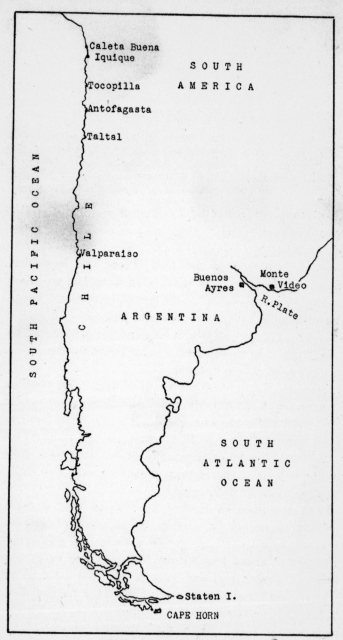

MAP 2.—SOUTH AMERICA.

months—we were sixteen weeks in Taltal—while the crew discharged the cargo they had brought and loaded another of saltpetre.

An eight-hour day was no more dreamed of in our simple windjammer philosophy than a Short-Wave Set or a Flying Flea. We worked from 6 a.m. to 6 p.m., with forty-five minutes for breakfast and one hour for dinner. During those weeks and months we were allowed one day ashore on liberty, though beyond getting drunk on the native "stagger juice" and being locked up in the local gaol there was nothing to do when we were there.

For the first day or two after arriving in one of those ports the crew was employed in mooring the ship, and in unbending, or sending down from aloft, the sails.

Then work was begun on the cargo. Lighters, capable of carrying from 50 to 100 tons, were rowed alongside by the "lancheros." We carried about $1\frac{1}{2}$ million feet of timber. It ranged from small pieces, 2 inches square and 12 feet long, to heavy baulks, 12 inches square and 40 feet long. All these had to be passed down over the side by hand, one by one. A dolly, or hand, winch was rigged on deck. With it, four men hove up from the hold the heavier logs.

Meanwhile the apprentices were "week and week about," half of them working on the ship, and the remainder doing the boat-work. The latter had to be ashore each morning at half-past five to bring off a tally clerk in readiness to start work with the men at 6 a.m. After breakfast they rowed the Captain ashore and landed him on a small jetty. In Caleta Buena, on account of the swell that continually rolled in, he had to swing himself on to it by means of a rope, hanging from a beam overhead. Having but one hand, this was no easy job either for him or for the apprentice in the stern-sheets who had to assist him.

While he was there they laid off at a safe distance to wait for him, and "swopped lies" with boats' crews from other ships. On days when the swell was not too bad two or three boys looked after all the boats and the remainder landed on the jetty. That usually resulted in a fight with the native loafers, who called them "gringos" and whom they chased off the pier and up the one and only street.

Sometimes there was a very heavy swell, what was known locally as "surf day," and then the boat-work was not only difficult, but at times dangerous. Here is a description of one such day, taken from a letter written in Antofagasta in May, 1904:

"Saturday was what is known here as 'surf day.' There was a tremendous surf and we had a narrow escape. We rowed the Skipper ashore safely, but on the way back, while another fellow and I were pulling and the steward was coxing, we saw a tremendous breaker coming in. It was at least fifteen or sixteen feet high, and our gig is only about two feet above the water. We could not get out of the way, of course, so put her head on to it. If it had been just a swell, it would have been all right, but the crest was curling over. I tell you, my heart was in my mouth. When we looked ahead all we could see was a wall of water rolling towards us.

"At last it came, and goodness knows how we got over it. We did, though, and were congratulating ourselves when we saw another. There were three, one after another, and they broke behind us with a terrific roar. We could not hear each other speak. What with the noise and the anxiety of getting over them, it was not exactly pleasant.

"We were fairly close to the shore and the people shouted like billy-ho. They thought we were goners. If we had been twenty yards later and it had broken on us, it would have smashed us to pieces. I tell you, I was thankful to get on board.

"But we had to go ashore again, to fetch our Skipper and the Skipper of another ship. When he is not in the boat the senior apprentice coxes and is in charge. He has only been to sea a year longer than we have and we did not like trusting ourselves to him. We asked the Mate to let somebody with experience steer the boat. At first he did not want to. We told him that if he did not, we would not go, so he let the steward come with us again.

"We did not meet such big seas as before, but once or twice we had to turn round and head them when an extra whopper came along. When the Skipper came on board the Mate told him that we would not go in the boat without someone who understood handling a boat in the surf. He said: 'Don't blame them. It was as much as four hands could do to bring her off, and there were only two then.'

"I tell you, I was glad to get on board for the night. It was a near go."

The work of passing over the side 1½ million feet of timber lasted from six to eight weeks. When it was all out about 400 tons of sand ballast, which was carried underneath it to "stiffen" the ship, had to be discharged. Men in the hold shovelled it into baskets, and others on deck hove them up with the dolly winch.

Both in Cardiff and Acapulco the cargoes of coal, about 3,000 tons, were handled in this manner. The apprentices' job, whether discharging sand or coal, was down in the hold. They caught the empty basket as it was lowered and swung it out to the side. Then they hooked on the full one and steadied it into the square of the hatch to prevent it from upsetting.

In a climate like that of Acapulco, twelve hours a day of such work for weeks at a time in the stifling heat and coal-dust down below was very hard and caused a lot of sickness. I had a touch of dysentery, due partly, in all probability, to eating too many pineapples. It started on a Friday, however, and as I was going ashore the following Sunday on liberty, I did not "go sick." By that time I had learned that if I were too sick to work, I was too sick to go ashore.

When all the ballast was over the side the ship was empty and the men were usually given a liberty day. The apprentices who were doing the boat work at the time had to row them ashore. At half-past five the following morning they brought them back.

Whether or no the experience of getting a crowd of drunken men from a rickety jetty into a small gig and ferrying them safely on board in a heavy swell trained a boy to be an officer, it certainly taught him how to handle a boat under difficult conditions.

While the apprentices were also allowed a day on shore, their favourite break in the monotony was to give a "send-off" to a homeward-bound ship. Several captains went on board her, taking with them the apprentices and two or three of their men who helped that crew break out their anchor and set sail.

On one occasion a homeward-bounder, down to her "marks" with a cargo of saltpetre, was about to sail, and we, as well as apprentices and men from other ships, had rowed our Captain on board.

While the skippers hobnobbed in the cabin over a fare-well drink and cigars, and laid bets on the quickest run home to the Channel, the twenty or more apprentices crammed themselves into the half-deck. There they perched on the edges of bunks, on sea-chests, table, and doorstep, like swallows collecting on telegraph wires prior to their migration southward, raising a thick "fug" with their evil-smelling native cigarettes and lying unblushingly about the sailing qualities of their respective ships.

Much the same thing was going on forward, where all the men were crowded into one fo'c'sle, smoking plug tobacco and giving a home to the contents of a few bottles of the local fire-water, "pisco," that they had saved from their liberty day for the occasion.

When the captains came up the companion-way to the poop there was a shout: "Man the capstan!"

That was a signal for the half-deck and fo'c'sle to disgorge their respective swarms. These made a bee-line forward and clustered on the capstan bars.

"Start the wagon!" shouted the Mate of the ship; and we commenced to "walk her round."

To an accompaniment of a clanking of the pawls, one of the men began to sing a homeward-bound chantey; and the words of the chorus, sung by about thirty men and heard all over the anchorage, informed the other vessels and the people ashore that the ship was bound down to "Mother Carey" and up again on the other side of the American continent to the paying-off office and home:

> " Rolling Home,—rolling Home,
> Rolling Home across the sea.
> Rolling Home to good old England;
> Rolling Home, dear land, to thee."

By the time the anchor was awash and we had helped them sheet home we had been carried some miles to sea. There was a shout to get the boats alongside, and we scrambled down the side-ladder into them. After shoving off clear and giving them three cheers the order " Give way!" started a race back. We were heavily handicapped in this by the huge size of our coxswain, the Old Man, who encouraged us between puffs of his cigar with such remarks as: "Put your backs into it! D'you want the *Nonesuch* to pull across your bow?"

A day or two after the last basket of sand ballast was tipped overboard lighters full of saltpetre were rowed alongside. We carried about 3,000 tons. It was in sacks, and the crew hove up one of them at a time with the dolly winch. That exercised the muscles of the arms and back for a further six or eight weeks.

Finally, the last one was hooked on in the lighter and a man with an ensign sat on it. The rope was taken off the winch, and when all hands had "tailed on to it" both man and sack were chanteyed up "two blocks." While they were being lowered down to the words and tune of "Whisky Johnny" the steward arrived with bottles and a tot was served out to all hands.

There was usually a jamboree in the fo'c'sle the same evening. The ship was loaded and ready to sail from the West Coast, and the men celebrated the event by having a glorious drunk with the "pisco" they had treasured up since their liberty day.

Although we were not homeward bound, the following letter gives an example of that. It also tells of the passage of seventy-six days from Caleta Buena round Cape Horn to Cape Town.

That was my worst trip during the five years I served on the *Aristomene*. In many of the ports we eked out our pocket-money by exchanging shirts and other clothing for curios and fruit. I had done so much of this payment-in-kind business (changy for changy, we called it) that when we left Caleta Buena my sea-chest contained more curios than clothes. We were off the Horn in the middle of winter, and bad weather drove us a long way south. By that time I only possessed two shirts, neither of them fit to wear. For some time I was half-frozen, having nothing but a vest under my coat and oilskins. Then I managed to sew one shirt inside the other, so that the holes in one were covered by the pieces of the other. That remained intact until we arrived in Cape Town, where I received a parcel of clothes and money from home.

"The last night we were in Caleta Buena there were high jinks on board. That was the day we finished loading and the Skipper gave the men four bottles of grog. Besides this they had a lot they had saved from their liberty day, and about 7 p.m. most of them were drunk.

"The carpenter and one of the men, who are very quarrelsome when in drink, started fighting, and by-and-by there was an awful row forward. The carpenter had got an axe and a cold chisel from his shop, and had chased most of them on to the top of the midship house. The boatswain, who was also three sheets in the wind, waited for him round the corner with an iron belaying-pin, and, when he passed, struck him on the eye and stunned him.

"Next morning he was an awful sight. His face was smarmed with blood, and both his eyes were closed. One was stuck with blood, and the other is gone altogether. He was almost bent double from the effects of the drink and the wound.

"On July 7th we unmoored ship and were towed out. Several of the men were drunk all day. We sighted a four-masted barque on the 16th and for six days we were in sight of her. She was the *Marion Fraser* of Glasgow, bound from Tocapilla to Hamburg with saltpetre.

"We had a strong breeze on the 26th, and that night it increased to a gale. For three days we were hove-to under three lower topsails. There was a very heavy sea running and a lot of water came on board. We had about six inches of it washing about in the half-deck all the time. Our door won't shut nearer to the door post than an inch.

Every two hours we bailed out twelve or fourteen big buckets of water. We have no fire, so it *is* nice having to turn out of a warm bunk into the cold air and put on wet clothes, oilskins, and sea-boots. Then as soon as you go on deck you may have to pull on the braces and a few seas wash over you, while the temperature is below freezing, it is snowing, and you have to wait four hours before you can go below to get warm again.

" This is usually the case in bad weather, and as we were driven by head winds down to between 58 and 59 degrees south, it was very cold, being winter.

" This is what is commonly called the romance of the sea life. Some of the poets, or whatever kind of people talk like that, ought to try it and then see what they would say about it. Should not I make a fine old growler? But I am wandering. As Dan Leno says: ' Whither am I whithering? Wherefore am I why?'

" Still, I am not complaining. If it were always fine weather and no excitement, it would soon be monotonous. *I have not repented coming to sea yet.*

" 29th, wind decreased, so we set sail again. From then until the 5th of September we did nothing much except make sennit. We were getting down south and the weather was becoming cold. It was a dead calm on August 12th, and we had a very heavy snowstorm. On the 20th we had some more bad weather and were hove-to under three lower topsails for two days. It was bitterly cold. We were then off the Horn, or, rather, a long way south of it. It was a south-east gale and snow! Ugh! I shiver to think of it.

" At last, on the 22nd, we could start to head up towards finer weather. From then until the 31st we had a steady south-west breeze and did ten knots all the time.

" We started scrubbing paintwork on the 6th, to smarten her up ready for going into port. From the 6th until the 10th we had dirty weather, but scrubbed every day. The next three days we were painting and cleaning brass-work.

"I am now up to date, as I commenced this letter at sea. We have a fine breeze, and, if it holds, shall arrive in Cape Town tomorrow. I am afraid there is no chance of coming home yet. I must close now until we are 'safe at last, the harbour past,' and at anchor in Table Bay."

As a result of that farewell binge in Caleta Buena, the carpenter lost an eye and was off duty during the whole passage. In Cape Town he was sent to hospital and persuaded to sign the pledge.

Later on, after he had rejoined the ship, we were ashore one evening and saw a crowd standing round two men who were drunk and fighting. We looked over the heads of those in the ringside places just in time to see one of them go down for the count.

It was our one-eyed "Chippy!"

CHAPTER VII

"IRON MEN"

" In them days it was ' Wooden Ships and Iron Men '; now it's
' Iron Ships and Wooden Men.' "

THAT "little Spark of Holy Fire" was handed down to
me and the other apprentices on the *Aristomene* by the
Captain and Mates when they wished to "make our souls
dwell low in the Valley of Humility."

When and where it originated I cannot say. I only
know that it was well matured when I was a young vintage
and that it is still going strong. In fact, during moments
of bad temper, caused by a three-day fog on the Grand
Banks, I have quoted it to my young Wooden Men; and
some years hence in all probability, when Britannia rules
the Four Winds of Heaven as well as the Waves of the
Seven Seas, the captain of an aerial-ocean greyhound will
still be passing it or its aerial equivalent on to his first-
voyagers.

That, however, is meandering, as the old lady said of
the sailor's life, so I will start this chapter again by intro-
ducing one of the " Iron Men," Davy, as he was known
to all of us on the ship.

My first recollection of him is when the crew, most of
them drunk, joined the ship in Cardiff. The other apprentices and myself were watching them come on board, and
listening to the quarrels and curses as they milled round
the gangway with their sea-bags. Suddenly one of them
left the crowd and clambered on to the main hatch. He
was a man of about 35 years of age, of medium height,
stockily and powerfully built, with the fair hair and blue

eyes peculiar to the Scandinavian races. He was dressed in a dirty, nondescript suit of clothes, with no hat, collar, or tie. He proceeded to take off his coat and, in a drunken voice, to broadcast to all and sundry his readiness to fight any unmentionable so-and-so in the I-forget-what-he-called-it ship. One or two cuts and bruises on his face testified that that challenge had been offered and accepted before he came on board.

Such was Davy, as You-Who-Live-Ashore would have seen him in places like Tiger Bay, Cardiff.

At eight o'clock that night, while we were towing down the Bristol Channel, all hands were called aft and, as was the custom at the beginning of a voyage, the Captain made a speech. He informed them that if they behaved themselves, he was a good man to get on with; if they didn't—I forget what he said he was in that case, but to my fifteen-year-old ears it sounded pretty bad.

Then we were divided into watches: the Mate and Second Mate called a name in turn, and that man moved to the port or starboard side accordingly. Davy and I were both picked for the port, or Mate's, watch.

My next contact with him was about 3 a.m. that same night when we were setting sail. To me this consisted of being pushed hither and thither in the dark by a crowd of more or less drunken men, and of a prolonged chorus of shouts, curses, and orders to do various things with a bewildering maze of ropes. One of them was occasionally stretched along the deck, and as I tailed on to the end of it I heard sea-chanteys sung for the first time.

In the middle of this seemingly chaotic pandemonium a huge powerful hand grasped my shoulder and pushed me violently to one side, while a drunken voice shouted: "You Goddam boys better get to hell outa my vay!"

That was Davy, outward bound.

I can remember no more of him until I was making my

first attempt to wash clothes during a Sunday forenoon
watch on deck. I was stooping over a bucket in the lee
scupper, struggling to wash coal-dust out of a shirt, when
a voice behind me said: "Yesoos! That's a helluva vay
to vash close!"

I straightened myself up and looked round, to find
Davy gazing disapprovingly at my laundry work. This
time I saw the man as he was known only to his
shipmates at sea, away from the drink and filth of sailor-
town. He was barefooted, and although he was only
wearing a grey flannel shirt, dungaree trousers, and belt
complete with sheath-knife without which no "Iron Man"
was decorously dressed, they, like himself, were spotlessly
clean. The cuts and bruises had disappeared from his
face, which had obviously been shaved that morning
before taking the eight to ten trick at the wheel from
which he was returning. Being by that time in his right
senses, he had a fresh, clean complexion. He picked a
shirt out of the bucket and examined it.

"Who teach you to vash close, anyvay?" he asked.

"Nobody," I answered. "I've never done it before."

"Looks like it," he said, grinning. "You vash close
like an old varmer: 'First the arms and then the breast,
damn and b——r all the rest!' You never be clean like
that. You bring it forud to the fore hatch in the dog-vatch
und I show you."

"I can manage it all right," I assured him.

"Like hell you can," he assured me. "You put it
avay now und bring it along at two bells."

"Right you are," I said. "Thanks very much."

As I was walking away with the bucket and soap he
asked, "You goin' to leave the deck like that?" adding,
when I looked enquiringly at him and at the deck, which
was wet and soapy, "You get a broom und a bucket of

vater und vash off them soap-suds, else they leave vhite marks on the deck und the Mate raise hell vith you. Vait! I show you! My Gott! Who bring you oop, anyvay?"

I stowed my laundry away while he fetched a broom and a bucket of water. Swilling a little on the deck, he scrubbed it and washed the soap-suds into the scupper.

"That's good," he remarked. "Vat's your name, anyvay?"

I told him. He rolled it round his tongue for a moment, grinned at me and said, "Hell! Guess I call you Micky."

At five o'clock I took the bucket of dirty shirts forward to the fore hatch where he was waiting for me. We both squatted on the edge of it and he placed the bucket on the deck between his feet.

"You don't vant to stand oop ven you vash close," he told me. "You only make your back ache und you can't see vat you doin'."

There was silence for a few moments while he vigorously rubbed a shirt.

"Vhy you go to sea?" he asked presently.

"Because I like it better than staying ashore," I replied. "I don't want to live in one house all my life and never see anything."

"You von't like it long—it's a dog's life—better go to gaol. Say! How long you vear this shirt?"

"I don't know." I thought a moment. "A few days, I expect."

"Few days!" he retorted. "Looks like you vos born in it und never take it off yet."

"That's only the coal-dust in Cardiff," I said.

"If you keeps dirty close like that layin' round the half-deck, you gets bugs ven ve gets into hot veather." Pause. "Say! That a clean shirt you got on today?"

"Yes."

" Vell, you vear it this veek vhile you vorks, and have
a clean vun for the dog-vatches.   Next Sunday you vashes
it und vorks in the other vun and puts on another clean
vun for the dog-vatches."   Pause.   "Boys don't know
nuttin' now-days.   I bet you can't fix a hole in your
socks."

"I bet you couldn't when you first went to sea," I
retorted.

He dropped the shirt into the bucket and for a moment
looked at me almost indignantly.   Then he burst out
laughing and said, "Say, Micky, that ain't no lie.   Some
day I show you how to do it."

"When did you go to sea?" I asked.

"I run avay from home ven I vos tvelve."

"In a British ship?"

"No, in my country ship; but they don't pay much
money und by-n-by I clear out in 'Frisco und ship on
a 'merican ship."

"What are they like?"

"That vun vos a son of a bitch.   The Mate kill a man
vun day.   He knock him down und he split his head on
a bitts und die."

"What happened to the Mate?"

"Oh, nuttin'; but afterwards he disappear vun night."

"How d'you mean, fell overboard?"

"No, yoost disappear vun dark night."

"Well, he must have fallen overboard."

"I'm tellin' you he diden'.   Ve shorten sail vun night,
und ve go aloft to make 'em fast, und ven ve get to the
cross-trees ve hear a voice vot said: 'Don't come no
higher!'   Ve vos scared und come down, but the Mate raise
hell und chase oos oop agen; but ven ve get to the cross-
trees the voice tell oos agen not to come no higher, so ve
all come down und refuse to go oop agen.   Then the Mate

say: 'You Goddam varmers! I show you the vay oop!' und he vent oop und ve never see him no more."

"He must have dropped overboard and nobody saw him go," I persisted.

"I'm sayin' he diden'. He vos a bad man und he kill a sailor, so sump'n vos vaiting for him oop there."

"But nobody can disappear like that. One of the men must have been waiting for him."

"Goddamit, Micky! I vos there. I know. Ve vos all on deck. It vos yoost sump'n oop there 'cos he killed a sailor. I tell you, I seen lots o' things like that. Maybe you be Mate of a ship vun day, so you 'member vot I tells you."

I did not learn until later on that the superstitious belief of the "Iron Men" was one of their "blind spots"; but I realised that he was perfectly serious, so said no more. By then the shirts were washed, and while we were tying them with bits of twine on a rope, stretched across the fore hatch, he said, "Say, Micky, you eat all your sugar? I svop my vhack of marmalade for it."

"Right you are," I replied.

At that moment we heard a shout from the poop: "Lay aft the watch! Square the crojick yards!"

"Goddam vind ain't shifted any," Davy growled, glancing aloft. "These lime-juice Mates is alvays friggin' about vith the yards. You vanta sail vith a 'merican Mate."

We hurriedly tied the last shirt on the line and trotted aft together, in time to freeze on to the weather crossjack brace.

Davy evidently had such a poor opinion of my "bringings oop" that he decided to take me in hand himself. During the whole of that three-year voyage he kept an eye on me, teaching me among other things, as he had promised, how to "fix a hole in my socks."

6

Up aloft he taught me to use "one hand for myself and one for the owner," which, being interpreted, means that when the sail was bellying out and flapping one should hold to the jack-stay* with one hand and drag the canvas up on to the yard with the other. Occasionally, when it was very heavy and stiff, he broke that rule by lending me "his" hand, with some caustic remark such as: "Couldn't pull a sodger off'n your sister!"

On deck in heavy weather, when a sea broke on board and swept us all into the lee scupper, I sometimes felt his hand grab the collar of my oilskin coat and heard him shout: "Goddam, Micky, yoomp oop the fife-rail!"

With his help I did, to find most of the other men also there, holding on to ropes, and jeering and laughing at one or two luckless ones who had not "yoomped" in time, and who, in sitting or lying postures, were washing from one side of the deck to the other as the ship rolled.

In port, however, one discovered his other "blind spot": drink.

After being "adrift" for two days in Yokohama he was eventually brought back by two Japanese policemen, drunk, dirty, his clothes torn, and his upper lip cut and swollen.

The following extract from a letter describes one of his exploits, he being one of the Principal Boys in the Pantomime:

"Yesterday, Sunday, we had quite a pantomime. Two of the men went ashore in the morning, filled up with American Red Top Rye whisky, and came back aboard before dinner, gloriously drunk.

"At dinner time they got their food from the galley, but it was not good enough for them, so they took half

* See small sketch, top right-hand corner of diagram "Yards and Sails," p. 39.

each and marched aft to the cabin, where the Old Man
and the officers were at dinner, one of them shouting:
' Hi, Skipper! Look at this soup!'

"They walked right in, planked it down in front of
him, and began to call him anything but a gentleman.
He, to put it mildly, got slightly annoyed, and, with the
officers, tried to put them out. He happened to hit one
of them on the head with his wooden stump, whereat the
man became wild and threw his coat, waistcoat, and collar
out on deck (it was raining pretty heavily at the time) and
told ' Pa ' and the officers to come out and fight.

"At last they quietened down and went away. A little
while afterwards they came back and wanted some dinner.
The Skipper would give them none, so they poured bless-
ings on his head and departed once more.

"The Skipper then went to get his after-dinner nap.
He was dozing when aft they came again. They walked
right into the cabin, put a bag of peaches and apples in
their pockets, and woke him up to ask for a dollar to go
ashore and buy a dinner. After an argument he gave
them a dollar between them. That wasn't enough, and
they sat down and refused to leave unless he gave them
one each. Eventually, to get rid of them, he gave it.

"Needless to say, today, Monday, they have done no
work. They were ashore all the morning and came back
aboard after dinner, just as drunk. The Skipper was
having forty winks and nobody was around, so they
walked into the cabin, locked him in and took the key
into the fo'c'sle. When ' Pa ' was liberated he 'phoned
for a policeman, and at present they are enjoying Uncle
Sam's hospitality.

"It was really very funny and we had a good laugh."

Then from another letter, written a week later: " Those
two men who made all the trouble last Sunday were tried

on Wednesday. One was fined £7, and the other £6, both to be kept in gaol until the ship sails. Poor beggars!"

Another of his "performances," this time at sea, may be said to take one from the ridiculous to the sublime. In this case he "starred" in a one-act melodrama and was supported by a cast consisting of the apprentice, Mac, and myself.

Mac was afflicted with "moon-blindness": though perfectly normal during the day and at night when there was no moon, his eyes were affected when there was one. At the "full" he was completely blind. In view of the fact that defective eyesight bars one from sitting for one's certificates, he was afraid to tell the Captain and Mates and swore us all to secrecy. Only Davy, who was in the same watch and whom we all liked, was taken into our confidence. He shared with us as far as possible any jobs that fell to Mac during these periods of blindness, and we arranged that one of us should always be near Mac on deck, to prevent him from falling or hurting himself.

During our watch on deck, one night near to the full moon, we had to take in some of the lighter sails in a squall of wind and rain. All the watch was required aloft. Mac therefore had to go up with us. As usual he came with Davy and me. I went first, he followed, and Davy brought up the rear.

Climbing from the lower rigging out over the cross-trees was the most difficult part. When I was over them I guided his hands on to the topmast shrouds, while Davy placed his feet on the ratlines. Arrived at the yard, we saw his hands safely on the jackstay and his feet on the footrope, and then he felt his way out between us. On this occasion it was quite a hard squall. The sail was flapping heavily and, owing to the rain, was stiff. The footrope was wet and slippery.

Davy was master of ceremonies and we took our cue from him.

"Grab it, Mac!" he shouted; and we reached out together, pulled some canvas on to the yard and lay on it.

"Un' agen, Mac!" he continued; and we dragged in another armful.

In this manner we had gathered in about half of it, when suddenly it gave a violent flap and bellied right out again. It nearly knocked me off the yard, though I managed to hold on to most of my share. At the same time I heard Davy's voice.

"Yeesoos Christ!" he shouted.

As I stood there, clinging to the jackstay with one hand and to the flapping canvas with the other, the moon began to shine through the edge of the squall and it became a little lighter. I turned my head to see what the others were doing. I could see Davy faintly, but not Mac. I looked again. There were no signs of him. He had disappeared!

"Davy!" I cried. "Mac's over the side!"

"Keep that Goddam sail qviet!" I heard him shout.

It was still too dark to see anything clearly, but I could not understand that. Mac was overboard, and all Davy thought about was the sail. When the German sailor fell off the mainyard after leaving Port Tampa we shouted "Man overboard" and hurried down on deck. To hell with the sail! He wasn't going to leave Mac like that!

"Man overboard!" I shouted frantically, though, as I discovered later, nobody on deck heard me.

Then, while those thoughts were jostling each other in my mind, and when I was on the point of letting go the sail to shin down on deck, the light improved sufficiently to enable me to see that Davy also was in trouble. He was clinging to the jackstay with both hands, and had only one foot on the footrope. There seemed to be a heavy weight on the other that was dragging him off the yard! As I peered down to see what it was the last bit of cloud drifted clear of the moon which shone directly on the "weight," showing it up distinctly.

I was looking at Mac! When he dropped from the yard he had clutched one of Davy's ankles. He was hanging from it, swinging from one side to the other at the end of the leg like a pendulum as the ship rolled in a long slow quarterly swell!

I understood then why Davy wanted the sail kept quiet: if it flapped, it might knock one or both of them over the side. Never mind what he had taught me: "one hand for myself, one for the owner." They needed both of them. I let go the jackstay and clung desperately to the sail.

For the next few minutes I lived through an eternity in what might be called a world of two dimensions, they being the length and breadth of the canvas that was dragging at my arms and almost lifting me off the wet, slippery footrope. I distinctly remember talking to it, alternately cursing it and begging it to be quiet.

Davy eased one hand off the jackstay to see if the other could support the weight. Evidently he decided it could, for he reached slowly down.

"Lift oop, Mac!" he gasped.

Mac began literally to climb up the leg. The hand descended lower and lower until at last it was level with his neck. The ship rolled, and as the "pendulum" swung across the fingers tried to grasp it. They missed it! Again she rolled, and this time they managed to grip it. Mac gradually clambered and was lifted higher and higher. He got one leg over the footrope. The other followed, and for a moment he sat there, gasping for breath, Davy still holding the collar of his coat. There was one more brief struggle. Then he was standing between us again, breathless but unhurt. Davy wiped the perspiration off his face with the back of his hand.

"Get a Goddam move on you!" he growled, reaching out and gathering in an armful of canvas.

That brought Mac and me back to a normal three-dimensioned world once more. We followed his example, and in a few minutes the sail was rolled up and secured.

We were the last to arrive on deck and there was nothing more to do. Mac, white and shaky, felt his way to the half-deck. I stood there with Davy, wondering if I should say anything, and, if so, what. He solved the problem for me.

"Goddam vind droppin'," he grunted, after a look aloft. "Ve be settin' sail agen yoost now."

With those words the "Iron Man" rolled hurriedly forward to get a smoke while there was time. The incident was closed.

His departure from the ship at the end of the voyage was merely a reversal of his arrival at the beginning. Our homeward-bound passage was to "Queenstown for orders." For a few days we laid there at anchor, and then proceeded to Cork to discharge the cargo of wheat from Wallaroo*; and in Queenstown the Davy as known to his shipmates at sea began to degenerate into the Davy who was seen by You-Who-Live-Ashore.

In those days it was the custom for "runners" to come on board and sell goods to the crew. To encourage sales, many of them gave a drink of whisky for each ten shillings' worth of merchandise bought by the men. The result was, "Iron Men" being what they were, the merchants disposed of their stocks and the men were loaded with drink and a lot of junk that was of no earthly use to them. When we left Queenstown Davy was decidedly

* See sketch-map, p. 97.

"under the influence," and possessed, among other things, two alleged gold watches and chains.

A few hours after the crew was paid off in Cork we saw him in town, very drunk, his waistcoat adorned with his two gold chains, and a lady on each side of him, yardarm to yardarm.

About noon the following day, when we were sitting down to our dinner in the half-deck, he appeared at the door, looking sick, dirty, and unshaven. He gazed round until he saw me.

"Say, Micky," he said. "Gimme a drink!"

He had worked three years for the pay he had received the previous afternoon, and of that and his two gold watches nothing remained!

Before he went ashore, however, he remarked, "Say! I had vun helluva night!"

That was probably his way of saying what the little boy who had stomach ache after eating too much Christmas pudding said: "It's worth it!"

CHAPTER VIII

LETTERS FROM FOREIGN PORTS

(First Voyage. August, 1902, to July, 1905.)
" All work and no play makes Jack a dull boy!"

I AM beginning to wonder whether my "grousing" in previous chapters about the hard work, bad food, and discomforts on sailing-ships has led you to believe that there was no other side to the life. That, of course, was by no means the case. Doubtless my working hours were longer and harder than those of a boy ashore; but on the other hand my opportunities for play far exceeded his. A sailing-ship, going to any part of the world where a cargo could be picked up, enabled me to see something new and intensely interesting in every port I visited.

It can be likened to a seven-league boot by means of which, during the passage from Port Tampa, Florida, to Yokohama, for example, I stepped from an electric tramcar in the United States to a dug-out canoe in the East Indies where I could buy a monkey for a few ship's biscuits, and from there into a rickshaw in Japan—countries as far apart in customs, speech, racial peculiarities and appearance as they were in knots or nautical miles.

The following extracts from letters, written in the places I saw during those five years in sail, will, I hope, enable you to share with me some of the amusement I have had and the things of interest I have seen in a playground upon which, like the British Empire, the sun never sets.

MONTE VIDEO.
(Aged 15 years.)

" Last Sunday for the first time we were allowed ashore. On Saturday afternoon the Captain told the senior apprentice and he told us, so in the evening we were in a fine muddle, getting our clothes ready. Next morning we were up at 5.30 and got the boat out and cleaned her. After breakfast we went to the *Elginshire* for two of her apprentices, and then rowed ashore.

" There are very funny-looking trams. They have a floor, seats, and ceiling, but only posts from the floor to the ceiling, with no windows. They are drawn by three horses, and the driver blows a horn.

" The roads are paved with square stones, and in the best houses the doors open into a sort of courtyard which is filled with palms and ferns. Creepers grow over the walls. There are policemen at nearly every corner and they wear overcoats and swords.

" Near to where we landed is a big fruit market, and most of our money went there: large oranges and bananas, 1od. a dozen; apples, 2d. each; big eggs, 6d. a dozen. Further in the town is a fine cathedral, with two steeples and two bells in each. Opposite this is a kind of recreation ground, called Plaza Independencia, with flowers and surrounded by palms, bamboos, etc.

" Then we saw a big place, called Museo Nacional. We looked inside and saw some stuffed animals, so guessed it was a museum and toddled in. It was not up to much. We had not to pay to go in.

" Next we saw a restaurant, labelled: ' English Café, attendance by waitresses, English spoken.' We went inside and had some lemonade. The attendance was by two very ugly Spanish girls, and nobody understood a word of English.

" Then we came to another recreation ground, called Plaza Libertad. We sat on a seat and a crowd of people came and stared at us. Some shoe-blacks wanted to clean our shoes. Several little kids followed us and asked us for cigarettes, so we bought some and made them scramble. In the middle of the fun a policeman charged into them and they disappeared in a second. Then the bobby laughed at us as though he were quite pleased with himself.

"Going back to the boat a big, fat, double-chinned woman stopped us. Her waist was six feet at a rough guess. She told us she came from Bristol thirty-seven years ago, and said it was hard times at Monte Video. Then she said: ' Now, boys, goin' to stand us a wet?'

"I gave her two cents, and another fellow a threepenny bit. Then we rowed back to the ship."

PORT TAMPA, FLORIDA.
(Aged 16 years.)

"We are laying at a wharf on an island in the bay until we have discharged our sand ballast. There are railway lines on it and we have to shove trucks, carrying a ton of ballast, about 400 yards. The beach is covered with all sorts of shells. They are very pretty and I shall bring some home. There are cactus and woods of palms, and of animals there are turkey-buzzards, a kind of crane, and coons (a sort of fox that lives in hollow trees).

"On Sunday we went ashore with a nigger who took us all over the island, coon hunting. We looked in all the hollow trees, and at last found one. The nigger told me to get up the tree and poke it out. I did so, but a branch gave way and down I came. I climbed up again, though, poked it out and killed it with a whack on the head. The nigger gave me the skin. It is a beauty, thick fur. I shall bring it home. We had a bathe in the afternoon. Mosquitoes are awful here. I have got one, $1\frac{1}{2}$ inches long and 1 inch wide. I have spread out its wings like you do butterflies. I shall bring it home.

"On Friday I caught an inside chill or something. All day I had pains in my inside that nearly doubled me up, but I did not lay up. Next day I had some castor oil and was much better. On Sunday I was quite well.

" There is a canteen at the fort, close to us, but we are not allowed to go there. We should be run in if we were caught. On Saturday night, though, two other apprentices and I went there and brought back some jam, etc. We caught enough fish on Sunday morning for a good tea. It is always a treat to get something fresh to eat."

" At 4.15 a.m. on Sunday the tug came and we were towed up to Port Tampa, but anchored out and went alongside the wharf the next day. There are three Tampas: Port Tampa, where we are; Port Tampa City; and Tampa City. In the evening we went ashore to Port Tampa City station. The fare by train to Tampa City was 35 cents, so we went by electric tram-car for 10 cents and had a feed with the other 25 cents. Bananas are five cents (2½d.) a dozen. We saw several shooting booths, three shots for five cents. I had three, and got one bull; one, half an inch away; and another, an inch and a half away. We got back at 1 a.m. and were tired today, so stopped on board tonight."

" Since my last letter I have done nothing extraordinary. On Saturday night the Skipper gave the men some money. The result was that eight out of fourteen were imprisoned and fined five dollars (just over a pound), two were chased by the police but escaped, and one was stabbed just over the heart, but not dangerously.

" I forgot to say that there are swarms of pelicans here. They fly up to a good height, and then flop down head first into the water.

" The gentlemen of colour who trim the cargo in all the dust get about two and a half dollars a day (about 10s. 6d.). One of them told me that they have to spend

fifty cents (2s.) of that on whisky or gin, as water is
very injurious to them while working in the dust.   They
get very thirsty, so as they can't drink water, it's no
wonder they booze so.   The little kids smoke big pipes,
chew tobacco, and swear like troopers—only more so.

"The fellow who was stabbed is in a bad way.   He
can't use his arm or hand, and is afraid he never will.   I
hope he will, for he is a decent fellow—Irish, comes from
Belfast, very red hair and moustache, and covered with
freckles.   He can't keep away from drink when once he
sees it.   He had none for three weeks, and then he went
ashore, got drunk and was stabbed.

"I got the photo of the family safely, and will send one
of myself in Japanese costume to you from Yokohama."

YOKOHAMA.
(Aged 16 years.)

"The first three days we were in the boat, rowing the
Skipper ashore and waiting there for him all day, so did
no work.   As we have not yet been allowed ashore except
in the boat with the Skipper, I can't tell you much about
Yokohama in this letter.   The town is divided into two
parts: the English part, and Japanese Town as it is
called.

"The Japanese, both men and women, wear long
cotton gowns and sandals.   Some sandals are merely flat
bits of wood, with other pieces underneath, like this:
‾|‾‾‾‾‾|‾ .   It makes them shuffle along instead of walk.
In the streets are long rows of rickshaws.   The men who
pull them wear large, round, straw hats, and each has
his number on it.

"Every day men with boxes of curios, china, silks,
etc., come on board.   I have got an exact model of a rickshaw, and of a sampan with oars, sails, anchor, etc., in
tortoiseshell."

"Last Sunday I went ashore on liberty, and the first thing I did was to jump into a rickshaw. It seems funny to sit in a kind of mail-cart and have a man to pull you along.

"The Japanese town is nothing but small shops of curios and chinaware, etc. It looks just like the pictures you see: people with umbrellas, walking about in long gowns and sandals. The Japanese women can give the English women a lesson in hairdressing. It is done quite differently from the English style. They roll it up as snugly as anything.

"I wish you could see the silk shawls, sashes, etc. They are fine and so cheap. I bought a silk shawl for one yen (about 2s.). The colour is gold, with gold flowers in the corners. There are also good curios such as wooden writing-paper and envelopes. The paper folds up, the envelopes close, and you write on it just like ordinary paper, but it is solid wood. I have got a packet of each to bring home. There are fine writing-desks, tables, etc., but I could not afford much. I have got a tea-set of pure china: 12 cups, plates and saucers, a milk-jug, teapot, and sugar-jug—42 pieces altogether. The cups ring like a bell when you tap them."

"On the 12th we rowed the Skipper ashore. There was a White Star liner, the *Doric*, alongside the wharf, so we went on board to have a look at her. The Third Officer and one of the quartermasters had served their time on the *Aristomene*, so we had a good time. We had our dinner there: beef, bread, pie, and tinned peaches. A slight difference from salt junk and hard tack.

"We saw her sail. There was a crowd of Koreans on board. They are the wildest-looking people I ever saw, worse than the Malays in Java. They had long, black hair, dirty, yellow faces, and any clothes they could get hold of. One of them—I don't know if he was a man or a woman, I could see no difference—had on a woman's dress and a man's jacket.

"We weighed anchor on the 15th, and set sail with a good breeze and a fair wind."

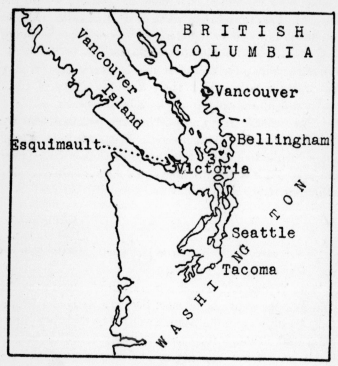

MAP 3.—VANCOUVER, ETC.

ROYAL ROADS, ESQUIMAULT (for orders).
(Aged 16 years.)

"We are anchored two miles from Esquimault, the naval headquarters of the Pacific, and four from Victoria. Esquimault is only a small place and there are only about two streets, namely: Bowling Alley and Skittle Alley. There is a first-class cruiser here, the *Grafton*, and a sloop, the *Shearwater*. A bluejacket showed us all over the sloop. He was captain of a gun, a 4-inch quick-firer, and he showed us how it worked.

"We have a fine time here. There are heaps of salmon in the Sound, and every morning from six to eight we go fishing with the Mate. He does the fishing, we do the rowing! You tie a bright piece of tin on the line close to the hook, tow it over the stern as you row slowly along, and the salmon kindly attach themselves to the hook. We have salmon for breakfast and tea every day. Today we caught a large cod. There are also plenty of crabs and crayfish, and we dig up clams on the beach.

"The scenery is grand. Wherever you look you see high hills, covered with forests. There are houses built snugly at the foot of the hills, and small boats dotted over the bay. As it is autumn now and the leaves are changing colour, it is like a picture."

VALPARAISO.*
(Aged 17 years.)

"I am sorry I did not write last week, but the Skipper was sick, so we could not post.

"On Wednesday one of our company's ships came in. The Skipper went out to meet her, and as it was a long pull, I had to go in the boat as well. She had six apprentices, and although they have not been to sea as long as we have, all but one are second voyagers. They left home a month after we did and have been home and out again, while we have not been home yet. Our Skipper and theirs and the Skipper of the *Elginshire* go aboard each other nearly every night until 11 p.m. or midnight. We have to wait up for them to row them back, and we have concerts with the other apprentices and tell them exaggerations about how our ship can sail.

* See Map 2, p. 58.

"The cruiser *Grafton*, the one we saw in Esquimault, is here, and on Thursday there was a ball on board. We were ashore in the boat, waiting for the Skipper, and saw all the visitors go off. There was a big swell running, and you should have heard the ladies squeak.

"Yesterday a German ship came in with part of her bulwarks smashed and her hold half-full of water."

"On Monday I had a fit of biliousness. I laid up all day and had some pleasant draughts of castor oil and quinine. Next day I was all right.

"On Good Friday we all had a holiday and I had a liberty day ashore. I went with the apprentices from the other ship of our company that is here, and we had a fine time. There is a park with a botanical garden in it, called Victoria Park, and a square, called Plaza Victoria.

"Most of the roads are very bad—big stones and very narrow pavements. Many of the carts are drawn by two horses, and the driver rides one of them instead of sitting in the cart. His stirrups are made of wood, and his feet go right into them like the toe of a boot. When they get off their horses to go anywhere they tie its front legs together so that it can't run away.

"That day there was a tremendous bonfire on the hills. We found out that it was the burning of Judas Iscariot. Something to do with their religion, I suppose. At Easter they have a holiday from Wednesday night to Monday.

"The trams have women conductors. The policemen wear a kind of sea-boot, and have a whistle made of bone which they blow all day, making an awful row. Only a very few houses have chimneys."

"On Wednesday I was in the boat again, as the Skipper went out a long way to a steam boat. The *Elginshire* sailed on Thursday, and as our Skipper went out

7

some distance on her, I had to go as well. We had to race all the way back with the boat of another ship. We beat them, so the Skipper gave us fifty cents to buy some fruit. He is having a tea-party on board today with the captain of the other ship of our company and some people from ashore.

"I don't think there is anything else to say, so good-bye for about a week."

ANTOFAGASTA.*
(Aged 17 years.)

"Of all the God-forsaken, miserable, filthy holes that a human being could think of, this is it. It is not a harbour at all, just a village on the shore, exposed to the whole of the Pacific Ocean. All the time there is a heavy swell rolling in, and as we have to row the Skipper ashore every day, it is not very nice.

"The town stretches for about two miles along the shore and half a mile inland. Behind it is a range of mountains, about 3,000 feet high, so close that the ends of the streets go up it. Rain is never known on this coast, so there are inches of dust on the roads, and everything is filthy. The houses are one-storied, and they and the shops are just as dirty. Dust is thick on the floors, as though they have never been swept. Everything—streets, houses, etc.—smells terribly. Fruit and other things are very dear and very dirty. If we come home from here, we shall be in quarantine, as there is bubonic plague. I am going up the mountain if I get liberty.

"There are one or two trams. Take an ordinary English tram, cut it lengthwise down the middle, chop each half into three pieces, and stick four wheels on each piece. Put three mules in front, side by side, add a driver and a woman conductor, and you have an Antofagasta tram."

* See Map 2, p. 58.

"At last I am able to write another letter. On May 2nd the Skipper fell down the hold on to the cargo and was pretty badly hurt. Blood was coming from his mouth and ears. A boat was immediately sent for a doctor to a Chilean man-o'-war that is lying here. Two doctors and a midshipman came, but there was nothing serious. He hurt his left arm and shoulder, and until a few days ago did not go ashore, so no letters were posted.

"On Saturday there were schools of mackerel round the ship, and we caught about three hundred. That is fine sport, better than Royal Roads salmon fishing. We sent a lot over to another ship, who had not been able to catch any. She was not far from us, but no mackerel were near her.

"Ashore we have seen a lot of dead swordfish that the fishermen have caught. They are about fourteen feet long from tip of sword to tip of tail. The sword is about five feet long. There are also sea-lions here, with heads like dogs.

"We have caught several squids, or devil fish. They are awful-looking things. The body is about two feet long, and it has a fan-shaped tail. The head fits into two bones, like shoulders. If you pull the head and body fairly hard, they come apart. The back of their head is something like a rabbit's when skinned. Extending from the front of it are ten arms, about a foot long and covered with suckers. If you separate the arms you can see the mouth. It is the same as a human being's when pursed. Is that the right expression? I mean, when it is screwed up round. Inside the mouth is a kind of tooth, like a parrot's beak. They swim at a terrific rate, either forwards or backwards. When they catch hold of anything the arms spread out, cling to it with the suckers, and draw it in.

"Our boatswain put his hand in the water one day

when he was in the boat, and a squid caught his arm. He had quite a job to get it clear. We bathed when we first came here, but since there are sharks as well as the squids, we have stopped it. There are pelicans here also.

"On the 9th we tarred decks. That is a grand job. Get a tin full of coal-tar and a bit of rag. Then go on your knees and tar the whole deck.

"Some time ago one of our owners died, and on the 10th I painted a blue line round the ship. That is a sign of mourning. When the crew of the other ship of our company that is here heard about it they solemnly shovelled some coal overboard. I suppose it was to give him as warm a time as possible down below, as he feeds us pretty poorly.

"I think I must belay now, as the midnight hour is not far away and I have to be out at 5.30 a.m."

CALETA BUENA.*
(Aged 17 years.)

"We left Antofagasta on Wednesday night and had a hard night. We worked as usual all day from 5.30 a.m. until 6 p.m., and started to heave up the anchor about 8 p.m. The tug came at 9 o'clock. She was brand new —we were the first ship she had ever towed. She managed to tow us out a little way, and then broke down. For a long time we drifted about until she was repaired. We were setting sail from 3.30 a.m. until 4.45 a.m., and then the other watch went below. My watch was on deck until 8 o'clock, so for twenty-seven hours we had no rest or sleep.

"This is an awful hole. I thought Antofagasta was pretty bad, but this is the last place God made and He forgot to finish it. The same range of mountains, 3,000 feet high, comes right down to the water's edge, except

* See Map 2, p. 58.

that just here there is a space of about fifty yards in width on which is one short, narrow street and a few houses. That is the town of Caleta Buena.

"A cable car, which brings the saltpetre down to the ships, runs up the side of the mountain. The full car, as it comes down, pulls the empty one up. To get ashore, you row alongside a little pier and swing yourself on to it from the boat with a rope.

"We shall have finished loading by about the end of June, and shall arrive home about the middle of October. I am beginning to count the days now.

"Last Sunday we had liberty, and started to go up the mountain. We climbed up about a third of the way to where there is a cemetery, and then rested and went no higher. The cemetery is a curious place. The tombstones are only wooden crosses, and as the ground is sand and rock, it has a most malodorous effluvium. There were a lot of beer and wine bottles lying about, and bits of candles on the graves.

"On Monday there was an earthquake close to this place, and about dinner-time we had a terrific hurricane of hot wind and sand. The sand was so thick that you could not see fifty yards. We and all the other ships here dragged our moorings, and next day had to be moored again. Some houses and most of the railings round the cemetery were blown down. In Iquique, eighteen miles from here, it was worse. Eleven ships either dragged their moorings or broke adrift altogether."

"We are now loaded and ready to sail, so this will be my last letter from here. All hope of coming home is gone. The Skipper has given us the Cape Town address. It will be a year or more before we get home. It is hard luck!"

CAPE TOWN.
(Aged 17 years.)

"Last Monday we knocked off at 3 p.m. to go to a review of all the volunteers, and saw Princess Christian give the Colours to each regiment. There were Cape Highlanders in kilts, Horse Artillery, Kaffrarian Rifles, Cape Mounted Rifles, Engineers, and several more.

"On Wednesday the Princess sailed for England on the *Kildonan Castle*, which was lying close to us. About 4.30 p.m. a regiment of Cape Highlanders marched by. They were to guard the gangway. At 5 o'clock the Princess drove past with an escort of Lancers and Cape Mounted Police. All the ships were decorated.

"The other day the Skipper bought a second-hand gramophone for £4 10s. The owner said it cost £16 16s., but I greatly fear that that was a falsehood. Every evening, and at the present moment, there are sundry weepings and wailings and gnashings of teeth, and other discordant caterwaulings, floating from the cabin in melodious discords."

"At last we have left the dock, and shall lay outside for about a fortnight, waiting for stores from home. Yesterday a Yankee whaler came in, so we asked the Skipper if we could have the boat to go aboard the 'spouter.' He said 'yes,' so away we went. It was worth seeing, and I wish you could all have been there. It was just as Bullen describes it in the 'Cruise of the Cachalot.' She was the *Josephine*, of New Bedford.

"Right forward is the windlass for heaving up the anchor, and, when whaling, for hoisting the blubber on board. Close to that is the fo'c'sle scuttle, leading down to the crew's quarters in the 'tween deck. Ordinary merchant vessels such as the *Aristomene* have a house built on deck for the crew, so that it is well lighted and

aired.   We are 1,662 tons register, and only carry fifteen
men.   She was only 384 tons, and carried twenty black
and five white men.   As they had hardly any ventilation
down there and it was dark and dirty, you can imagine
what sort of a place it was for twenty-five men to live in.

"At the topmast head on the foremast is a crow's-nest
where there are men on the look-out day and night.
Right abaft the foremast is a platform with boats on each
side.   One of the boat-steerers—the man who throws the
first harpoon—showed us all the gear in the boat, the
harpoons, lances, etc.

"A harpoon is just an iron rod about three feet long, one
end of it being fixed to a wooden handle.   At the other
end of it is a piece of steel, shaped like this:
The curved edge is as sharp as a razor, and it is secured
to the iron rod at the dot, so that it can be swivelled to
and fro.   Before the harpoon is thrown into a whale that
piece of steel is placed in this position on the iron rod,
being held there by a small peg, marked A.

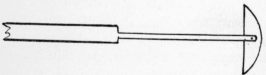

When it strikes the whale it cuts right through the skin
and flesh, and as the whale swims away and jerks on it
the peg is broken and the piece of steel opens out, so that
it cannot be withdrawn, like this:

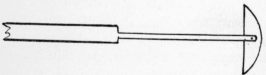

"That sort of harpoon is used for small whales.   For
big ones, they have a harpoon like that, but with a tube,
resembling a rifle barrel, fastened to the iron rod.   In the
tube is a powerful cartridge, and at the side of it is a

thin rod. When the harpoon enters the whale this thin
rod strikes the skin and is shoved back, releasing a spring
that fires the cartridge into the whale.

"There is another gun, I believe, which is fired like
an ordinary rifle, but we did not see it. The lances are
used for killing the whale, and are thrust into it time after
time when the boat hauls up alongside it.

"At first the officer in charge of the boat steers, and the
boat-steerer throws the harpoon. Then they change
places, and the officer lances the whale while the boat-
steerer steers. There are two tubs of rope, one end of
it being bent on to the harpoon. The rope leads through
the bow of the boat. One man takes a turn with it round
a logger-head aft, while another stands by to cut it if
necessary. They told us that they had to throw water
on the rope because it smoked with the heat as the whale
dragged it out of the boat. Bullen says you don't, so
they may have been stuffing us.

"Abaft that boat platform is a hatch with a strong
fishy smell. We went down. The steam donkey is there,
and the barrels of oil.

"Amidships was the try-works where they boil the
blubber. This is a place built on deck of bricks so that
a fire can be lighted inside.

"A little further aft is where they heave the blubber
on board. Over the side is a platform which is lowered
down level with the whale. An officer stands there with
an instrument shaped like a shovel, but very sharp. He
cuts the blubber diagonally, while tackles heave on it and
turn the whale over and over—just like you peel an
orange, all in one piece.

"Right aft at the stern was a kind of house with both
ends out. Under this was the wheel, and, on one side,
the hospital and galley. There were stairs on the other
side leading down to the cabin. We went down a few

steps and came to a sitting-room with easy chairs. That
opens into the dining-saloon.   On one side of it is the

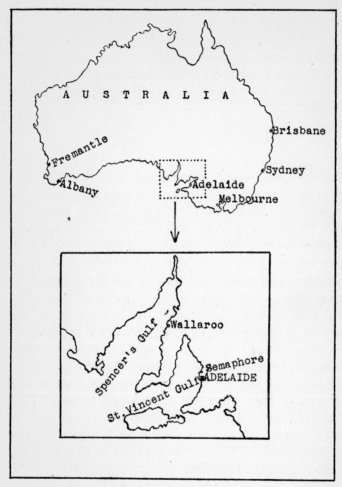

MAP. 4.—AUSTRALIAN PORTS.

Skipper's room, and on the other the officers'. On the
forward end of it are the boat-steerer's and cooper's
rooms.

"The mate was a huge nigger, nearer seven feet tall than six, and broad in proportion. He looked a hard case. He asked us to have a glass of wine, so we said we would. He poured us out nearly a tumblerful, and I took a good drink. It was pure Jamaica rum and nearly suffocated me. He only laughed.

"In case I can't write again from here, Merry Christmas to you all. This year I shall be home in time for tennis."

WALLAROO, SOUTH AUSTRALIA.
(Aged 18 years.)

"We spent Saturday cleaning up the ship for the New Year and the annual Regatta. Our ship is to be the flag-ship. The judges, refreshment stalls, and a brass band will be here, and people will have to pay a shilling to come on board. We pay nothing, of course. Four of the men are pulling in a special race for ships' gigs. I hope we win. Last year it was won by one of our company's ships.

"Sunday was a lovely day, but in the evening there was some thunder and lightning, which did not look well for Monday's regatta. Monday morning it rained like old boots—only worse. Still, we hoped against hope. The people began to come down, and soon the deck was full of them. They were wet through and looked a sight. One lady was wearing a white dress and a straw hat with red flowers. The dye came out of the flowers and ran all down her back. The half-deck was filled with people we know, trying to keep dry.

"At 1.30 p.m. our boat race came off, and then there was some excitement. Unfortunately our boatswain, who was coxing, had been drinking not wisely but too well of the cup that cheers and—er—does something else, but it is a long word and I can't remember it.

" For one-third of the way our boat led by two lengths. Then, as it was rounding a buoy, the boatswain apparently saw several buoys, and another boat came level with it. It got away again, though, but rounding the last buoy, the same thing happened and we lost by one length. Still, we had the worst boat and a coxswain three sheets in the wind, so we didn't do so badly.

" Just as we were getting tea we heard a commotion on deck and came out to see what it was. Some men were bringing an unconscious man on board. He was drunk and had fallen overboard from the wharf. They picked him up just in time. They laid him on the after hatch, rubbed him, and poured a drop of whisky down his throat. Presently he began to groan, and by-and-by muttered: 'Oh, God! Come home, Jack. I've never been beaten before, but I'm beaten this time.'

" As soon as he came round two men carried him to the police station. That was the first New Year's Day it has rained for sixteen years. Hard luck!

" Yesterday, Sunday, as it was our only chance, we all had our photos taken. They won't be ready for this mail. After that we hired bicycles from 11 a.m. until 6 p.m. for 1s. 6d. We first of all rode to Kadena, a town six miles inland. We stopped there and had some lemon squashes. Then we continued on to Moonta, twelve miles down the coast from Wallaroo. More squashes, and back to Wallaroo, about 28 or 30 miles altogether.

" Kadena is a pretty little town, hardly as big as Wallaroo, with a nice park and better buildings. Moonta is a good-sized place and very pretty.

" I must say good-bye now. We are going to Queenstown for orders, so shall be home at last."

CHAPTER IX

AND SO HOME

" As homeward she turns her questing bowsprit toward the sea."

" At last we have arrived in the Old Country once more, but with rather a wet welcome. We passed the Fastnet Rock on Sunday morning, Mizen Head at noon, and Old Head of Kinsale at midnight. A pilot came off at 9 p.m., and at 3.30 a.m. on Monday we passed Daunt's Rock, outside the entrance to Cork Harbour. A fair wind took us right up to Queenstown and we dropped anchor at 5.45 a.m.

"I think the Irish element is entering into me, as I am beginning at the end of the passage. We left Wallaroo on the 31st of January, expecting to be here by the end of May at the latest; but we have had bad luck all the way, light winds and head winds. We were 56 days to the Horn, 96 to the Line, and 139 to Queenstown. The average is about 100 or 110 days.

"We had the usual bad weather round the Horn, the worst being seven consecutive days of swimming and washing round the deck. We had one very bad night, after we had been running before a hard gale for four days. Of course, there was a very big sea running, and once, when the ship would not answer her helm, she broached to. While she was broadside on to it the seas swept right across the deck. As we had to go down there and brace the foreyards to get her before the wind again, they were tumbling us about good-oh. It was pitch-dark and bitterly cold, and we were washing from one side of the deck to the other, wondering if we were over the side or not, occasionally banging our heads and other tender parts of our anatomy against hatches, etc. which reminded us that we were still on board.

"Ugh! Who would sell a farm and go to sea? Still, it's all in the day's work and relieves the monotony a little.

"Before we got to the Horn we caught three albatrosses, ten or eleven feet from tip to tip. To catch them you get a piece of tin or copper, triangular in shape and with the middle cut out. Make a fishing line fast to one apex, and tie a piece of 'salt horse' to the hypotenuse. It pecks at the meat, its curved bill hooks in the triangle, and you haul away and pull it on board. When on deck they cannot fly away and can hardly walk. After a little while they are seasick!

"This time we had a fair wind and sighted the Horn. It is only a barren rock. We seemed to be really homeward bound when once round that corner. We had very light winds until we got the south-east trades which took us to five degrees north of the Line. Then we had two days of doldrums: dead calm, torrents of rain, and broiling heat. After that the north-east trades took us past thirty degrees north.

"In the south-east and north-east trade winds there is a lot of work to be done when homeward bound. All masts and yards have to be painted, the rigging is tarred, everything down below where there is no cargo is painted, all habitations are scrubbed and painted, bulwarks, etc., are scrubbed and painted, teakwood is scrubbed and varnished, decks are holystoned, and then the poop deck is oiled, and the main deck tarred.

"After we lost the north-east trades our real bad luck commenced, no wind at all, and even that was dead ahead. At last we crawled to the latitude of the Azores. There the ship felt tired and wanted a rest, I suppose, for we had a few more days calm.   One day we were in sight of seven other vessels, all becalmed like we were.

"By degrees we got to within 150 or 200 miles from here, and then easterly winds set in.   They wholly and entirely flabbergasted us.   While there we sighted a ship called the *Dartmouth*, also bound to Queenstown, so of course it was a race.   We were a fortnight doing the last 150 miles, when with a fair wind it is an easy day's sail. We have done 900 miles in three days.

"At last we got a fair wind, and anchored, as I have said, at 5.45 a.m. on Monday.   At 6.30 a.m. who should come in but the *Dartmouth*.   We had beaten her by three-quarters of an hour—a good race.   We gave her three cheers as she passed in, though we nearly had a smash up.

"To get to her place, she had to pass us where we laid at anchor.   Her pilot was not looking what he was doing, and she headed directly towards us.   They managed to get her helm hard over in time, but her foreyard fouled and knocked a hole in our crossjack yardarm.   Our Skipper was down below at the time and heard the noise. He came running up in very much deshabille to see what was the matter.   If our crossjack yard had come down it would have fallen on him.

"The sea-boots you sent to Wallaroo are all right, never leaked a drop.   My old ones were in a more holy than righteous state.   In fact, the only good thing about them was that the water ran out of them as fast as it ran in.   Japs seem to be giving the Rooshuns beans.   Will you cable my congratulations to the Mikado?

"I shall be home in a few days now, so expect me when you see me."

CHAPTER X

SECOND VOYAGE

(November, 1905, to October, 1907)

Two days after the letter quoted in the last chapter was posted in Queenstown the ship was towed up to Cork and I came home on leave, looking, I have since been informed, a weird little specimen.

That probably is no exaggeration. I was wearing the same uniform in which I had left home three years previously, but my age had increased from 15 to 18, and my "tonnage" proportionately. The result was that only the lower button of the coat would function, a couple of inches of leg and forearm were exposed, and, having been kept in my sea-chest with all my curios and soaked several times in salt water, both coat and trousers were stained and creased.

Considerable interest was shown in my hands which were very calloused after all the "pully-hauly" on ropes. As they were being examined and felt, some yellow stains on one or two fingers roused the family's curiosity.

"I thought in Cardiff that those tarry ropes would stain the hands," said my father; and turning to my mother, he added, "but it will soon wear off."

"Not unless I give up smoking cigarettes," I remarked, grinning at the old man, who was a non-smoker.

My sea-chest was also the worse for wear. It had been taken upstairs on arrival. Later we went up to unpack, and as I took the lashings off it my mother, father, and two sisters gathered round, eager to see all the curios I had brought home. When I lifted the lid they all peered inside—and out hurried a number of healthy, sailing-ship-bred cockroaches, anxious to discover wider and more open spaces!

When the panic subsided the sea-chest was carried downstairs again and unpacked in the garden.

I leave this first holiday to your imagination, and pass on to the play-time of my second voyage.

ACAPULCO.
(Aged 19 years.)

" This is a fine harbour, surrounded by hills. When inside you cannot see the entrance. The town, only a small place and very primitive, lies at the foot of them. The people are a very dark yellow, and by no means handsome. Most of the men wear white trousers and shirt, with a black sash, large straw hat, and no coat or boots. The streets are very badly kept, and pigs with very long snouts run about loose on them. The only horses I have seen are mules (Irish again). The only good thing is the fruit. Cocoanuts grow all along the beach, and mangoes, bananas, and pineapples grow wild.

" We get ashore sometimes with the Skipper, but, of course, can't go far. There is a plaza—a kind of recreation ground—with mango trees in it, and the fruit lies about on the ground. We have to buy bananas and pine-apples, as we can't go far enough for them. Still, for a few ship's biscuits we can get as many as we want.

" On Saturday nights and Sundays there are prize fights and cock fights. A week before we came in there was an eight-day bull fight which is held every year.

" Last Sunday seven of the men got some drink on board, and at night went ashore on hatches. These are made of wood, about six feet long, two feet wide, and three inches thick. One, who was drunk, fell asleep on his hatch, drifted three miles away, and was three hours

paddling himself back with his hands. Another tried to
swim off to the ship on Monday morning, but was fagged
out before he got on board. Luckily we saw him in
time and sent a boat to pick him up. The rest have
deserted.''

"There has not been much excitement this week. The
boatswain managed to get drunk this afternoon. He told
us that he had a great depression of mind and feared he
was going loco, another way of saying crazy. We sympa-
thised with him. He said he did not expect to live many
years and would go to gaol tomorrow.

"The first three days we were here we bathed, but then
the police came off and stopped us. They said there were
sharks, and two days ago we caught one, two feet long.

"We don't know where the ship is going to from here.
Certainly not home from this port, as no cargoes are ex-
ported from here. We are hoping to go to Iquique or one
of the nitrate ports and load for home. I hope we
do, because my apprenticeship expires in thirty-four days.
Sydney and Melbourne are the only two ports away from
England where I could get my ticket. If the ship does not
come home, and if they don't pay me off and get me a
berth in a homeward-bound ship, they have to pay me
£3 a month.''

"We had our liberty day last Sunday and had a good
time. After breakfast Mac and I went ashore. First of
all we explored the town, and then went out into the
bush. It is a wild place. The houses (?) are made of
bamboos, stuck into the ground about an inch apart.
We could look between them right into the house. The
roof is made with leaves. There is only one room for
eating, sleeping, and having their being.

"We saw lots of banana trees, but they had no

8

bananas on them; and any amount of cocoa-nut trees, but did not fancy shinning up a fifty-foot trunk, with no branches.

"Later we met some people we knew and went to a cock fight. It is not much sport. A narrow, curved knife, about three inches long, is fastened to the left spur, and a man holds each cock. When they begin to get savage they are let loose. The one that kills the other first, wins; or if one runs away, it loses.

"At 5 p.m. we were told that there was to be horse racing, so of course we went. There were several horses, and one of the streets was the race course. The races consisted of two men, each on a horse, galloping side by side along the street with an arm round each other's neck.

"At 6 p.m. the second mate with the first-voyage apprentice came for us in the boat. We persuaded him that it was too early to go back, so leaving the first-voyager in the boat to look after it, he came ashore with us. We did not go on board until after 8 o'clock. The men, who also had had liberty, came off at the same time, and most of them were drunk. One of them was very much so and had fallen over a cliff, about twenty or thirty feet high. He only bruised himself.

"Good-bye now for a month or so. Hope you are all alive-o and kicking."

ROYAL ROADS, ESQUIMAULT (for orders).
(Aged 19 years.)

"We were a week in Royal Roads and had a pretty good time. We laid at anchor, so had to row the Skipper into Esquimault* every day. We did pretty well, too, only got into one scrape.

"Esquimault is not very far from Victoria, which is a

* See Map 3, p. 87.

fine city. The Skipper went there every day, so we thought we should also like to go. One day we rowed Pa, otherwise the Old Man, otherwise the Skipper, into Esquimault, and as usual he told us to go back to the ship. Instead of doing that, we left the first-voyager to look after the boat and took the next tram to Victoria. It takes about twenty minutes and the scenery is very pretty.

"After changing a money order that another apprentice had received from home we had some dinner and then walked round. There are some fine buildings, especially the government building and a museum. We were peacefully walking along a street when someone said: 'Look out! there's the Old Man!'

"We scooted round a corner and continued our walk, but ten minutes later ran into him again. We scooted once more. By-and-by we returned to Esquimault and waited for him, trying to look innocent. Presently he came down with a frown on his manly brow and asked us what we were doing in Victoria. He did not growl much, though, not nearly as much as we expected he would.

"On Saturday morning a tug came for us at 4 a.m. and towed us into Port Townsend.* The doctor and customs examined us, and we came on to Bellingham.

"I have heard nothing about being paid off, and don't expect to. Men are scarce here. We shall most likely come home from Chile with saltpetre, and arrive about June or July. What-ho!"

BELLINGHAM.
(Aged 19 years.)

"This Bellingham† is not much of a place. There is hardly anything to do. There is one fairly good theatre.

* Port Townsend is opposite Victoria. See Map 3, p. 87.
† See Map 3, p. 87.

Yesterday, Sunday, we went out to Lake Whatcom, a good way into the country. It is a pretty ride, but there is not much to do when you are there. In several places clearings were being made in the forest, and in one place a man and his wife were both working. It looked pretty hard work, and if starting a farm in Canada is like that, I'd rather go to sea.

"Last week one of our fellows saw a man stabbed in the street. He came out of a saloon and four others started to hammer him. Then one pulled out a knife and stabbed him. Nobody seemed to take any notice. It is quite a common thing here, that and revolver shooting.

"By the way, you remember our worthy boatswain's racket in Acapulco—getting gaol, etc. Last Monday night he went ashore, and nobody knew where he was until he came back on Saturday. He had been in chokee again, and the Skipper had had to pay twenty-seven and a half dollars to get him out, about £5 10s. Of course the Skipper charges him for it. He went ashore again on Sunday, and today, Monday, is still absent.

"Today we have a general holiday. It is Labour Day, and is to celebrate an eight-hour working day or something."

"We have spent a most delightful week chipping rust over the ship's side. You sit on a plank that is slung over the side, tap the iron ship's side with a hammer, and whichever way you turn your head the rust insists on entering your eyes, ears, and nose.

"The other night we went to Beck's Theatre and saw 'Jesse James, the Missourie Outlaw.' It was not bad, plenty of revolver shooting and 'Hands up, pard!' To-morrow some Georgia Minstrels are coming and we are going to patronise them."

"Our plans last week for going to the Minstrels were rudely frustrated. We were chipping the ship's side close down to the water, and one man knocked a hole right through it, large enough to put three fingers in. Orders were sent for it to be repaired, and the workmen came at 7 p.m., so midst wails and lamentations we resigned ourselves to our fate, fervently blessing the ship, the man who designed her, the man who built her, and the man who knocked a hole in her.

"There is a theatre here which gives two performances every night, and after the first show tonight there is to be a wedding on the stage, for advertisement, I suppose. All the big shops have one or two presents in their window, with a notice on it.

"The Skipper was in Tacoma last week for three days, and as the Mate was on the wharf, tallying, and the boatswain was *non est*, there was only the Second Mate to look after us, so we had a peaceful time."

"This week has been the same as the last—nothing special. We did not go to the wedding in the theatre, as there was no room. I expect we shall be loaded by this time next week. Then we shall tow to Port Townsend, about forty miles from here, for a crew, as all but five men have deserted.

"We are going to Taltal,* Chile, and if the ship does not come home from there, I shall try to be paid off and come back in another ship. I should only be wasting my time here. At home I might get my ticket and a good job, as we hear there is a shortage of officers now. By the way, did I tell you that I got a sextant from the Skipper for £2 10s. just after we left Cardiff? It is a jolly good one and worth a lot more.

"Au revoir now for two or three months."

* See Map 2, p. 58.

"The saltpetre freights are very low now, so there is
not much chance of coming home yet. Still, we shall be
here two or three months and they may rise. We shall
most likely go to Sydney or Newcastle, N.S.W., in which
case I shall try to get leave in Australia. I could pass
for my Second Mate's certificate there and get a ship as
Second Mate.

"Yesterday a steamer, called the *Anglo-Australian*,
came in. Our Second Mate had been Third Mate of her
and he went on board in the evening. Two other apprentices and I went with him. We stayed until 11 o'clock,
and they gave us a pile of books. She is a fine boat and
the Second Mate speaks well of the company, so if you
meet anyone connected with it, you might give them a
hint that a young officer with a brand-new certificate will
be in London next October and might be willing to accept
a berth in one of their boats."

"We have got our orders at last. We are going to
load for Europe. We don't know what port yet, but it
will be home for us and we should be there about the end
of September. You can imagine there was jubilation in
the camp when we heard about it. We shan't be sorry
to leave this place, having already been here twelve
weeks—twelve weeks in a sand pit. We will have a reaction when the prodigal son arrives home with a fifty-
pound pay-day in his pocket.

"By the way, great excitement about a fortnight ago.
We have a pair of pigeons and they hatched two young
ones. Mother and children are progressing favourably,
which is rather surprising because everybody thinks it
his special duty to look at them and stroke them a dozen
times a day.

"Last Saturday some officers and engineers from a steamer asked us and the officers and apprentices of the *Scottish Lochs* to play football with them against a shore team. Pa, the Skipper, gave us leave, so on Sunday they came for us in their boat and we all toddled bravely to the football *field*. This was a square place, ankle-deep in dust, and a crowd of Dagos were kicking a ball around. The captain of their team made arrangements with ours, and then took us into a room to change, after which we mustered our thin red line on the field of glory. Our goal-keeper, the second engineer of the steamer, had played at home for the Rangers. I played outside-right.

"The first half ended 0—0, chiefly owing to our goal-keeper. In the second half we broke down altogether, out of practice and the heat. They scored three and we retired crestfallen. They played a good game and had some combination.

"When this reaches you we shall be well round Cape Stiff—the nautical name for our old friend, the Horn—and up by the Falkland Islands, getting into warm weather. I must say au revoir for about four months, and shall think of you, warm and cosy, when we are freezing aloft off the Horn."

CHAPTER XI

OFFENCES AND PUNISHMENTS

" If any seaman lawfully engaged or an apprentice to the sea service commits any of the following offences, in this Act referred to as offences against discipline, he shall be liable to be punished summarily as follows : . . ."—*Merchant Shipping Act.*

An account of the life and training of us ordinary men would not be complete without a brief description of the way in which punishment was meted out to offenders on shipboard, though this does not mean that you will be inflicted with a long, legal homily. Should you be desirous of delving deeply into the matter, you can do so by procuring a copy of the Merchant Shipping Act and turning up " Provisions as to Discipline."

This subject can be divided into two categories: official offences and punishments within the meaning of the Act, and those not provided for by it that may be called unofficial.

Omitting actual crimes, which would be dealt with by the law on shore, the former includes drunkenness, insolence to an officer, disobedience to a lawful command, etc. These are punishable by the captain, and he has the offender brought before him to be " logged."

That last word requires an explanation which introduces another section of the Act: " keeping of the log-book."

Actually two of them are kept on a ship. One, known as the Chief Officer's, or Mate's, log-book, is nothing more or less than a ship's diary, and should be written up every four hours by the officer of the watch and signed by him. It has columns for speed of ship, courses

steered, variation and deviation of the compass, direction
and force of wind, state of weather, etc.   All alterations
of course and points of land passed are entered in it, as
is at noon the latitude, longitude, and distance run since
the previous noon.   It is a complete record of the voyage
from the port of departure to the final port of discharge,
where it is handed in to the owners.

The other, that referred to in the Act, is called the
"official log-book," and at the end of the voyage it is
given to the superintendent of the Mercantile Office before
whom the crew are discharged.   It must contain a complete list of the crew, stating the conduct, character, and
qualifications of each, offences with the punishment inflicted, cases of illness or injury, marriages and deaths
on board during the voyage, together with various other
things.

When therefore a member of the crew is "had up
before the Old Man" for drunkenness or some similar
offence his punishment, usually a fine of five shillings,
as well as anything he may have to say for himself, is
entered in this log-book, and he is said to be "logged."

I will now put the Merchant Shipping Act away with
my other deep-sea curios, and give two examples of how
the way of transgressors was made hard in an unofficial
manner.   These concern crimes committed by, and the
consequent retribution meted out to, apprentices on sailing-ships.

One of them is to fall asleep in your watch on deck at
night.   Imagine that you are about 16 years old, that
you are watch and watch and had the "eight hours out"
last night, thereby only sleeping from midnight until
4 a.m.   During the day you have been running up and
down from aloft, unbending one suit of sails and bending another.   When you turned in at 8 p.m. you were
dog-tired.   You were called again at 11.45 p.m. and

came on deck more asleep than awake at midnight to keep a four-hour watch. Your duty is to strike the bell on the poop every half-hour, though between-whiles you may spend your time on the after hatch.

As soon as your watch has been mustered and the other has gone below you make yourself comfortable on it. It is a drowsy, tropical night, and the long, slow roll of the ship and the creaking of the yards are a lullaby that in a few minutes causes your head to nod and your eyes to close. Suddenly you come to with a start. You rush up to the poop and look at the clock in the companion-way —to find that it is only ten minutes past twelve.

The Mate, also sleepy, calls you over to the sacrosanct weather side, and passes away some of his time by asking you seamanship questions. At half-past twelve you strike one bell and go back to the after hatch.

Habit and your subconscious self get you up there in time to strike two bells at one o'clock, and then the Mate tells you to fetch him his sandwiches. You bring them up to him, get a drink of water for yourself, walk up and down a few times, sprawl on the hatch once more—and you suddenly hear the Mate shouting to you and asking you the time.

You tumble half-asleep up the ladder, trip over your feet as you run along the deck to the clock, and as it is 1.35 a.m., you hurriedly strike three bells.

By this time you are weakening fast. Five minutes after that bell your adversaries, the lullaby and the warm, sleepy night, give you your quietus so effectively that eventually the Mate has to come down and shake you to restore you to consciousness.

The consequences of that misdemeanour are: four bells are struck at five minutes past two, the wheel and look-out reliefs which should take place at two o'clock are late, and the Mate sends you for a spoon and two buckets. He makes you fill one of these with water from over the side, seats you on the poop deck under his eye, and tells you to transfer the water from the full one to the empty one with the spoon—and to let him know how many spoonfuls there are.

A sleepy-headed apprentice requires about one hour and twenty minutes to accomplish this. There is therefore no opportunity to fall asleep during the remainder of the watch.

Another method of keeping a boy awake was to give him a capstan bar, make him shoulder arms with it and walk up and down the poop for an hour.

This unofficial justice usually made the punishment fit the crime. During a forenoon watch on deck I had been working in the lazarette, and had managed to fill my pockets with sugar. I came up at noon and stowed it in an empty Harriet Lane tin in the half-deck. Ten minutes later, when we were eating our dinner, the Captain appeared at the door.

"Which o' you boys was working in the lazarette?" he shouted.

"Me, sir," I answered, jumping to my feet.

"Then what the hell d'you mean by stealing sugar?" he asked.

I gazed at him in wonderment. Even Conan Doyle's hero had never placed his hand so quickly and so surely on the criminal. I was utterly at a loss to understand his method.

"Me, sir?" the words were repeated, but not their intonation.

"Yess'r—yous'r—look 't this"—this sentence shot from his mouth in the form of three sharp barks.

I stepped out on to the deck. He pointed to a line of brown sugar grains. We both followed them. They led us across the deck and into the entrance on the other side, along the alley-way past the Mates' rooms, into and across the saloon to the lazarette hatch. At the end of that long, winding trail we stopped and gazed at each other for a few moments.

" Better patch that hole in your pocket!" he remarked.

Realising that I " had it coming to me," I merely grinned sheepishly and said nothing. At last, much to my relief, he took his eyes off me.

"Where are you, stooard?" he shouted.

" 'Ere, sir," replied a voice off; and the steward's face appeared at the door.

" Get a dustpan and brush!"

Exit face, while I stood there, wondering uneasily what was in store for me. The steward returned with that instrument of torture.

" Get a hold of it!" said the Old Man to me. " Sweep up every bit of that sugar. Bring it in here when you've finished!"

I carefully swept it all up and brought it back to him in the saloon. Then in a voice that the king of the jungle might well envy he roared the invitation: " Siddown!"

I sat in a chair at one end of the table. He seated himself opposite me, shouting again, "Where are you, stooard?"

" 'Ere, sir."

" Get a spoon!"

" Aye, aye, sir "; and as it made this second exit the face glanced at me with a smile that was in itself sufficient punishment for my crime.

When the spoon was brought and served to me the Captain leaned forward, placed his elbows on the table and his chin on his hands.

" Go to it!" he said. " Make a meal of it! Don't leave a damn bit of it!"

I did—just what he said. I spooned that sugar from

the dustpan into my mouth.   He watched every grain of
it disappear.

As I was leaving the saloon he remarked: "P'raps
that'll teach you boys not to steal ship's stores!"

P'raps it did; it most certainly taught us to repair holes
in our clothes.

CHAPTER XII

SEAMEN'S MISSIONS AND FRIENDLY SOCIETIES

" The evil that men do lives after them ;
The good is oft interred with their bones."

SHAKESPEARE.

ALTHOUGH at first sight Seamen's Missions and Friendly Societies may not seem to come within the scope of this "yarn," they were nevertheless closely related to the early life and training of many Merchant Service officers. In fact, a large number of us probably owe a great deal to those Chaplains who used to come on board sailing-ships as soon as they arrived, meet the apprentices and take them up to the Institute for teas, suppers, games, and concerts.

Take my own case: from the age of 15 I lived for five consecutive years in close contact with the roughest and hardest type of men, much of whose conversation was about drink and the sailor-town pleasures that follow in its wake, and who looked upon that sort of thing as being perfectly natural.

During those five irresponsible and impressionable years I was away from all home influence and restraint, and nobody knew or cared what I did or where I went. All the ports were full of temptations to men and boys, strangers to the place, going ashore after long voyages, and there was no difficulty in finding those pleasures—there was far more in getting away from them. Had there been nothing else to do, I should probably have been led into them as were many other youngsters of my age.

Tacoma, where we loaded a cargo of lumber for Val-

paraiso, was no exception, and we were not only alongside a wharf where I could go ashore every night, but I
was also well supplied with money.

When the indentures were signed a premium was paid
to the owners. This was returned to the apprentice as
pocket-money by the captain when the ship was in port.
In Tacoma I had this allowance from the "Old Man" as
well as a money-order from home. Before we had been
there many days we discovered another method of "raising the wind." The crew was allowed a ship's tailor and
could order clothes from him up to a certain amount.
They signed for what they had and the bills were paid by
the captain. He deducted that sum from their wages, or,
in the case of the apprentices, from their premium. We
found, however, that we could sign a bill for, say, ten
dollars' worth of goods, but that the merchant would give
us about six dollars in cash instead of clothes.

I was then nearly seventeen years old, had been to sea
for sixteen months, and was beginning to consider myself
quite a man of the world. If there had been no Seamen's
Institute, I should have gone ashore with boys from other
ships, and in all probability we should have wandered
into some saloon. There a few drinks would have been
consumed, including the inevitable "one on the house."
When we made a move towards the door this would have
been handed to us by the hail-fellow-well-met bartender,
together with some such cheery remark as: "Drink
hearty, boys! Hell! Ye're no good as y'are now, yuh
might jes' as well be drunk!"

When, after another "round" or two, we left him, he
would have come to the door with us, to direct us to the
next "port of call."

"Walk three blocks down that street, boys, and turn
to yer left. Jees! They's some dandy French and
Japanese women there!"

I met apprentices, one or two of them younger than myself, who had followed those "sailing directions." In some cases I saw the results. These hardly bear thinking of; but they might have happened to me or to any other boy, had not those Chaplains spent their days walking round the docks and on the ships, and their evenings in the Institutes, where they gave us such a good time that we never thought of going elsewhere.

There also we met residents of the town. They gave up an evening or two a week in order to help the Chaplain entertain us. Sometimes they invited us to their homes. I remember two families in Tacoma who, although I was a total stranger, treated me as though I were one of their own boys and I thoroughly enjoyed myself with them.

All the above applies equally to Cape Town, where we were also alongside the dock, and where again I had sufficient money to get myself into trouble—though I obtained it by a more legitimate method than from the ship's tailor. In Yokohama I paid about five yen (10s.) for a china tea-set. I sold it for thirty-five shillings in Cape Town, where, as in Tacoma, the Seamen's Mission looked after me.

I only mention Tacoma and Cape Town because I am able to speak from experience, and can follow on, as I have done in previous chapters, with details written by myself at the time, thus eliminating any exaggeration that might creep in after an interval of so many years.

That same work, however, was, and still is, done all over the world: from Tacoma down the Pacific coast to Valparaiso, where, although we laid out at anchor, the "Padre" visited the ships in his launch and distributed books and magazines; in the Continental ports, in India, in Japan—like the British Empire and my playground, the sun never sets on it.

The following extracts from letters will give you an insight into what was done to amuse apprentices. It probably saved many of us from such results as I have referred to earlier in this chapter.

TACOMA.

" This town, Tacoma,* is just like an English town. There are several theatres, and every second or third house is a saloon.

" Last Sunday morning we went to St. Peter's Church, and in the evening to the Seamen's Mission. St. Peter's is a small Church, and instead of a tower there is a big tree, covered with ivy, standing at one corner. It looks just like a tower, and has a bell hung in the branches. One of us had to ring it, but we managed to break the rope, so no bell was rung that morning.

" There is a fine Seamen's Institute here and we go there nearly every night. We have tea there every Sunday, and concerts and socials every week. There is also ping-pong, bagatelle, quoits, chess, etc., so we have a good time.

" The Chaplain, Mr. Bernay, is a jolly nice fellow and everybody likes him. We went to a concert last Wednesday, and at the end of it sang one verse of the American National Anthem and one of ' God save the King.' There were twenty or more apprentices sitting together on one side, and we did not half sing ' God save the King.' The American National Anthem and ours are both the same tune. One of our company's ships has sunk in 'Frisco."

"Last Sunday afternoon we went all over the town, then had tea in the Institute and went to the service afterwards. For the evening service Mr. Bernay always lets us choose our own hymns. Some fellows had their tea there, chose a hymn, and then went to a theatre (theatres

* See Map 3, p. 87.

9

are open here on Sundays). Mr. Bernay said in his sermon that he had been to some ships that day and that some people were too lazy to go to the service. Others, he said, were willing to come to the tea, but did not think it worth while stopping for the service.

"Monday night we went to a theatre. Tuesday there was a fine concert at the Institute. One old sailor sang 'Santiano,' a song sailors sing when pulling on ropes. It was very long and we got sick of it, so some fellows shouted: 'Belay!' 'Make that fast!' and 'Heave pawl!'

"He got so mad that he stopped and said: 'Gentlemen, there is a pair of boxing gloves in the next room. If I am interrupted again, I shall insist on putting them on with the person who interrupts me!'

"He soon finished, though, so there was no boxing match. I got the money Dad sent to the owners and bought all the clothes I want.

"Thursday was Thanksgiving Day and a holiday all over the country. We did no work and went to a football match between Tacoma and Seattle. Tacoma won by 7 to 0. At 7 p.m. there was a turkey dinner at the Institute. We had a fine time: turkey, potatoes, cake, etc., then a short Thanksgiving service and a social evening.

"The Second Mate celebrated the occasion by getting dead drunk. It took three men to bring him on board.

"Tonight we are going to a tea and concert at the Institute, and to a tea and social evening tomorrow.

"I must close now. I am having a fine time and don't want to leave yet."

CAPE TOWN.

"Last Sunday evening I went to the Institute to church, and on Monday we had a fine day. All the work we did was to wash down the deck before breakfast. At 1.30 p.m. we all congregated at the Institute and got our

railway tickets. We only had to pay sixpence, which included food as well. The ordinary fare alone is seven-
pence-halfpenny. The train left Cape Town at 2.5 p.m.
and arrived at Rondebusch at 2.20 p.m. We had about
half an hour's walk to the grounds of the Diocesan
College. The scenery was very pretty.

"There was cricket and football, and, after that, sports.
I played football, and after half an hour of it I was tired.
It is summer-time here, so you can imagine it is very hot,
hotter than an ordinary summer at home. It took about
twenty pounds of fat off me. Going back to the station I
weighed myself. I am 145 pounds.

"I did not go in for any races, nor did anyone who
played football. There was 100 yards scratch, three-
legged race, 500 yards, thread-needle race, and tug-of-
war. The tug-of-war was first between *Briton* and *Goth*,
and then sailing-ships versus steamers, the winners to pull
against each other. As there was only one sailing-ship
here besides us, and only two off her pulled, nearly all
were from our ship.

"At five o'clock we had tea: bread and butter, cakes,
and lettuce. At 7 p.m. there was a concert. The train
left Rondebusch at 10.30 p.m. and arrived at Cape Town
at 10.35 p.m. It was a fine day and I enjoyed myself
immensely. If you could have heard the cheers we gave
the committee, you would have said that everyone did.
We paid for it next day, though. We were so stiff and
tired we could hardly walk. We weren't used to football.

"Thursday was a social evening with light refresh-
ments. Today I was going to the Cathedral, Princess
Christian was to be there, but I fell asleep at 8.15 a.m.
and only awoke at noon. Am going to the Institute tonight. Tomorrow we are going to see the Princess give
the colours to the Volunteers, and on Tuesday she lays
the Foundation Stone of the new Institute."

"On Tuesday at 11 a.m. Princess Christian laid the Foundation Stone of the new Institute, and apprentices from all the ships were there. Two of us were sent on to the platform to present a purse to her. The others stood at the entrance to it. I don't know how the other fellow felt, standing there in front of a crowd, but I feel more comfortable and at home on a royal yard. The Archbishop and several other big bugs were there, and also a choir. I am sending you a programme.

"Wednesday night we said good-bye to everyone and got some reading matter from the Institute."

The good that is done by all the Mr. Bernays is interred not with their bones but in the memory of those of us who have eaten their bread and their salt—and huge helpings of their Thanksgiving turkeys!

CHAPTER XIII

TIME-ON-PASSAGE

" We were towed out of Monte Video on November 12th. We hoped to get away next day, but laid outside ten days waiting for a fair wind."—*Extract from letter, dated January 28th, 1903.*

SOME time ago I read an article in the paper " from our Special Correspondent on board the *Queen Mary* in the Atlantic." In it he stated that one of the Powers-That-Be in the Cunard-White Star Line said to him: ". . . all that we needed for schedule time was 28½ knots. . . ." There followed comparisons between that ship and the *Normandie*, together with their respective speeds and times-on-passage.

That same evening I was looking through those letters and happened to read one from which the above caption is an extract. The contrast is so striking—" 28½-knot schedules " and " laid outside ten days waiting for a fair wind "—that the *Aristomene's* time between ports while I was on her from 1902 to 1907 may be of interest to you, she being typical of windjammers.

Sailing-ships are so near to complete extinction and one hears so little about them nowadays that many of you in all probability have but a vague idea of the length, in time, of their passages from port to port, or of the time lost while hove-to in heavy weather, at anchor waiting for a fair wind, during calms, and when driven back long distances by head winds.

Then, it was not an uncommon thing for a ship to be hove-to in a gale, and therefore stopped, for five days. Now, you walk up the *Queen Mary's* gangway in Southampton on Wednesday, sure of being able to keep **a** business appointment in New York on the following Monday afternoon.

Were you to come straight back in that ship, and had the *Aristomene* been due to sail from Southampton with you but been delayed ten days waiting for a fair wind, you would return from a round trip to New York almost in time to hear us sing an outward-bound chantey as we weighed anchor to begin our voyage.

During the passage of 169 days from Cardiff to Acapulco, described in Chapter V, we were becalmed on one occasion for seventeen consecutive days. In that time you would have made your round trip to New York, and your ship would already be west of the Grand Banks on her following voyage.

On that same passage we sighted and signalled the lighthouse on Staten Island.* After getting to within 19 miles of the Horn, head winds drove us back, and we sighted it for the second time exactly one week later. You would have completed your business in New York and be sailing for home that same day.

While away on your voyage you would never be out of touch with your family, not only by radio, but even by telephone. When you sailed you would know almost to an hour the time of your return.

Had you sailed with us in 1905 on the *Aristomene*, there would not only have been that lapse of 169 days, about five and a half months, before reaching your next port, Acapulco, but also a further six weeks or so before your first letter arrived home. For about seven months therefore your family would have received no word from you. Neither you nor they would have known until the last minute where you were going from Acapulco, or how many years, not days, would elapse before you returned home.

In spite of all those delays, there were times when

* See Map 2, p. 58.

strong fair winds sent us staggering along at a speed of
13 or 14 knots. That was to us what thirty-one point
something is to the present-day "fly-away vessels."
Here is a description of one "strong" breeze, taken
from a letter written in October, 1903. It was so strong
that we were doing almost our top speed without the help
of either sails or engines. My esprit de corps prompts
me to defy even the *Queen Mary* to run to schedule time
under those conditions.

"On the 7th the wind freshened and we reduced sail
to lower topsails and reefed foresail. We set all sail again
next morning, but at 7 p.m. the wind increased so rapidly
that the Skipper called all hands on deck to shorten sail.
By midnight we were scudding under bare poles. The
wind was awful. The Mate says it is the worst he has
ever been in. You could not stand up without clinging
to something—you would be blown over. To give you
an idea of it, not a bit of sail was set except the fore topmast staysail, a small three-cornered sail like a jib, set
right forward to help the steering, and the wind, just
striking on the stern, masts, and rigging, sent us along
at 10 or 11 knots—or about 12 miles an hour.

"Only two of the men were allowed to steer. The
two best men were picked for it. One of us had to be at
the other side of the wheel to help him. When you had
been there two hours, clinging on like grim death, you
weren't sorry to go below.

"There was a tremendous sea. Standing at the wheel,
they seemed to curl right over your head. Twice we
were nearly lost. The ship broached-to a little—that is,
got the wind and sea sideways instead of right aft—and
nearly rolled right under. The Skipper was on the poop
and the officers were at breakfast. They came running
out, thinking she was gone.

"The Skipper did not leave the poop from 7 p.m. on Thursday until 2 p.m. on Friday, except for meals. The gale broke at two o'clock, and at tea-time we set the lower topsails. Next day we set all sail except the royals.

"If it had lasted two or three days instead of only fourteen or fifteen hours we should have been lost. The seas would have been so great they would have swallowed us. All the men say she is a splendid sea-boat or she would not have lived. I don't want to see a blow like that again in a hurry."

And now, after all that preamble, here are the *Aristomene's* times-on-passage.

FIRST VOYAGE.

Cardiff to Monte Video	56 days (approx.)
Monte Video to Port Tampa ...	68 ,,
Port Tampa to Yokohama, via Cape Town	167 ,,
Yokohama to Royal Roads ...	29 ,,
Tacoma to Valparaiso	69 ,,
Valparaiso to Antofagasta	6 ,,
Antofagasta to Caleta Buena ...	4 ,,
Caleta Buena to Cape Town ...	76 ,,
Cape Town to Semaphore (Adelaide, S. Australia)	32 ,,
Wallaroo to Queenstown	139 ,,

SECOND VOYAGE.

Cardiff to Acapulco	169 ,,
Acapulco to Royal Roads	43 ,,
Bellingham to Taltal	88 ,,
Taltal to Fiume	165 ,, (approx.)

CHAPTER XIV

PROMOTION

" One's life resembles a road,
    And its milestones are the years."

ONE of the best-remembered milestones on my road down
to the sea in ships is the fourth, when my apprenticeship
expired. I was then eligible to sit for my Second Mate's
certificate, but there was a clause in the indentures to the
effect that if the ship were at sea when they expired, or
in a foreign port and I were not released and sent home,
I should sign on the ship's articles as able-seaman at the
rate of pay pertaining in the port of departure—in this
case, £3 a month.

By the end of the first year I had adapted myself to the
new life, and there followed a couple of irresponsible ones
with no thought beyond getting ashore in the next port,
seeing all there was to be seen, and having a good time.

At the end of my apprenticeship, when I had signed
on the articles as able-seaman, I was beginning to understand the significance of my father's words when, four
years previously, he left me on the ship in Cardiff: " I
have done all I can for you, old chap, now you must
learn to look after yourself."

That fourth milestone, at which I began to realise the
necessity of acting on my own initiative and of relying
on myself, may be said to be the boundary between my
boyhood and manhood; and a few months later, when I
had the good fortune to be promoted to Third Mate and
given charge of a watch round Cape Horn, this sense of
responsibility was greatly increased.

Before saying any more about that I will insert an extract from a letter which describes how I became a man.

"At 4 a.m. on the 14th a heavy squall struck us before we had time to take in any sail. With the exception of the mizzen topgallantsail, everything was blown away. We looked like an old rag shop up aloft.

"By the way, that was the day I finished my time, a fine way of celebrating it. The other fellows told me that the next time I finish an apprenticeship, or anything else, to send them warning and they would give me a wide berth.

"On Sunday, the 22nd of July, Pa, or Uncle, as we sometimes call the Old Man, invited us into his cabin and informed us that we had finished our apprenticeship. We quite agreed with him. He went on to say that we were the most backward lot of boys he had ever seen. We could not second that resolution; you would not expect us to. We resented that blot on our escutcheon. Then, after a long speech on our merits and demerits, especially the latter, he told us to sign on the articles, which we did; and the small exertion of signing my own name made me at one bound a man earning £3 a month. I have already earned £3 10s., which, with the remainder of my premium, makes a sum of £15 12s. 6d. due to me.

"This had not been a pleasant trip. There has been a good deal of sickness after leaving a climate like that of Acapulco. Luckily I have been well all the time. Nearly half of the men have been off duty most of the passage, which makes it harder for the rest of us.

"If the ship does not come home from here, I shall try to be paid off and get a ship homeward bound, to get my ticket, which I cannot do here."

There only remains my promotion to Third Mate before

leaving the "Iron Man Age." This occurred during my last passage on the ship, from Taltal to Fiume. No Third Mate had been carried that voyage, and when we were getting down towards the "umbrella and goloshes weather" the Mate was taken sick and had to be put off duty.

We boys were sitting in the half-deck one evening and suddenly heard the Captain's voice.

"Where's that boy Making?" he shouted from the poop.

I, the boy Making in question, was sitting on my sea-chest, doing my best to wangle music from a badly tuned mandoline. Leaping to my feet, I placed the instrument tenderly on my bunk, chocked it off with a pillow to prevent it from rolling out, ran up the poop ladder and halted in front of the Old Man, wondering which of my crimes was responsible for this audience.

There were a few silent and, to me, embarrassing moments while he gazed down at and through me "with eyes of microscopic power that could discern the population of a dewdrop."

"Mate's sick!" he said at last.

"Yes, sir."

"Got no Third Mate this voyage!"

"No, sir."

"Have to find somebody to keep the Mate's watch!"

"Yes, sir."

"Don't know who's fit to do it!"

"—Er—no—sir." I didn't quite agree with him that time.

"S'pose I'll have to promote one of you boys!"

"Yes, sir!"

"Don't know which one to choose. One's as no good as the other!"

On the spur of the moment I could think of no suitable

" come-back " to that scandalous statement. I therefore remained silent.

" Well! You'd better have it! " he continued.

" Thank you, sir."

" You can take over the middle watch tonight! "

" Yes, sir; and—er—shall I get the extra ten shillings a month for Third Mate?"

" Don't know. I'll promote you on the articles, it'll help you with your ticket. The owners 'll decide about the pay when we get home."

" Thanks very much, sir."

" Now don't imagine you know all about it, 'cos you don't; so don't blow the sticks out of her in a squall because you are scared to call me and ask me what to do. When I was your age I didn't know much. When you're mine you'll still be learning. If you can get that thought through your skull, you may be some use to somebody in a few years. You're in charge of the watch—and the ship. Don't stand any slack from the men, and come to me whenever you want anything."

" Thank you, sir."

" All right! That's all! Take over the middle watch! "

" Aye, aye, sir." I hesitated a moment. " Shall I shift into the Third Mate's room, sir," I added, " and— er—eat in the cabin?"

He was then going down the companion-way, but stopped for a moment and glared over the top of it at me.

" All right! " he shouted at last. " DON'T EAT TOO MUCH! "

He was right! I did *not* know it all! To be an apprentice, sitting in the half-deck and criticising the Mates, was one thing. Standing alone on the poop in charge of the ship during heavy weather off the Horn was another. It was an excellent schooling for me, but I spent some anxious watches in the course of it.

One night we were running before a moderate westerly gale. The Skipper was cracking on, dragging what he couldn't carry, to make the most of the fair wind, and when I took over at midnight the ship was staggering along under three topgallantsails, foresail, and mainsail. Ten minutes later he came up.

"Goin' to bed now," he said. "Carry those tuhgansels as long as you can, but don't let 'em blow out of the bolt-ropes!"

"Aye, aye, sir," I replied, casting an anxious glance at those sails, which seemed to be on the point of doing so.

About 1 a.m. there was a squall, and as the ship lay over to it I shouted: "Stand by the tuhgall'nt halliards!"

For the next ten minutes my sensations resembled those of a cat walking on hot bricks. I could see the dim outline of those huge spreads of canvas against the black masses of clouds; and as I watched them dragging at their sheets some words, said to me months previously by the Mate, came to my mind: "Any damn fool can set sail. It's a good man who knows just when to take 'em in!"

I began to argue with myself: "There's too much canvas on her."—"It's only a squall and won't last."—"Ships have had the sticks taken out of them in a squall."—"The Skipper'll think I'm an old woman if I call him to say there's a squall."—"He'll raise merry hell if I blow anything out of her." . . . And then the squall passed and the wind eased. With a sigh of relief, I shouted: "That'll do! Keep handy the watch!"

Half an hour later there was another squall, harder than the previous one. Without any hesitation that time, I shouted: "Lay aft the watch! Clew up the mizzen tuhgansel!"

The rattling of the patent sheaves and the noise of the men's boots on the poop deck woke the Captain, who came up to see what was happening. After a glance aloft he growled, " What're you taking in sail for?"

" Rather a hard squall," I answered. " I'm clewing up the mizzen tuhgansel. They're standing by the fore and main tuhgallant halliards."

" Humph!" he snorted; and he walked aft to look at the compass.

Apparently I was wrong. I hadn't enough nerve. He came back and asked, " Had any more squalls?"

" One," I replied, " not so hard as this one."

He had a long look to windward, then another aloft. Finally he said, " Bit more weight in the wind now. Make that tuhgansel fast. If you get any more squalls, take in the fore tuhgansel. Goin' to bed."

I heaved another sigh of relief. I was right after all.

When we were round the Horn and getting up towards the south-east trades the Mate returned to duty, and for the remainder of the passage I was merely his right-hand man.

Easterly winds outside the Straits of Gibraltar kept us beating to and fro for six weeks before we could get through them. In the Mediterranean we had to stop a passenger ship for provisions. I was in the boat that went to her, and the contrast between our Mates and her brass-bound officers was the cause of my leaving sail and going into steam as soon as I obtained my Second Mate's certificate.

We arrived in Fiume after a passage of, I believe, 165 days. I was paid off immediately and went home over-land. In due course I presented myself at the Board of Trade examination room; and three days later was able to inform the family that I had my " ticket."

The time has now come to draw a veil over those wind-jammer days and to pass on to a totally different world.

My elementary training was finished. I was to begin another schooling, which would teach me the meaning of responsibility in a profession that does not recognise a mistake and rarely allows a second chance.

I have listened to, and taken part in, many discussions as to whether that sailing-ship experience is of any benefit to the present-day navigator, and I agree that the ability to do fancy knots and splices has been of no assistance to me when bound up Channel in thick traffic and low visibility.

Nevertheless, if he were properly nourished, a training such as that of the *Aristomene* fitted a boy for the situations which arise at sea far better than that of a steamship. The rough life and hard work built up a tough constitution. Equally important was the influence of the men with whom he lived and worked: the Captain, whose fore-topsail-yard-ahoy voice made him jump to it; the hard-bitten Mates, who marched him up and down the poop one night with a capstan bar, and gave him their bread and butter another; and all the " Davys " of those days, drunken wastrels ashore but " Iron Men " afloat. Between them they instilled something into his ego that is not found in steamers.

Rough-hewn, hard-cases, as they would be considered today, they put something into my make-up during those early receptive years that has helped me over many rough places on the road when with only my own feet to stand on I have had to carry a load of responsibility on my shoulders.

I do not wish to reopen the " for and against sailing-ship training " controversy here, though, and I will now close this period with the last thing given to me by that Old Man when I said good-bye to him in Fiume: my testimonial, which had to be presented to the Board of Trade.

Ship *Aristomene*,
Fiume *Oct.* 23/07.

This is to certify that the bearer Victor Leslie Making as served four years Apprentaship also fifteen months AB, and Third Mate for last 5 months on board above vessel Trading the following parts of the world namely N and S America West Coast America Australia Japan and Mediteranean

During the said term. He as always conducted himself in a Sober Dilligent and Attentive manner, And as given me entire satisfaction

Signed ———
F. Young
Master *Aristomene*
L,pool

Shiv Shrutamani
Junior Ou-22/07

This is to certify that Mr. Brown Vivit Leslie Manney as served for your Appreciatory also fifteen months 2,13 + Third Mate for last 5 months in board above name during the following part of the union named MTS America West-Coast America Australia Japan & Mediterranean during the said time. He as always conducted himself in a sober diligent attentive manner, And as given me entire satisfaction

Signed J. Young
Master
Shrutamani
Spark

PART II

" The thranite now and thalamite are pressures low and high,
  And where three hundred blades bit white the twin-propellers fly ;
  The God that hailed, the keel that sailed, are changed beyond
      recall,
  But the robust and brass-bound man he is not changed at all !"
                    RUDYARD KIPLING : *Poseidon's Law.*

CHAPTER I

SECOND MATE

" The goal of yesterday will be the starting point of tomorrow."—
Ibid.

MY passing from a life on a sailing-ship among the " Iron
Men " to begin a new one on a steamer was another uprooting, as revolutionary in character as the previous one,
when I was transplanted from my home to the *Aristomene*
and from the status of eldest child and only son to that of
" one o' them bloody boys." It was accompanied by
equally numerous emotions and impressions, and for the
first few days the disappointments and disillusions were
quite as great. In this case it was preceded by the depressing experience of looking for a ship.

To be eligible to sit for my other certificates later on,
it was necessary to serve as an officer in charge of a watch.
Instead therefore of seeking employment in a large
passenger-ship company where I should only be a junior
and not a watch-keeper, I looked for a berth in a cargo
boat or small passenger ship. Knowing nothing about
offices, I began by entering them timidly and asking
respectfully whether there was a vacancy for a Second or
Third Mate.

" Sorry," was the invariable reply. " *I* have nothing
for you now, but *I* will keep your name before me."

After a few of these rebuttals I was beginning to lose
heart. Then I happened to meet a man who obtained his
Master's certificate the same week that I passed for Second
Mate.

" Hullo! " he said. " Got a ship yet? "

"No!" I replied. "I can't find a vacancy anywhere."

"Who did you see about it?" he asked.

I described my method of approach and the reception given me by the haughty and supercilious Personages in the offices.

"Good Lord!" he exclaimed. "Did you let *them* scare you off? They're only the office boys! D'you want to go out East?"

"I don't care where I go," I answered.

"I heard the *Swaledale* wants a Third Mate," he said. "Those ships are all right. Go and see the Marine Superintendent."

He came with me. When we arrived at the company's office he led me in. The usual Personage greeted us with the usual supercilious look.

"Marine Superintendent in?" asked my friend, without bothering about a good morning.

"He's in his office," was the reply, "but I think he's busy now."

"Tell him there's an officer applying for the job as Third Officer on the *Swaledale*! He's got a square-rigged ticket and been Third Mate in sail."

"Yes—sir," answered the Personage.

Apparently this method of handling him had the effect of erasing the last three letters from that word. At all events, the six that remained knocked timidly at a door and vanished from sight.

"Come this way, please," he said when he reappeared a minute later.

I followed him into a room that had the name-plate on the door: Marine Superintendent.

"'Mornin', young fellow!" said that official. "Looking for a command?"

His eyes belied the gruffness of his voice, and I grinned.

"Not yet, sir," I replied. "I heard there was a vacancy for a Third Mate on the *Swaledale*."

"Got a square-rigged ticket?" he asked.

"Yes, sir. Second Mate. I was Third Mate in sail after I finished my time."

"Humph!" he grunted, looking me up and down. "When can you join?"

"Today, sir!" I answered eagerly.

"All right. Collect your dunnage and join her to-morrow morning."

Thus I obtained my first ship as an officer. She was a small steamer of 2,347 tons, and carried cargo and a few passengers to ports on the east coast of Africa, thence to Bombay to load for home. When I arrived on board the following morning I was almost deafened by the clatter of her steam winches, nearly brained by ton-slings of cargo that hurtled across the deck, and completely bewildered by discussions about double-bottom tanks and other mysteries.

What impressed me more than anything was that apparently nothing I had learned during those years in sail was of the slightest help to me. I had literally to begin all over again. What good did it do me to know how to cross a royal yard? A steamer had no yards, and only two stumpy masts! What was the use of knowing how to rig a dolly winch for four sailors to heave up a sack of saltpetre or a basket of coal? Here there were derricks and steam winches by means of which stevedores from ashore hoisted in a ton of cargo at a time!

I even had to learn another language! "Main top-gallant halliards" had to be deleted from my vocabulary and "No. 4 derrick topping lifts" inserted in lieu thereof; "fore topmast staysail sheet" was erased to make room for "No. 1 starboard inner derrick guy"; and so on *ad infinitum*.

Within twenty-four hours I was sitting on the settee in my cabin, suffering from an ailment that would have been diagnosed as first-voyage-apprentice-inferiority-complex: five years at sea, four times round the Horn, Third Mate of a wind-bag, Second Mate's square-rigged ticket—and I didn't seem to know one damn thing about anything!

On the second or third day, however, I was introduced to the Captain, a very robust and brass-bound gentleman. He said he was glad to hear I had a square-rigged ticket— those damn steam-boat sailors knew nothing. He even shook hands with me and called me *Mister* Making; and after five years' service as " the lowest form of animal life " on a sailing-ship that magic word *Mister*, spoken by a Captain, was such a pick-me-up for my morale that my complex depression moved rapidly away. Common sense reminded me that I was every bit as good as the average man, that that Captain had been through the same mill and so there was no reason why I should not become just as robust and as brass-bound as he. I left his cabin with my spiritual barometer at " fair " once more, and in a short time had shaken down.

This first voyage both as an officer and on a steamer was just as big a step for me as the corresponding one in sail. The conditions, duties, and my new associates were equally strange to me. The last passage I had made in sail was 165 days from port to port. As a contrast, this first complete voyage in steam was only a week or two longer than that, and during it we called at fifteen ports. There was also the novelty of having passengers on board. For those reasons I will give an account of it, beginning with an extract from a letter:

" We stopped in Gravesend to take on explosives, and then really started. It did seem queer to go to sea and have no sails to mess about with; but it was all right just the same! We kept watch and watch down Channel, I being on the bridge with the Chief Officer. Then we commenced the ordinary watches—four hours on and eight off. That also is all right!

"What beats me is that I have absolutely no work to do! While on watch I merely walk up and down the bridge for four hours and take sights for finding the ship's position. Then I have eight hours below! I keep the eight to twelve watch every night and morning. At 7.30 a.m. a quartermaster calls me, and the boy brings me tea and toast. I take over from the Chief Officer at eight o'clock, and am relieved again at half-past eight for breakfast, at which there are four courses. Lunch is at one o'clock, five courses; tea and cake at 4 p.m.; dinner at 6.30 p.m., seven courses; and supper at 10 p.m., cocoa and sandwiches. The boy looks after the rooms, makes the beds, cleans our shoes, etc., so we have not much to grumble at.

"We had fine clear weather down Channel, a moderate gale in the Bay of Biscay, and fine weather since. We have not worn sea-boots at all, which speaks for itself. . . . A fortnight passage is a bit different from 165 days. We shall be a few hours in Port Said, I expect, and the same in Suez. The next ones are Port Sudan, Suakim, Aden, Mombasa, Kilindini, and Zanzibar."

Our expectations of remaining only a few hours in Port Said were not realised. My next letter, written after we arrived, says:

"We discharged all the Port Said cargo on Sunday morning, and, of course, expected to go right on through the Canal to Suez. Then news came off that the owners were bankrupt, so here we are, awaiting orders. The people ashore won't give us coal for our bunkers or allow us through the Canal until they get the money.

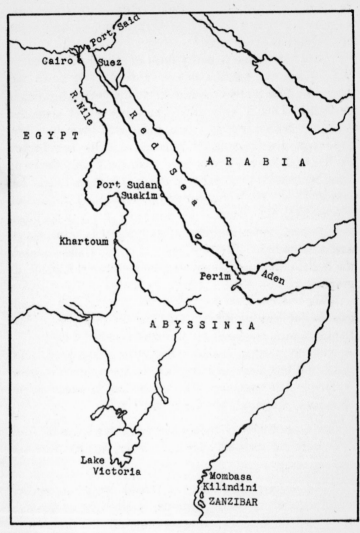

MAP 5.—AFRICAN PORTS.

"We are having a ripping time. We get up about 8 a.m. and do nothing all day except eat, sleep, and smoke cigarettes. If we don't go ashore in the evenings, we have good fun on board. Last Sunday we had a concert in the saloon with the passengers, and I was at the piano all the evening, playing for songs.

"The passengers are a jolly crowd. One of them, a Scotchman about 20 years old, has bagpipes, and the others dared him to walk through Port Said in Highland dress, playing them. Next morning he came to breakfast in his kilts, etc., and then he and the others went ashore and all round Port Said, playing the bagpipes in the cafés. The Captain would not give us leave to go with them. Another passenger, who was very well oiled, was chasing rats (imaginary ones, I mean) out of the saloon with a revolver the other night."

We were held up a month before money was forth-coming to enable us to proceed through the "Ditch." There for the first time I saw strings of camels in their natural setting—squadrons of ships of the desert, proceed-ing in single line ahead along the banks of the Canal.

A few hours were spent in Suez to discharge a little cargo, and by the time we arrived in Port Sudan I was beginning to consider myself a one-hundred-per-cent. steam-boat officer. The speed of a steamer no longer awed me while in charge of the bridge nor gave me an urge to put the helm hard over every time I sighted a light on the horizon. I had also quite lost the feeling that the engine-room telegraph might bite me if I touched it.

Port Sudan is memorable because of two events that occurred there, one during the discharging of a consign-ment of heavy steel rails. The Chief Officer and I were standing at the hatch, watching the natives heave up a sling of them. Suddenly one rail slipped out. With a deafening clatter it fell back into the hold among the men, ripping out on the way down the ends of some cases of dynamite.

For one breathless second we instinctively clung to the hatch coaming, waiting for the "bang"; but thanks to the special providence that looks after drunks, and also, it would seem, Sudanese stevedores, I was able to go ashore the following afternoon to take part in the other event: a cricket match, *Swaledale* versus Port Sudan.

The result, as reported in my letter home, was:

"Strictly speaking we lost, but actually we had decidedly the best of the game. We went in first, made 128 for 7 and declared. One passenger and I were in together for nearly an hour. He made 65 not out; and I, 29 not out. They knocked up 134 for 9 wickets. Of course, we ought to have played longer, but it was getting late and we hoped to get them all out in time. Hard luck!"

Going into the next port, Suakim, the ship ran aground. She was floated again in a few hours, however, and little or no damage was done.

While we were there the Second Officer had an opportunity to become pilot in Port Sudan. The Captain agreed to release him. He was therefore paid off, and left the ship. As he could not be replaced in Suakim, I naturally got in the Captain's way as much as possible, to remind him that there was no actual necessity to continue on the voyage without a Second Officer—although one of the company's rules was that that officer must hold a Mate's certificate.

For some days this had no effect, and I was beginning to wonder if he were incapable of recognising a good man when he saw one. At last, when the increasing mileage behind us was rubbing out the smudge on the horizon that was Aden, he came into the chartroom where I was writing up the log-book and leaned over the table beside me. He watched me sign my name; but before I could add my rank, Third Officer, he took the pen from me, elbowed me out of the way, and himself wrote " Second Officer "—his method of promotion, as unceremonious as that to Third Mate of the *Aristomene*, but which had the effect of raising my pay from six to eight pounds a month.

As we proceeded southward down the African coast our latitude gradually decreased until eventually it was time to make preparations for Neptune to hold his court on board. The Rites and Observances connected with the Ceremony of Crossing the Line, as related by myself at the time, were as follows:

" Two days before we arrived in Mombasa we crossed the Line and had a great day. Father and Mrs. Neptune came on board and all the passengers were shaved. A bath about five feet deep was rigged up and pumped full. A throne was built and decorated with flags. The barber's razor, made of wood, was two feet long. The shaving-brush was a whitewash brush, and the shaving-soap a bucket of soft soap.

" The *Dramatis Personæ* were:

Father Neptune ...	Mr. ——,	Chief Officer.
Mrs. Neptune ...	Mr. Making,	2nd Officer.
Barber	Mr. ——,	2nd Engineer.
Constable ...	Mr. ——,	3rd Engineer.
Magistrate ...	Mr. ——,	Passenger.
Barber's Boy ...	Mr. ——,	Apprentice.

" Mrs. Neptune, your humble, was a charming young lady, about 21, dressed in a grey skirt, white bodice, auburn wig, a thingummy hat that I had an awful job to stick on, a veil, gloves, and a pair of corsets. These were buckled on in front, the strings at the back being hauled taut by two men, to give me a waist. Praise the Lord I am masculine! I also had a pair of white lace drawers and long black stockings. When my face was touched up and powdered I promptly fell in love with myself.

" At 9.15 a.m. the Chief Officer and myself slipped over the bow, covered by a canvas screen, and when all was ready we rang a bell and shouted: ' Ship ahoy!'

" The Captain, who was on the bridge, blew the whistle and answered us, and when we crawled over the bow as though we had just come out of the sea he came down with the Magistrate to greet us. He led us to the throne and politely helped me on to it, for which I gave him a very fetching smile. Then the Magistrate made a speech, welcoming our Majesties on board. Father Neptune replied.

" All the passengers were gathered on the saloon deck, the men in pyjamas or flannels, ready for their ducking. Speeches being over, the Magistrate summoned the Constable and Barber to do their duty. The first name was called, and as that passenger came forward the Constable, in boots sixteen inches long with wooden soles, flew upon him, arrested him and dragged him before us. After being presented to us by the Magistrate he was led away and perched on the edge of the bath. Then the Barber did *his* duty with the whitewash brush, the bucket of soft soap, and the razor, after which the victim's legs were tilted up and he fell head first backwards into the bath. The next name was called. . . .

" After the same performance had been gone through with each one it was our turn. The passengers seized the Constable and Barber and threw them into the bath. Then they advanced upon me. Four caught me, two at each end, lifted me up, and threw me in head first. Unfortunately, my head being under water, I could not see it; but the others told me that as I went in my legs flew up and exposed to the vulgar gaze of the public a dainty pair of legs, encased in black stockings and white lace unmentionables.''

We were seven days going from Aden to Mombasa. There the somewhat uneven tenor of our lives was disturbed by such rumours as this: ''By the way, we hear that we are all sold (the ships, I mean) since the owners have bankrupted (good word, that), so don't know what will happen to us when we get home.''

In Zanzibar, our last port on the coast, the rumours began to assume a more concrete form:

'' We were two days in Zanzibar, and worked day and night to hurry out the cargo, because there is a man in Mombasa who is owed £1,000 by the owners. He had got a writ, or whatever you call it, out. We escaped him by an hour.

'' The second and third engineers and I went ashore there. We hired a carriage and drove out into the country. It was splendid. We went along a narrow winding road through plantations of cocoanuts, etc., occasionally passing a native village.

'' I fancy each village must have its own trade mark, so to speak, for in every one the people wore different-coloured clothes. In one of them the women had rings in their noses and large ornaments hanging from their ears. There is one thing that is common to them all, though: the women were working, making fishing nets, baskets, etc., while the men lay around, doing nothing.

'' I suppose you know that this place used to be the centre of the slave trade. The slave market is still here, also the house of a man named Tipputip who supplied the explorer, Stanley, with stores and men.   It is a hotel now, kept by a German.

"We had orders this time to proceed to Murmagoa instead of Bombay."

In Murmagoa, a port in Portuguese India, south of Bombay, we loaded a cargo of manganese ore for Aberdeen and Antwerp, and then went on to Bombay for bunkers.

Hitherto we had carried a Lascar crew, but by this time the Mombasa rumours had become facts—the ships were to be laid up in Jarrow Slacks, Tyne—and we had orders to discharge them and to sign on a white crew for the run home.

Although our stay in Bombay was quite short, I was able to see a little of the place to satisfy my inquisitive mind:

"I was ashore yesterday and saw a Hindoo cremation, for which you have to have a permit.   I managed to get one.   I saw the body carried in.   There was no coffin; it was just in its ordinary clothes, its face uncovered and partly decomposed.   There were four small iron posts, about four feet apart one way and three feet the other, with logs lying between them.   The body was placed on those logs, and more were piled on top of it.   A small fire was lighted at a distance, and when properly burning it was placed underneath.   Then paraffin was poured over it, so that it blazed up. . . .

"What I like especially are the contrasts.   You may be in a fine road with large hotels, electric tramways, motor-cars, etc.; and a hundred yards away you come to a dirty narrow street, swarming with natives, and with bullock carts in place of motor-cars. . . ."

There is little more to say about my first voyage as an

officer in steam, although in the letters I wrote I waxed eloquent on the subject of the white crew, signed on in Bombay. They were typical specimens of the human flotsam and jetsam that drift ashore on the beaches out East: beachcombers and deserters from other ships; down-and-outers who were ready to ship in any capacity on anything that would float, and who had no intention of working unless they were driven to it. The engineers were in despair. For a day or two our speed was three knots an hour; and the average from Bombay to Perim,* where we put in for coal, was 4½ knots.

We bunkered again in Malta. There, in accordance with the traditions of the simple-minded sailor, I invested some of my pay in a Maltese canary. It sang beautifully, I heard it; but in accordance with his traditions, the any-thing-but-simple-minded Maltese canary merchant appar-ently switched birds when my back was turned. At all events, after he left the ship it never again so much as uttered a chirrup.

At the end of the voyage the ship was laid up and I returned home, my baggage including a cage in which was a feathered friend that in the U.S.A. would be called beautiful but dumb!

* See Map 5, p. 146.

CHAPTER II

STORM

" Then home, get her home, where the drunken rollers comb,
  And the shouting seas drive by,
  And the engines stamp and ring, and the wet bows reel and
    swing, . . ."

RUDYARD KIPLING : *The Long Trail.*

WHEN I left the *Swaledale* I still required about six months'
sea-service in charge of a watch before I was eligible to
sit for my Mate's certificate, and I therefore embarked
upon another offensive campaign against the haughty and
supercilious office boys. Six months' experience as a
watch-keeper had dissipated my awe of them, and I had
no difficulty in reaching my objective, the Marine Superintendents. Although one or two of the latter failed to
realise the desirability of acquiring my services, it was
not long before I strolled on board the *Indiana*, a cargo
boat of 2,508 tons, and informed the Chief Officer that I
was the new Third.

His reception and half an hour's conversation with him
were sufficient to make me realise that the *Swaledale*, with
her passenger frills, had merely been a pleasant interlude
between sail and steam. My real steamship training was
about to begin. In fact, it did so there and then, with a
foreman stevedore coming to the door and asking for one
of the Mates to go and see to something down in No. 1
hold.

The *Indiana* might be described as a typical cargo boat
of those days, just as the *Aristomene* was of sail. The
Captain's and officers' quarters were amidships under the
bridge. I had to share a room with the Second Officer,

154

and supply myself with such necessities as bedding, towels, etc. The food, though plain, was good. Meals were served to the Captain and officers in a small saloon adjoining the cabins.

Work was as plentiful as the food. During my watch on the bridge at sea I found that in addition to the usual navigation I was also expected to sew canvas, repair tarpaulins, and do odd painting jobs. A portion of my eight hours below was similarly occupied.

In port, my days, and sometimes my nights, were spent in running up and down ladders to the holds, watching the loading and discharging of the cargo, and taking copious notes of any damage done to it.

The three years that I served in this and other vessels of the same company were probably the least interesting of all those spent at sea. The ships were employed in the North Atlantic trade, with an occasional outside run down to the River Plate, and the letters I wrote contain very little fresh interest, either from the point of view of adventures or sight-seeing.

Of the former, with one or two exceptions, there were only the usual incidents encountered on the Lawful Occasions of small cargo boats. These include being awakened by a violent racing of the engines, owing to a blade or two of the propellor having dropped off. One sits up in one's bunk, expecting to see all the rivets fly out and the ship fall to pieces; the alarums and excursions when the ship shudders and stops altogether, her way of registering protest at being taken out of her natural element and run hard and fast aground; and the shout: "Fire!" which is followed by a rush along the deck with hoses, to dowse it before it gets out of control.

The latter happened on one occasion in a South American port. One of the cargo holds was so badly on fire that we could not handle it and had to call in assistance from the town. In due course the fire brigade arrived, and the captain of it walked on board. He was very short and very stout, and in his gorgeous uniform resembled a character from a comic opera rather than a fire-fighter.

He did not leave us under that impression very long. He first of all greeted our Captain with an elaborate salute and a hearty handshake. Then he waddled to the hatch where we were struggling with our inadequate hoses. For a few moments he solemnly contemplated us with eyes that seemed on the point of popping out of his plump, red face. After clicking his tongue disapprovingly and shaking his head disparagingly he proceeded to hoist one very short, fat leg over the coaming. When that foot had found a step on the vertical iron ladder he gave a mighty heave and grunt, and succeeded in getting the other one over. Then, with no knowledge of the construction of the ship or of the disposition of the cargo, he clambered down out of sight in the thick smoke.

In a minute or two he reappeared, his face blackened and his eyes streaming. Coughing and spluttering, he beckoned to his men, showed them how to rig their hoses to the best advantage, and in a comparatively short time the fire was under control.

I can only recall one instance of sight-seeing during those three years. I was ashore in Boston, Mass., with an engineer, and we joined a "rubber-neck" party that was making a tour of the town and its surroundings. The raucous-voiced guide, who was explaining the points of interest, evidently noticed that we were Britishers, for when eventually we came to a large monument he stopped the car at the foot of it. Then in a loud voice, looking directly at us, he said something to the effect that that was the Bunker Hill monument, it was so many feet high, it cost so many dollars, it was erected in such-and-such a year to commemorate the battle of Bunker Hill—where *we* drove the British into the sea!

Although the "keel that sailed had changed beyond recall," the men with whom I sailed on those ships bore out Kipling's words: "They had not changed at all."

Davy of the *Aristomene* had his prototype in a fireman of the *Indiana*.

I met him for the first time one Saturday night in Liverpool. We were to sail at midnight, and when the crew began to roll on board after the pubs closed the Captain stationed me on the gangway with instructions not to allow them to bring any bottles with them. By about half-past eleven there was a crowd of them and their pals on the dock and on deck. The majority of them were drunk, and they were arguing and quarrelling in most of the European languages and dialects.

Presently a fireman, a sea-bag on his shoulder and a bottle of whisky visible in his pocket, emerged from the mob that was standing round the shore end of the gangway. His nationality was Liverpool-Irish; height, about 6 ft. 3 in.; weight, about 200 lbs.; and he was sufficiently drunk to enjoy a fight.

Among the crowd at the other end of it was, of course, myself: height, 5 ft. 7 in.; weight, 144 lbs.; sober and of a peaceful disposition, but acutely conscious that it was my duty to deprive that fireman of his bottle.

I watched him stagger up the gangway. In the middle of it he stopped and turned round to shout another farewell to two lady friends, neither of them sober, and the charms of one sadly impaired by a very obvious black eye. As he stepped on to the deck I reached for the bottle, snatched it out of his pocket, and smashed it on the iron rail.

That action was seen from the dock as well as by the men on deck, and the noise instantly died away. Instinctively they formed a ring round us, while we faced each other in what was to me an ominous silence. It was only broken by the lady with the discoloured eye, who shouted: "Knock the little barstid's 'ead orf, Jack!"

Jack carefully deposited his bag on the deck, straightened himself up again and glared down at me. I stood by to collar him low. There was an interminable pause that almost made me wish he would hurry up and get it over. Suddenly a grin began to register on his face. Slowly but surely it spread until eventually he burst into a loud laugh.

"God damn you!" he shouted. "You little son of a bitch!"

Still laughing, he picked up his bag and staggered away to the firemen's fo'c'sle. To the disappointment of the spectators, but to my great relief, the incident was closed and babel broke out once more.

That was Davy's prototype, Jack, as he would be known to You-Who-Live-Ashore.

We on the ship knew him in his natural environment— the stokehold, where, like Davy in his, he was a very different man. When we were banging around in the Atlantic gales he was to be seen down there, balancing himself on the slippery "plates" while the ship did everything but stand on her head. As he opened and shut the furnace door to tend his fire he could be heard exchanging reminiscences with his mates about their amorous and drunken adventures in Liverpool. After cleaning his fire he would scoop up a drink of water from a bucket and wipe the perspiration and grime off his face with his "sweat rag." Sometimes, when a very heavy sea broke over the ship and cascades of icy-cold water poured down the stokehold ventilators over him, he would throw his iron "slice" down on the steel plates with a clang and look up, calling on the Almighty to bear wit-

ness that that ship was the ——est box he had ever ——
well fired, and that the —— Skipper and Mates couldn't
handle a —— London Bovril boat. In an emergency he
could usually be trusted to carry on down there until he
was ordered up to the boats. If the ship had to be abandoned, he was as useful on an oar as any of the "deck
crowd."

Much as one may complain about his behaviour when
the ship was in port, he was not easily replaced. During
a strike of sailors and firemen on one of my ships we
sailed with a black-leg crew. The firemen had been
brought from the North of England, and doubtless were
excellent men at their job—firing factory boilers. When
they came on board they were sober and gave no trouble.
For a day or two in fine weather they maintained quite a
good head of steam. Then we ran into a heavy gale, and
they promptly retired to their bunks, violently sea-sick.
After the engineers had finished their four-hour watch in
the engine-room they had to begin another in the stokehold, in order to keep sufficient steam for us to handle the
ship in the heavy sea that was running.

Drunk or sober, with or without bottle, Jack would
have been welcome.

Having served the requisite time in charge of a watch,
I left the *Indiana* to sit for my Mate's "ticket." Owing
to a new regulation that had come into force, it was first
of all necessary to obtain a First-Aid certificate, and I
therefore crammed some knowledge of emetics, compound
fractures, and arterial hæmorrhages into a brain that was
already seething with cosines of various things, jury
rudders, and red lights on my starboard bow.

In due course I was one of a party of successful candi-
dates who emerged jubilantly with a "blue paper" from
the Board of Trade examination room. From there we
proceeded to a more westerly and cheerier district of

London, where in accordance with the time-honoured custom we could "wet our ticket."

My ambition was to get into passenger ships as soon as I had my master's certificate, and knowing that those superintendents look askance at a man who has been in the habit of jumping from company to company, I went back to the same owners. I am not sure to which ship they appointed me. My discharges, together with the ship itself, were lost shortly after this, and although I obtained duplicates from the Board of Trade records, there is some confusion in the new book. I think, however, that they sent me back to the *Indiana* for a few voyages. I remember quite distinctly that during the first homeward-bound passage after obtaining the First-Aid certificate I had occasion to put into practice some of that newly acquired knowledge.

Loaded "down to the scuppers," we were bound from Newport News, Va., to London, and as we approached the region "Fifty North and Forty West where the whale got his throat" the bottom was dropping out of the barometer and a heavy confused swell was already causing the ship to give an occasional "wop (with a wiggle between)." The sun set behind a dense bank of clouds. There was the sickly green glare in the sky that together with the falling barometer invariably elicits the same question from every "Old Man" as he gazes anxiously from the bridge at it: "Everything snug around the decks, Mr. So-and-So?"

When I was called at 11.45 p.m. I was told that I required my oilskins, and I clambered up the bridge ladder to take over at midnight in dense rain and spray.

Some of you who read this may have visited one of the "luxury ships" and had an opportunity to see round her bridge. It would be fifty or sixty feet above the sea, and more than half of it would be covered in, windows

across the front, and a roof (deck-head, we call it) overhead. Only the wings would be exposed, and they would
have strongly built wooden or iron sides and front, almost
as high as yourself.

Bridges on 2,000-ton cargo boats were quite different.
They were less than half that size and only about twenty
feet above the sea. They were completely exposed, mere
platforms, with only an iron rail round them on which was
lashed a piece of canvas. A heavy spray was sometimes
sufficient to rip that off the railing.

On such a bridge I spent the next four hours trying to
keep a look-out ahead and watch the helmsman. It was
pitch dark, raining heavily, and a gale of wind was driving sheets of spray over me.

The Captain also was there, already regretting that he
had not turned the ship round in time and hove her to.
She would have been easier to handle, and would probably have ridden it out safely and more or less comfortably. As it was, it was impossible to turn her in the sea
that was then running, and there was no alternative but
to run for it, keeping the wind and sea as nearly astern as
possible. When I was relieved at 4 a.m. they were still
increasing. At eight o'clock it was howling, and there
was a mountainous sea. I went on watch again at noon.

It is difficult to conceive, and even more difficult to describe, the forces that are let loose in one of those " disturbed areas." Wind is no longer air in motion. It is a
solid, invisible something that throws one about, and
against which one can only stand with difficulty while
clinging to the rail with all one's strength. It does not
whistle or even scream in the rigging, as some sea books
declare. It roars—one long continuous roar that deafens
one and tires one's brain. It is a thousand intangible
devils, roaring in one's ears, pushing, hitting, trying to
tear off one's clothes. After an hour of it one wants to

curse it and hit back; but one can only carry on and struggle to keep a look-out ahead, or, when a heavy sea causes the "wet bow to reel and swing" off the course, to shout in the helmsman's ear: "Give her helm, man, give her more helm!"

The seas, I think, inspire one with wonder and awe rather than with fear—monstrous offspring of those thousand intangible devils, grown so tall that from the bridge one looks over the stern and *up* at them; mountains, sixty or seventy feet high, running amuck, tripping over each other and falling with a roar and a scrunch, rearing up again and racing ahead; one's brain can hardly grasp the fact that they are real.

It is no less difficult to believe that thousands of tons of steel can be kept afloat and manoeuvred in them. When one notices the first upward movement of the barometer after one of those disturbances one can understand the exaltation of Bligh as he shouted in the *Bounty's* launch: "By God! We're beating the sea itself!"

Such were the weather conditions when I arrived on the bridge at noon. The Captain was still there. He was slightly over 60 years of age, and had been standing there for about twelve hours. Wedged by the force of the wind against the rail near the wheel, he was looking aft at the seas. Each one lifted the stern out of the water and swung it to one side, while the engines raced violently and the ship began to roll over 30° or 40°. As it rose he motioned with his hand to the helmsman to put the wheel over to counteract that swing. The sea roared along the length of the ship, and when it passed the midship section she became horizontal again. Then she rolled over the other way, and while the bow was reeling wildly upwards and sideways he motioned to ease the helm. Hour after hour he stood there, knowing that if that swing were not checked in time, he would lose control of her and she might be battered to pieces in the troughs. Many of the crests broke on board round the bridge and over a cargo hatch just abaft it. So far, beyond bending a rail and washing off a ventilator, they had done no damage.

They were also having their troubles in the engine-room, owing to the violent racing of the engines when the propeller was lifted out of the water. An extra engineer was standing by the throttle, and his action of closing it when the stern rose and of opening it again when it sank synchronised with the Captain's motion to the man at the wheel.

About 2 o'clock the thing we all dreaded happened. Three mountains came up behind her. The first one canted her stern and rolled ahead. Before the helm could take effect the second one caught her and swung her further still, its crest breaking over the rail amidships. We were practically at the mercy of the third and she rolled right into it. It curled over us and fell on the bridge and the cargo hatch.

I heard a roar of breaking water all round me, followed by a crash, and the bridge disappeared from under my feet. For the next few minutes I was washed hither and thither, not knowing whether I was over the side or not. Eventually I "fetched up" with a bump against some solid object. Most of the wind was knocked out of me, but I managed to hold on to it. When I could get my head above water once more and open my eyes I found that I was clinging to a steam-pipe on the deck below the bridge and about thirty feet abaft it.

Instinct rather than reasoning power made me start back towards it, and at the foot of the ladder I met the Chief Officer, who was hurrying out of the accommodation.

"What the hell are you doing off the bridge in this weather?" he shouted as soon as he saw me.

I must have been bumped rather heavily, for my mind was a bit hazy and I could not understand what he meant. He was talking about the bridge! Well! What about it? I looked up. Something did seem to be wrong!

"That's funny!" I remember saying.

He glanced at it. The ladder was still there, but that wing of it had disappeared.

"My God!" he shouted. "Where's the Old Man— and the man at the wheel?"

He dragged me up the ladder with him. The Captain and the man were still there, the former still gazing aft and motioning to the latter with his hand, and the latter still putting the wheel over in response. Fortunately, the full force of the sea had struck the wing of the bridge where I was standing, and had left them and the steering-gear uninjured. In the "smooth" which followed those three seas they were succeeding in getting the ship off before it again.

My wits were clearing then and I was beginning to notice things, the most important being that the Chief Officer was running down the ladder again, shouting for all hands: that cargo hold was completely uncovered and open to the seas that were rolling on board. Tarpaulins and wooden hatches had all been swept off it.

The task of covering it again was a Herculean one, even for all hands, which, under those circumstances, included the three officers, steward, cook, and any firemen who could be spared. A few wooden hatches that had not been swept over the side were picked up. Spare ones and planks were dragged along and fitted in place, the seas continually washing over us and down into the hold.

The work was perhaps half completed when the same thing happened again. It came so suddenly that I cannot recollect much about it. I remember that I was on the weather side, stooping to pick up one end of a plank, and as the ship lurched over the sky was shut out by a huge wall of water that toppled over and crashed down on us.

I made quite a lengthy submarine cruise that time. I could feel myself travelling in various directions. When I was banged against winches and ventilators I consoled myself with the thought that I was still on board.

Eventually my hands felt an iron object and gripped it. When I was able to look around I found myself lying in the scupper, clinging to an iron cleat on the bulwark. Something over my head, however, was preventing me from lifting myself out of the water. I tried to pull it out of my way, and it slid down on me. It was one of the sailors. The sea had carried him across the deck and left him stranded on the bulwark, half on and half overboard.

For a moment we sat there, nearly up to our necks in the water, gazing at each other in astonishment. Then he gripped my arm with both hands and fervently thanked me for saving his life.

That was no time or place to argue or to point out that I thought I was saving my own, so he probably is grateful to me to this day.

We struggled to our feet and splashed back to the hatch, which was once more completely uncovered. By that time all hands were collecting round it—all those who were left. There were three absentees. Two were never seen again, that sea had swept them over the side. A scream disclosed the whereabouts of the third, a Scotch seaman, named Macfarlane. As he was washed across the deck one leg had been caught and wedged between a steam-pipe and the fiddley* and the shin had been frac-

---

* The " fiddley " is an iron casing, about seven feet high, enclosing the funnel and vertical iron ladders that lead down to the stokehold. It is also used as an " uptake " ventilator from the stokehold. In the photograph of the *Parisiana*, page 170, it can be seen, painted white, as a continuation of the engineers' quarters round the fore side of the funnel.

tured. We found him there. He was lying in the water
and shouting with the agony of it. The foot and lower
half of the shin were held as in a vice. The remainder of
his body was swinging back and forth as the ship
rolled.

The boatswain, a sailor and I went to him. After free-
ing his leg the sailor and I took his shoulders, and the
boatswain, a powerful man, tucked both his thighs under
one arm.

I shall never forget the next quarter of an hour. We
only had to carry him about forty feet, but he was a
heavy man, and we were knee deep in the water that was
continually swirling about the deck as the ship rolled 30°
or more each way. We could only spare him one hand;
we had to cling to the rail with the other to keep on our
feet. His fractured leg, held under one of the boatswain's
arms, was swinging about and bumping against us and
against ventilators and stanchions! His screams and
curses were ghastly to listen to.

After what seemed an interminable time we got him
into one of the cabins and laid him on the settee. We
cut off his trouser-leg, placed the leg more or less straight,
and "chocked him off" with pillows as securely as possible. I left the sailor to hold him steady, and with the
boatswain returned to the work of covering the hatch.

I have no idea now how we did it. It was a long job—
slipping on the deck, falling in the water, dragging
planks, and lashing tarpaulins that wanted to belly out
like a windjammer's mainsail. I remember that, although
seas were continually washing over us, we shipped no
more of those dangerous ones and the work was eventually finished. As we made fast the last lashing the
Chief Officer asked me: "Where's that man?"

"On the settee in one of the rooms," I replied.
"There's a man watching him."

"Well!" said he. "You're supposed to be a doctor with that First-Aid certificate, you'd better fix it for him!"

"Lordy!" I thought to myself; unpleasant as it was on deck, I would have preferred to remain there.

I returned to the cabin, and as the ship gave a violent lurch and I saw him lying there, groaning, scraps of my first-aid lectures ran through my mind: *"No attempt must be made to move the patient until the limb has been rendered as immovable as possible!"*—"Draw the foot into its natural position!"

It sounds so easy in a lecture-room. It might not be so very difficult on a comfortable bed in a hospital, but there everything was complicated by the heavy rolling of the ship. I kept the sailor, a man named Smith, to help me, and set to work, first of all cutting off his clothes and drying him. I remember that he was very bow-legged, and that I managed to "draw the foot into its natural position"—an arc of a circle that matched the other. Before I could tie on the splints he muttered: "Is it straight, sir?"

"As straight as ever it was!" I answered proudly. "Exactly like the other!"

"You shut up, Mac," Smith said to him. "The Second Mate's doin' a good job on it."

"I want it straight!" he shouted.

At that moment the Chief Officer walked in, water dripping off his oilskins and squelching in his sea-boots. There was a bottle of whisky in his hand!

"This is what you want!" he said.

He took a glass from the bottle rack, poured out three-fingers, and held it to the man's lips. Macfarlane slowly drank it.

"Christ!" he whispered faintly. "That's good!"

"What about you?" the Chief Officer asked me.

"Can do!" I replied; and he handed me an appropriate "Second Mate's nip."

Noticing a glint in Smith's eyes, he said, "You a tee-totaller, Smith?"

"No! sir!" was the prompt reply. "Good 'ealth, sir," he added as he took his three-fingers.

"Gimme another, sir," whispered Macfarlane.

The Chief Officer held the glass to his lips again, and when he had swallowed it said, "I'm going on top to see what the Old Man and the Third are doing with this wagon. Glass starting to rise and those big fellows are flattening out."

He left the cabin, but before I could make another start on the leg Macfarlane said, "Let me 'ave a look at it, sir."

"It's all right, Mac," said Smith soothingly. "You keep quiet so's we can lash it up."

"I'm goin' to see it," he cried.

He was getting excited again, so I thought it better to humour him.

"Lift his head a little," I told Smith; adding as the ship lurched, "Easy! Take it easy!"

Macfarlane looked at it. "It's not straight, sir!" he exclaimed. "Don't leave it like that!"

"The damn leg's all right. I'm not going to move it!" The events of the afternoon had not tended to give me a bedside manner.

"It isn't set proper! I won't 'ave it like that!" he shouted, beginning to struggle with Smith.

"Hold him, Smith!" I cried; then to Macfarlane, "All right, Mac, keep quiet. Tell me what you want me to do."

"Slue it round that way a bit," he said, motioning with his hand.

I was beginning to realise that my first-aid lectures had been incomplete. They had omitted the setting of a leg of an almost delirious seaman on a heavily rolling ship in a gale of wind when one was feeling somewhat shaky oneself and was still soaked to the skin and bitterly cold.

It seemed obvious, however, that if I did not humour him he would struggle and jerk it out of place. I grasped the foot.

"Look out," I warned him. "It'll hurt you."

I began to "slue it round" as gently as possible. He gave a cry. Then, gritting his teeth, the perspiration rolling down his face, he watched me silently. Suddenly he held up his hand.

"Hold her!" he gasped. "Guess she's about plumb now!" and his head fell back on Smith's shoulder.

Praise be! He had fainted, and I could finish the job in my own way.

CHAPTER III

THE *PARISIANA*

CHARTER PARTY

" It is this day mutually agreed, between ———— Owners of the Good Steamship called the ———— of the measurement . . . .

" 1. That the said ship being tight, staunch and strong, and every way fit for the voyage, shall, with all convenient speed, sail and proceed to ————.

" Freight payable ———— as customary (The Act of God, the King's Enemies, Pirates, Robbers, Thieves, Barratry of Master or Mariners, Restraint of Princes, Rulers, or People, Revolutions, Riots, or Emeutes, Fire on Board, ... or otherwise howsoever, always excepted)."

AFTER making about two voyages on the *Indiana* I was taken out of her and appointed Second Officer of the *Parisiana*, a new ship of 3,083 tons that had just been completed on the Tyne. We made two trips to Newport News, Va., and then were sent out East. Our last port there was Calcutta, where we spent five weeks of the rainy season loading a cargo for New York.

It is difficult to imagine anything more unpleasant than that class of ship in that climate. Everything about her was iron, even her decks. The cabins were unbearable. After trying vainly for a few nights to sleep in the sweltering heat the horrors of the "Black Hole" which I made a point of visiting could be understood and appreciated.

In New York we loaded a general cargo for Australian and New Zealand ports, but it was written that the ship should never reach them. On December 12th, 1910, in that lonely expanse of water between South Africa and Australia, she made of herself her own funeral pyre—and very nearly ours.

At the risk of being tedious, in addition to the picture of the ship I will give a brief description of her and of the disposition of some of the cargo, in order that what follows may be more easily understood. For the same reason I give a sectional diagram of her. Both are from memory. There are some details missing, and others that are inaccurate. The essentials are there, however, and they will serve the purpose.

She had no poop or forecastle head, the upper deck being continuous from bow to stern. Between the bow and the bridge were two cargo hatches, known as No. 1 and No. 2 hatches. In the space between the bridge and the funnel was No. 3 hatch. Walking aft from there, one passed the engineers' quarters, close abaft the funnel. On the after-deck were two more cargo hatches.

Underneath the upper deck was a similar continuous one which I will call the shelter deck. At the forward end of it were the sailors' and firemen's fo'c'sles, the remainder being used as a cargo space.

The general cargo loaded in New York consisted of every kind of merchandise, most of which I have forgotten, though from my diary and from a newspaper cutting still in my possession I know the disposition of that which concerned us at the time.

On the shelter deck, underneath the engineers' quarters, were 20,000 gallons of turpentine and 1,500 cases of petroleum. In No. 2 hold were a number of motor-cars and a large consignment of resin in barrels. Somewhere in the ship was a " parcel " of cartridges.

Owing to the distance between coaling stations, No. 3 hold was used as a bunker and completely filled with coal. At the bottom of the steel bulkhead which separated it from the stokehold was a sliding steel door (*A* on the sketch) through which coal could be passed to the furnaces.

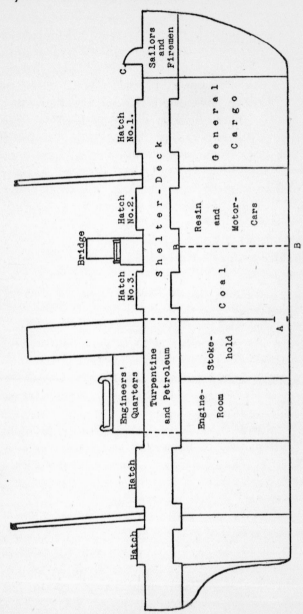

SECTIONAL DIAGRAM OF THE "PARISIANA."

A, sliding steel door; B–B, temporary wooden bulkhead; C, scuttle from crew's quarters to upper deck.

Instead of a steel, watertight bulkhead between Nos. 2 and 3 holds, a temporary wooden one had been fitted, to separate the cargo from the coal. (See B-B in the diagram.)

The ship carried four boats. There was a small one on each side of the bridge. Abaft the funnel, over the engineers' quarters, were two larger ones, one on each side.

Including the Captain, officers, and engineers, the ship's company numbered thirty-five. The Captain was about 65 years of age. He was a quiet and a rather religious man, of medium height, thin, and, though brass-bound, not very robust.

The Chief Officer was a complete contrast to him. He was an enormous Irishman, about 6 feet in height, broad and stout. His head was large and round, and was covered with a shock of bright red hair. His temper was what one would associate with those characteristics. He had had command in another company, but, having been involved in a collision with another ship, had had to leave it, and so was Chief Officer again. He was an excellent seaman, and feared neither God, the Devil, nor the Deep Sea. The right man in the right place on the *Parisiana*.

After sailing from New York on October 10th we called at Las Palmas in the Canary Islands to replenish the bunkers. That was to be the last port of call before reaching Melbourne, the first Australian port. The run down south was uneventful, and after rounding the Cape of Good Hope we began the long "reach" to the eastward—"running the easting down," as it was called in sailing-ships.

By a curious and unfortunate coincidence, there were not only no ports of call between Las Palmas and Melbourne, but we sighted no land where we could be reported, and we spoke no ships. When, therefore, we were overdue later on there was the whole of the Atlantic and Indian Oceans in which to look for us—not a cheering thought either for us or for those at home.

In that lonely stretch of sea that extends for about 4,700 miles from the Cape to Australia there are only two small islands in the vicinity of ship's tracks. Amsterdam Island, the larger, is the more northerly one, and about fifty miles south of it is St. Paul, which lies in latitude 38° 42' south and longitude 77° 34' east. Both are " Provision Depôts " and should have a store of food, blankets, matches, etc., supplied by certain governments, cached where it can be found by crews of ships who are cast away there. The Captain intended to take a course which would pass to the southward of St. Paul, but in view of the fact that we had made no landfall since leaving Las Palmas, he decided to haul to the northward and sight it, in order to check his chronometers before making the Australian coast.

About 11 a.m., December 10th, land was reported on the port bow, and at noon we were passing St. Paul Island. It was a most uninteresting place to look at.* From a distance of some miles it merely appeared as a huge rock. During the morning I had amused myself by looking it up in the Sailing Directions, and had read about the provision depôt for shipwrecked mariners. At noon I relieved the Third Officer, and I remember saying to him that it looked a devil of a place to be cast away on, one would be almost as well off in a boat. Exactly one week later I landed there, and as he helped me out of the boat he reminded me of what I had said.

After breakfast the following morning I took the usual " sights " and worked them up, had an argument with the Third Officer because our results differed, and then went back to my cabin to continue a book.

A little later I heard the Chief Officer shouting for the boatswain to bring along the covers for No. 3 ventilators.

* See drawing, p. 214.

I paid no attention to that. Captains and chief officers have all kinds of fads and fancies about the ventilation of holds and cargo, and it might have been any one of them. Almost immediately after that, however, I heard the Captain tell him to get all hands out and shift the coal in No. 3 hatch. He added "Get all the firemen the Chief Engineer can spare!"

I looked up from my book. All hands—firemen, too? That was no Chief Officer's pet theory. Things were happening! I slung my book on to my bunk, grabbed my cap, and ran out on deck. No. 3 ventilators were in my mind, and I looked at them. Quite thick smoke was issuing from them and blowing across the deck to leeward! The ship was on fire!

CHAPTER IV

FIRE!

" There's fire down below!"—*Sea Chantey.*

ONE'S sensations under circumstances such as those are as difficult to describe as they are unpleasant. It would come as a shock to You-Who-Live-Ashore were you to look up and see a cloud of smoke pouring from your bedroom window; but you can turn in an alarm, and in a few minutes an up-to-date fire-fighting equipment is there. If your house is completely burnt down, you have solid ground all round you and a friend's house to shelter you.

We were less fortunately situated. Our fire appliances consisted merely of some small canvas hoses, with but few connections on the pipeline. Instead of being upstairs, the fire was in some unknown locality under our feet, due apparently to spontaneous combustion in that mass of coal in No. 3 hold. In place of solid ground, we had some thousands of miles of almost unfrequented ocean all round us, and we had not been reported since leaving Las Palmas.

True, St. Paul Island was only about 170 miles to the westward, but in the weather conditions down in those latitudes it was a small place to find in a boat; and when we were looking at it the previous day it had not impressed us as being a very desirable seaside resort.

When I went out on deck some of the men were lashing canvas covers over the ventilators. The boatswain was running forward with others to collect shovels from the forepeak. Word had been sent to the Chief Engineer, and as we stood there the Second Engineer, with a pair of trousers pulled over his pyjamas, hurried forward to turn

176

out his firemen, shouting as he passed the Captain: "The Chief's getting shovels up from the stokehold!"

In a very few minutes all the watch below, "deck crowd" and "black squad," were elbowing each other up the ladder that led from their fo'c'sles to the upper deck, their costumes indicating the haste in which they had tumbled out on hearing the shout: "Fire in No. 3!"

As they were running aft to where we were standing a cascade of stokehold shovels poured down on the deck from the fiddley, while a fireman's voice above us shouted: "Stand from under!"

"Where's the carpenter?" the Captain asked the Chief Officer. "Get him along with a hammer to knock the wedges out."

"I've sent for him, sir," was the reply. "Knock 'em out with your shovels," he added, turning to the men.

While they were hammering at the wooden wedges that secured the tarpaulins on the hatch I saw the carpenter. He had been working aft and obviously had not heard of the fire, only that the Chief Officer wanted him. He was slouching along the deck with a what-the-hell-does-he-want-now attitude. Suddenly he caught sight of the smoke. I saw him "bring up all standing" and look at it, his mouth wide open. One could almost see the word "fire" slowly registering on his mind. Then, seemingly with an effort, he overcame his inertia and rushed forward. Without waiting for an order, he attacked the wedges with his hammer, and in a second they were flying in all directions and the hatch was being uncovered.

The Captain hoped that by shifting coal from the top it might be possible to work down close to that portion of it which was burning or smouldering, and then to pump water on it and extinguish it. The surface of it was level with the shelter deck, and a gang of men were sent down with shovels to pass it there. Another party, on the shelter deck, moved it from there out of the way to make room for more. The ship had already been stopped to lessen as far as was possible the draught, and at first the smoke was not very thick, most of it seeping up through the coal in the forward half of the hatch. The men had to be relieved from time to time, but they were able to work rapidly and were making good progress. Then suddenly the whole situation changed.

On the previous day the firemen had begun to use coal from this hold for the furnaces, passing it through the sliding door (*A* on sketch) into the stokehold. Presumably, as they had shovelled it away down below, a number of big lumps had jammed, leaving a hollow space somewhere in the middle of it. At 1.30 p.m. that jam gave way. Without any warning, the men working on the surface of the coal felt it collapse under their feet. There were terrified shouts for help as they struggled towards the side of the hatch. Some managed to reach it and grasped shovels that were held out to them by those standing on the shelter deck. Others fought against it, their faces terror-stricken as they felt themselves being sucked down with it.

Two firemen had no chance of escape. The coal caved in directly under them and they dropped into the cavity. We on deck who saw it happen rushed madly for ropes or for anything that could be thrown to them to hold them up; but while the first lines were being thrown down towards the two white, agonised faces that were looking up to us and crying for help the coal rushed in and down from all sides and completely buried them.

The ropes were caught by others, and while we clung desperately to them on deck they took turns round their arms and hung there, the coal running down past them and battering their legs and bodies. Eventually it settled and we were able to get them out. Some could drag themselves up, but others, who were waist-deep in it, had to be dug out, bruised and cut.

In addition to the task of locating and fighting the fire we were then faced with the urgent one of extricating the two firemen while there was a chance of them being alive. We only knew that they were buried somewhere in the middle of two or three hundred tons of coal, part of which we believed to be burning. One alternative was to dig down to them; but speed was imperative and we could not afford time to turn over coal gently to look for them. We must dig the pointed shovels into it with the utmost haste—and that meant there was a grave risk of driving them into the men themselves and of seriously wounding or even killing them.

The fire itself rendered that method impossible. Before we had finished digging and hauling out the other men the smoke became thicker, and in a few minutes clouds of it were belching from the forward end of the hatch. It was no longer possible to work down there.

There was then only one other alternative. By a fortunate chance, the run of coal had been on the after end, close to the bulkhead between No. 3 hold and the stokehold; and at the bottom of that bulkhead was the sliding door. In the forlorn hope of getting to them by shovelling coal through that door into the stokehold, the engineers rushed firemen down below.

I gathered afterwards from what was told us that the scene down there must have surpassed anything dreamed by Dante. In that cramped and poorly-ventilated space, in an atmosphere that was soon a thick fog of coal-dust through which the lights gleamed but dimly, and in the glare and heat of the furnaces one gang of desperate firemen frantically shovelled coal through the narrow door. Another shifted it from there out of their way.

I do not know how many tons they shifted. The en-

gineers were in charge of that, we were fully occupied on
deck; but later they told us that they could not have continued much longer, there would have been no more room
in the stokehold. As it was, towards the end they could
only work with difficulty. Gradually, however, as it was
cleared away at the bottom, the coal slid down and
brought the two men with it. Suddenly a shout was
heard from one of the men working in the doorway:
"Look out! There's a leg!"

Shovels were dropped on the iron plates with a clang,
and the Second Engineer looked through the opening, the
black-faced, sweating firemen crowding round him. He
saw two legs. The rest of the body was still buried in the
coal. He and a fireman picked up a shovel and carefully
scooped it away. More ran down over them and over
the two legs. They began again. The legs were uncovered, then part of the body. Gently they tugged at
it. It slid towards them in another cascade of "black
diamonds." They dropped their shovels and pushed coal
through the door with their hands until the face was uncovered. Slowly, to avoid another run, they dragged the
body clear and out into the stokehold. There was a loud
cheer, and as shovels were picked up again to carry on
with the search a huge fireman slung the unconscious man
over his shoulder and carried him up the iron ladder to
the deck.

We on deck heard that cheer, and a few minutes later
were lifting the limp form down from the fiddley to the
deck. His head was cut and bruised, and his mouth and
nose were clogged with fine coal; but he was still alive.
It was some time before he was brought round, but eventually wheezy sounds could be heard in his throat. Then
he began to groan, and finally was able to breathe naturally. His wounds were bandaged and he was made
comfortable on the deck.

Before he regained consciousness another cheer from below announced the recovery of the other man, who was also brought up on deck. His head and face were badly knocked about and covered with blood and coal-dust. The Captain sent the steward and myself to try to restore him to consciousness, but although we tried every means we could think of, it was hopeless and at last we had to give it up.

Meanwhile the remainder of the ship's company had been equally busy at No. 3 hatch. I have already said that clouds of smoke began to drift up the hatchway after the coal had run down and buried the two men. While the engineers and firemen were hurrying towards the stokehold to dig them out the Chief Officer suddenly burst into a loud laugh.

"That's done the job for us!" he shouted. "Get the hoses along!"

"I believe it has," said the Captain. "It's run down and uncovered the burning coal."

"Sure it has!" was the excited reply. "We'll get water on it and dowse it!"

A cheer from the men showed that they had overheard those remarks, and an instantaneous and complete change came over them. Instead of working feverishly in a grim silence, they began to laugh and joke as they ran the hoses along the deck to the hatch.

"Gorblimey!" exclaimed a cockney sailor. "This beats Guy Fawkes dye!"

"Hey! Cook!" shouted another. "Put yer bloody soup pot on this and give us a drop of 'ot stuff fer a change!"

"'Ope it chokes yer!" replied the "doctor," looking up with a black, grimy face from a kinked hose that he was straightening.

A similar change could be seen in the Captain and Chief Officer. They were standing together on the starboard side, looking down and trying to see through the smoke. The tense expression had left their faces, and they were already concocting an entry for the logbook.

This wave of optimism lasted for perhaps a couple of minutes, and then some freakish change in the draught caused a momentary rift in the cloud of smoke. Everyone was standing round the coamings, looking down. The surface of the coal was, of course, much lower since the jam gave way, and so for a second they not only saw that, but also the upper part of the temporary wooden bulkhead that separated the coal from the cargo in No. 2 hold. It was sufficient to enable them to notice that the smoke was coming through spaces between the planks. Not the coal, but the cargo in No. 2 hold, including hundreds of barrels of resin, was on fire!

The laughter and jokes instantly died away and were followed by a dead silence. All of us, from Captain to cabin-boy, realised then what we were up against. The men with hoses dropped them. Red, watery eyes in black, grimy faces gazed round uneasily, first at the Captain and then all round the deck and at the boats.

"Gawd!" I heard one man mutter.

"That's tore it!" said another.

For a moment the sudden realisation of the seriousness of the situation shook them. The Chief Officer promptly snapped them out of it. He talked to them in the language they best understood. What he said would not look well in print; but in a few seconds he had driven the furtive, uneasy look from their eyes, and the grim expression that had been there before returned.

"Don't stand there gaping at me! Get some axes!" he shouted at the end of his peroration; and then, after tying a wet handkerchief over his mouth and nose, he climbed rapidly down the ladder into the smoke.

He reappeared almost immediately. He had discovered that, as it was coming through the bulkhead and drifting *upwards*, it was not so thick right down on the coal. Provided one climbed down quickly, it was possible to remain there for a few minutes and work. He suggested that holes be cut in the bulkhead and hoses played through them directly on to the fire. The only other alternative was to open up No. 2 hatch; but as it would be necessary to hoist out a lot of cargo in order to get below with hoses, much time would be lost and the draught would be greatly increased.

While he was explaining that to the Captain the carpenter returned with axes. The Chief Officer looked at the men.

"I want somebody to help me down there," he said. "Who's coming?"

None of them replied verbally, but they all came forward, those in front picking up the axes.

"Don't be so damned greedy!" he remarked with a laugh. "I want one axe. You, Jones, get a life-line round you."

The end of a rope was secured round each of them and a wet cloth was fastened over their mouth and nose. Then they climbed down the hatchway.

In a few minutes Jones reappeared. He was lifted over the coaming to make room for the Chief Officer. They wrenched the cloths off their faces and gasped in some fresh air.

It was then the turn of another man and myself. Life-lines and cloths were fastened on us and we slid, rather than climbed, down the vertical iron ladder. There was just sufficient light to enable us to see where the Chief Officer had been chopping. It was very hot, and what

little air we could breathe into our lungs only hurt and
stifled us.   When we had completed one hole through
which a hose could be played I pushed the man towards
the ladder and followed him up.   At the top my eyes
were so painful that for a second I could not open them,
but I felt hands grasp my arms and lift me on to the
deck.

There was a wonderful moment while my lungs
breathed in real air, and then I gasped the information
that one hole was ready for a hose.

My recollections of what followed are very vague.
Time after time the Captain, or an officer, and a man
went down into that nightmare of heat and smoke.   They
reappeared a few minutes later with tortured eyes and
lungs and were replaced by others.

After holes had been cut in the bulkhead additional
smoke came through them and made conditions worse.   It
was so dense in No. 2 hold that we could get no idea of the
exact locality of the fire and could only play the water
blindly in all directions.   Soon after three o'clock it became impossible to work down there.   One man was over-
come by the smoke and had to be hauled up by his life-
line.   According to the diary: "At 3.30 p.m. the smoke
was so thick in No. 3 hold that it was impossible to get
down at all.   We battened it down and opened up No. 2,
to jettison the cargo and get at the fire that way."

No. 2 derricks had already been rigged, and as soon as
the hatch was uncovered men jumped down.   Cases of
goods were piled on to slings.   These were hooked on and
hoisted on deck to be thrown overboard.   The men had
to be relieved at frequent intervals owing to the smoke,
and as they worked the cargo out it became worse.

It was during that time that the steward and I were
trying to revive the fireman.   I therefore did not see much
of what was done.   The diary says: "They worked there

for over an hour, and then the smoke was so dense that they could not see across the hatch.''

The Captain gave orders for it to be battened down, and for another attempt to be made at No. 3. While this hatch was being uncovered he swung the ship, hoping to cause a draught that would lessen the smoke down there. It was utterly hopeless. Dense clouds of it rolled up and drifted round the deck. When he shouted to us to cover it again it was all we could do to get close enough to put on the hatches.

At half-past five he decided to proceed with all speed towards St. Paul Island. If a suitable place could be found there, he intended to beach the ship. Holes were also cut by the engineers in No. 2 ventilators. Steam-pipes were connected to them and steam turned on from the main boilers, in the hope of smothering the fire.

At 7.45 p.m. the ship was stopped for a few minutes to bury the fireman. He had been hastily "sewn up," and placed at the stern with an ensign over him. All those who were not on duty mustered there.

Considered as a funeral party, we must have presented a strange appearance, though there was no shortage of "black." The Captain, officers, engineers, sailors, and firemen were black with coal-dust and smoke from "truck to keelson." It was not easy to know who was who, though a fireman could be distinguished by his filthy black "sweat-rag" and an officer by his wet and coal-stained uniform.

So we gathered round what lay beneath the Red Ensign, looking at each other's black faces with red-rimmed, sore, and watery eyes. The Captain read the prayers: ". . . we now commit this body to the deep . . . until the sea gives up its dead. . . ." There was a splash; and as the engine-room telegraph rang " full speed " once more we walked forward. I heard one fireman remark

13

to his mates: "Well! That poor b——r's troubles are over!"

The routine of that night was similar to all others. We were proceeding at full speed towards the island and there was nothing to do but keep our usual watches and, if possible, get stellar observations to fix the ship's position.

Nevertheless, the smoke that was oozing from venti-lators, the smell of burning in all parts of the ship, and our sore eyes were reminders that that night did differ from previous ones: that while an officer walked up and down the bridge or worked out the latitude and longitude by stars; while an engineer watched his gauges and bear-ings, and the firemen cleaned their fires and shovelled on more coal; and while the officers and men off duty got some rest, a furnace was blazing underneath them in No. 2 hold.

And yet, so accustomed does one become to ship's routine, when the bell was struck on the bridge and an-swered by the look-out man no one noticed the irony in his cry: " All's well!"

The first entry in the diary next day, December 12th, reads: "7 a.m. the deck forward was almost too hot to walk on, and owing to the great heat down below, the ship's side close to the water was bulging out."

It was obvious then that in spite of everything being covered as securely as possible and of steam being turned on to the hold directly from the main boilers, the fire was gaining rapidly. This new development, the ship's side bulging, made it doubtful whether she would last until we made the land. The Captain therefore decided to make another attempt to get to it.

This time he did not stop the ship to lessen the draught in the hold. So far we had been favoured with fine weather—light breezes and the usual slight swell that is always felt in mid-ocean. During the night, however, the wind had settled in the north-north-west and was freshening, bringing with it a rough sea. The visibility also was deteriorating and at 7 a.m. there was a fine, misty rain. If we failed to reach the island, it was imperative to get as close to it as possible before the ship's side opened out altogether.

The first attempt was to be made by way of No. 3 hatch, and he gave orders for it to be uncovered. There was not much smoke down there, but any doubt as to the exact locality of the fire was set at rest. It had burned through the wooden bulkhead between Nos. 2 and 3 holds and was spreading from the cargo to the coal. When we took off the hatches we looked down at a blazing mass of hundreds of barrels of resin and tons of coal.

Owing to there being so little smoke, we were able to stand on the shelter deck for a few minutes at a time and play water directly on the flames. The diary says: "The Captain, Chief Officer, and I went down there in turn for about five minutes, taking with us a man to assist with the hose."

The heat was intense. It scorched our eyes, and before we dared venture near it we had to have a hose played over us. It was a hopeless task; the hoses were so pitifully inadequate, both in quantity and size.

"Might as well —— on it!" I heard one of the men say.

Probably a spark of the hope that springs eternal kept us at it, though the small streams of water that we splashed on what was literally a burning, fiery furnace did not have the slightest effect.

Eventually we had to give it up. Human flesh, especially the eyes, could not support such a heat.

At noon we were forced to stop the ship. The bulges

in the ship's side were becoming worse and looked like opening out altogether.

Our last despairing effort was made at No. 2 hatch; and then even the most obstinate of us had to admit that we were beaten. The tarpaulin and hatches were taken off, but I cannot remember all we did. Various methods were tried to shift some of the cargo and to get down with a hose; but although, as at No. 3, there was not much smoke, the heat was appalling. We could see the flames. They were coming towards us as we worked there, literally eating up the cases of inflammable goods that were in their path. At three o'clock they suddenly blazed up through the hatch-way, scattering us in all directions and driving us back abaft the bridge.

That was our Waterloo. At 3.30 p.m. the Captain ordered the boats to be provisioned and swung out in readiness for lowering. At the same time he proceeded once more towards the island, though, owing to the condition of the ship's side, at reduced speed.

There was then no chance of the ship reaching it, but probably no one worried about that—they were too worn out. Personally I was incapable of worrying about anything, I was so dead tired and my eyes were so painful. In fact, as I walked along the deck to the boat on the port side of the engineers' quarters there was no part of me that did not hurt. All my muscles were sore and aching, my skin was dried up by the exposure to the heat in No. 3, and felt like " crackling "; even the cool fresh air hurt my lungs. Worst of all were my eyes. If only I could have sat down somewhere and held my hands tightly over them to shut out the light and wind!

All hands were in the same state. Men not required to assist at the boats flung themselves down on the deck and buried their face and eyes in their arms. Those who were working moved about as though walking in their sleep, their eyes half, and sometimes quite, closed.

The boats in which we were to leave the ship were the two carried over the engineers' quarters abaft the funnel. We were fortunate in having plenty of time to get them ready. They had contained, of course, the usual Board of Trade requirements such as biscuits, water, compass, etc., but we were able to add much more gear that should be useful if we succeeded in reaching St. Paul. Some tinned meat, cocoa, brandy, extra biscuits and water were put into them, as well as rope, twine, canvas, fishing lines, carpenter's tools, and a considerable quantity of tobacco and cigarettes. From the chart-room we brought the chronometers, sextants, a chart, sailing directions, and nautical tables. Our dog was tied to the after thwart of the port boat. The ship's cat was placed in a box in the stern-sheets. Both boats were then swung out and placed in readiness for lowering.

At 4 p.m., when we were about 26 miles from the island, the ship was stopped for the last time. Not only was smoke coming through the ship's side between the steel plates near the water, but holes had been burned through the iron deck round No. 2 hatch. Suddenly a large section of it caved in, just on the fore side of the bridge. The flames and heat drove the Captain off it. He pushed the engine-room telegraph handle to "stop," and shouted to the Third Officer and the man at the wheel: "Get out of it!"

He followed them down the bridge ladder, and went to see the Chief Engineer about abandoning the engine-room.

There was then nothing more we could do until the time came to leave the ship. While it had still been possible to go forward to the fo'c'sles the Captain had instructed the men to bring all their clothes aft; and when the whole ship's company was assembled near the boats the deck

outside the engineers' quarters resembled a miniature
Petticoat Lane.

They were thankful for his foresight. Most of them
were soaked with water from the hoses, and all were black
with coal-dust and smoke. Some buckets were found, the
engineers gave them soap and they were able to wash
and change into dry clothing. There was, of course, no
room in the boats for their bags. They therefore put on
as much underclothing as possible and, most of them,
their shore-going suit of clothes.

At 5 p.m. some food was served out to them, and after
that they lay on the deck and dropped off to sleep from
sheer exhaustion. The Captain and officers were able to
use the engineers' bath, and we had something to eat in
their mess-room with them.

At six o'clock the ship began to take a heavy list to starboard, and it was time to get the boats away. The men
were roused, the boats manned and lowered into the
water, and both made fast to boat-ropes that had been
prepared on the lee side. With the exception of the Captain, Chief Officer, and myself, and the Chief and Second
Engineers, all the ship's company was kept in them.

When it became dark, although we were hardly able
to appreciate it, the ship must have presented a wonderful
spectacle. I quote the diary: "At 8 p.m. No. 1 hold
was on fire, and soon after that the saloon and bridge
also. The flames rose higher than the masthead. Several
holes were burned completely through the ship's side, and
blazing masses of cargo rolled out into the sea. About
10 p.m. two dozen rockets that were stored in the chart-
room exploded all together."

The fire was not only spreading forward, but also, of
course, aft. We who remained on board could follow its
advance towards the stern by the temperature of the iron
upper deck. After the bridge went it slowly crept along

underneath us, until eventually the deck was warm over the turpentine and petroleum that was stowed under the engineers' quarters.

That was the cue for our exit, and we went to the side-ladder. The last words spoken on the ship were while we were waiting for the boats to haul alongside. They were spoken, or, to be more accurate, sung by the Chief Officer, the " Red-headed Mick," as the men called him behind his back. Before stepping over the rail on to the ladder he gave a loud laugh and sang two lines of an old sailing-ship chantey:

" The food is bad and the wages low,
It's time for us to leave her."

His boat came alongside and he followed the Second Engineer down. It was dropped astern clear of the ladder. When the other had taken its place the Chief Engineer and I scrambled into it. For a minute the Captain stood at the top of the ladder, silhouetted in the glare. I saw him shake his fist at the blaze forward. Then he turned round and slowly climbed down into the stern-sheets. That was at 1 a.m., December 13th. The wind was still freshening, the sea rough, and the weather misty.

I will let the diary finish this phase: " 3.30 a.m., wind and sea increasing. We could no longer lay alongside, having twice been nearly swamped as the ship rolled. The Captain decided to abandon her altogether, and we pulled some distance to the north-west."

CHAPTER V

IN AN OPEN BOAT

" Bail, lads!   By God!   We're beating the sea itself!"
BLIGH of the Bounty.

I THINK we all dreaded the moment when the Captain shouted to the Chief Officer to cast off and pull to windward.   Much as he may growl at his ship, the British seaman, more perhaps than any other, looks upon it as his home, especially on long voyages such as this one.

The Captain has photos and pictures on the bulkhead, or wall, of his cabin.   Odd souvenirs of home are strewn about on his table and desk, and he has a shelf filled with his favourite books.   One drawer contains a lot of note-books, full of his fads on navigation and stowage of cargo. In another, that he always keeps locked, are his latest letters from home.

He is not a passenger who opens his steamer trunk for a few days during a cruise, and to whom the ship means nothing more than a comfortable way of travelling and of seeing the world.   Like the Englishman's home, that cabin is his castle.   All those things are part of his life and go where he goes.

One sees much the same thing in the officers' and engineers' rooms.   Their photos and all their "junk" are spread about and travel from ship to ship with them.

If you go forward you will see a room marked: "Boat-swain and Carpenter."   In it will be found the boat-swain's pet marline-spike, fid, palm and needles, and probably a half-completed sennit door-mat that he is making to take home.   The one drawer will contain his and the carpenter's shore-going suit of clothes. A few pictures, cut from the illustrated periodicals, will be pasted on the bulkhead.

The carpenter has his own chest of tools which he keeps in his shop. They cost a lot of money, and he will have spent years buying them one at a time out of his pay. In his shop, also, is sure to be a bit of furniture that he is making in his spare time for his home.

In the fo'c'sles the men will have picture-postcards of actresses and of amorous couples surrounded by flowers, pinned over their bunks. All their worldly possessions are contained in their canvas sea-bags.

When we were evicted by the fire, all that part of our life had to be left behind to burn with the ship, and it was in our minds as we laid alongside the blazing hulk in the heavily laden boats. In the port one were the Captain, Chief and Third Engineers, myself, thirteen men, the dog and the cat. The starboard one carried the Chief and Third Officers, Second and Fourth Engineers, and thirteen men. In addition to that complement were the stores and provisions. The boats therefore were very crowded and had but little freeboard.

We were laying near the stern, as far as possible from the flames, and although she was a comparatively small ship, her size was magnified by the darkness and mist until her black hull, silhouetted in the glare of the fire, seemed to tower over us. As she rolled away from us the boat-ropes, that were fast to her rail, were wrenched out of the men's hands, and it was necessary to fend off with boat-hooks and stretchers to prevent the edges of her steel plates from fouling the boat's planking and capsizing us. When she rolled towards us it was even more difficult. We were on the starboard side, towards which she had listed, and each time she seemed to be falling over on us. Her plate edges struck the gunwale and nearly pushed it under, while water slopped over us into the boat. Further forward blazing masses of cargo were rolling out through holes in her side.

During those two hours our morale was probably lower than at any other time. We were dead tired, hungry, cold, and wet, and after the exposure to the smoke and heat the motion of the boat was making many of us sick. It was an agony to look into the cold wind and mist with our smoke-sore eyes. The fireman who had been rescued from the coal was in the Chief Officer's boat, and was in a very weak condition. Others were suffering from such minor injuries as cuts and bruises.

"There goes the old woman's half-pay!" said one of the men when the Captain gave orders to cast off.

It did not help to cheer us up to be reminded that our pay ceased as soon as we abandoned the ship.

We experienced some difficulty in getting away clear of the ship's side, and as soon as we were out of the lee she had made for us we met the full force of the wind and sea. The diary states that we pulled some distance to the north-west, or windward, but actually we made little progress. We could hardly hold our own, and the ship merely drifted to leeward of us.

The force of the wind and sea was such as one sometimes sees from a sheltered corner on the boat deck of a large passenger steamer: a strong breeze, and a rising sea that is just beginning to give a gentle see-saw motion to the ship. As the bow dips one watches light showers of spray blowing across the fore-deck. If there are no clouds, these are magicked into small rainbows by the sunshine.

We were struggling to pull a crowded, heavily laden boat into the teeth of a similar wind and sea on a pitch-dark, misty night. Each of those waves was an enemy against which we had to defend ourselves. Some kicked the oars out of the men's hands. Others punched the bow and pushed it to one side or the other. The larger ones broke over the gunwale, and men, crouched on the bottom boards out of the way of the oars, were constantly bailing. Several of those breaking seas would have been sufficient to swamp us. Very few could have wetted and damaged irreparably our scanty store of provisions.

After a while this buffeting began to tell on the men in their exhausted state. Oars were knocked out of their hands more frequently. One man, who was jerked backwards off the thwart, lost his overboard. Then about 4.30 a.m. the wind began to moderate. The mist, however, became thicker. Before long we were enveloped in a dense fog and the ship was lost to sight. Both boats were turned round, and when we had pulled back about a mile in the direction we had last seen her we took in the oars and put out the sea-anchor.*

It may be wondered why, instead of waiting two hours alongside the ship and then rowing back to her after abandoning her, the Captain did not immediately make for St. Paul Island. The explanation is that he wanted to make sure she was a total loss before finally leaving her. It is not pleasant for a captain to abandon his ship

* A sea-anchor is a funnel-shaped canvas bag, sewn on an iron hoop about two feet in diameter. A " bridle " at the end of a rope is also secured to it, the other end of the rope being fast to the bow

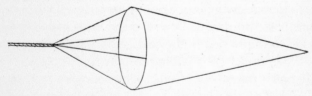

of the boat. When it is thrown overboard it acts as a drag as the boat drives to leeward before the wind and sea, and should keep her heading into it.

and, later, to learn that she has been picked up and towed or worked into port by another man.   There certainly seemed no possibility of this; but strange things happen at sea, and it becomes second nature to take nothing for granted.

The wind and sea continued to moderate, until at eight o'clock there was only a light westerly breeze, and we were shipping no more water.   Our first meal was served out then.   It consisted of one biscuit and a " Three Castles " tin of fifty, half full of water.

While we laid there in the fog the men were able to rest, and they huddled together for warmth in the bottom of the boat.   The dry clothing into which they had changed before leaving the ship was soaked, but no discomfort could have prevented them from sleeping.

The Captain, engineers, and I spent the morning taking stock of the provisions.   The biscuits and water were placed aft where we could watch them, and after wrapping canvas round the former the carpenter rigged a small platform which raised them clear of any water that might collect on the bottom boards.   We also rearranged a locker in the stern-sheets, to keep dry the chronometer, sextants, and books, and to prevent them from rolling about.

As we worked there, occasionally looking round to see if there were any signs of a break in the fog, the uneasy movements and mutterings of the sleeping men showed that they were living over again in their dreams the events of the past two days.   One of them, who had narrowly escaped being buried in the coal, suddenly sat up, shouting: "On deck!   It's pulling me down!"

He woke the others.   Half-frightened, they started up and looked at the Captain.

" It's all right, men," he assured them.   " We're not far from land.   As soon as the fog lifts and we see the ship I'll make a start. Get some rest now, I'll want you on the oars soon.''

Like children being put to bed by their nurse, they huddled more closely together, shut their tired, sore eyes, and went obediently to sleep once more—literally '' rocked in the cradle of the deep '' as the boat rose and fell on the high swell that was still running.

Towards noon the visibility improved and we saw the other boat. Gradually the fog cleared away altogether and we sighted the ship to leeward of us. She had a very heavy list and was blazing fore and aft, dense volumes of black smoke pouring from one of the after hatches. The men were roused, the sea-anchor taken in, and we rowed as close to her as possible. We found a lot of wreckage—hatches, partly burned cases, wooden fittings, etc.—floating round her, and heard several explosions, apparently due to the '' parcel '' of cartridges.

At noon the sun was visible, and I got out my sextant to make an attempt at finding the latitude. The mast had been stepped after leaving the ship. Standing on a thwart with one arm round it, a man holding each of my legs, I tried to '' bring the sun down.'' The difficulty was to find the horizon. When the boat was in the trough of the swell all I could see was a wave on both sides of me. Then it rose on the crest of the next one and I looked over an expanse of undulating water, trying to find a definite straight line against the sky that might be it.

Eventually I obtained a few ''sights '' that seemed fairly satisfactory, and I worked out the latitude with the mean of them. At 2.30 p.m. I was able to get other observations for longitude, and according to those calculations the island bore north-west, distant 30 miles. We pulled over to the other boat.

''She can't float much longer!'' the Captain shouted. '' I'm going to make for the land now!''

Neither fire nor water could depress the Chief Officer's spirits. He gave a loud laugh, and roared, "Aye, aye, sir! A month's pay we're there first!"

The boats' crews waved their caps and gave each other three cheers. The Captain shouted a final "Good luck to you!" and sat down.

"Give way, lads!" he ordered.

We were off! The race for a month's pay and for the lives of thirty-four men had started.

Our biggest handicap was the prevailing wind. It was westerly, and was therefore against us. Though the distance was only 30 miles, it would probably be a dead beat or pull to windward all the way. When we started there was so little breeze, and that westerly, that the sail was of no use to us and we had to resume rowing. Fortunately there were sufficient of us to double-bank the longer oars and to relieve each other every hour, though, owing to the lack of food, it was killing work.

The sleep had done the men good, however. They were in better spirits and lay back on their oars with a will. The wind remained light for some hours, and although there was still a heavy swell, we gained a few miles. At five o'clock we had supper: one biscuit and W. D. and H. O. Wills' demi-tasse of water.

As the evening drew on one could see the men's strength waning. They began to droop over, rather than to lay back on, their oars, and it became more and more of an effort for their aching wrists to lift them out of the water at each stroke.

At eight o'clock the wind backed to the north-west, dead ahead, and began to freshen. The sea rose with it. By 10 p.m. we were making little headway and water was slopping over the gunwale. At midnight we were hardly holding our own and were bailing most of the time. We had to struggle on, though. Even if we only held our own, it was preferable to laying to a sea-anchor and drifting to leeward away from the island.

The men were no longer able to rest. When they were relieved they slid off the thwart on to the bottom boards and sat there in the water, scooping buckets and tins of it over the side. As fast as it was bailed out more cascaded over the gunwale and over them.

Slowly those interminable hours passed, until at 4 a.m., December 14th, the wind had increased to a moderate gale with thick rain, and a heavy sea was running. It was no longer possible to hold the boat's head up to it and the sea-anchor had to be put out. Even then we were obliged to have an oar out on each side, to straighten her up when she was tossed almost broadside on to it.

About that time we saw what we believed to be the last of the ship. A faint glare was noticed on the horizon astern. Suddenly it brightened until the masses of black cloud above it were dyed a dull red. So it remained for the space of a minute or two; and then "night drew her sable curtain over it."

Daylight came at last and ushered in another day, December 14th. It was a relief to be able to see what we were doing. In the darkness the seas broke over the gunwale and pushed the bow round before we could see them—attacking us when our backs were turned, as it were. When dawn broke it became a more sporting fight. We could see them coming and anticipate their moves.

About nine o'clock we had some food. To the one biscuit and half-tin of water was added a thin slice of corned meat. That breakfast was a long time being served: the sail had to be spread over the stern-sheets to protect it from the spray that was continually blowing aft, and one by one the men crawled underneath it. Each

received his "whack," ate it quickly, and then backed
out to make room for another.

During the meal the wind shifted to the south-west and
began to moderate. At 1 p.m. we were able to take in the
sea-anchor, and although there was still a very strong
wind and a heavy confused sea, we managed to get the
sail on her. Close-hauled on the port tack, we were just
able to make the course, north-west.

In that wind, with no reef in the sail, we had literally
turned the tables on the seas. The boat then was leaping
at them. She pushed them, banged them, jumped over
some and ducked her nose under others. Every available
bucket and tin was brought into use to keep pace with
the deluges that were continually streaming over us.
Little we cared about that. We were on our way, and,
what was more, not using up what little strength was left
to us on those damnèd oars. For the time being at all
events we had beaten the wind and sea. We had captured
and harnessed our enemy, the prevailing westerly wind,
and were making it do the work for us.

One could read that thought in the minds of the men.
When you have sailed for some time with the same crew
there springs up a bond between them and you. In port,
when they get drunk, you wish to goodness you could get
rid of them. When they growl and "hang the latch" at
sea you call them a bunch of damned sea-lawyers. At
the same time you know the stuff that is hidden away
under their "scrimshanking." The fire afforded an
opportunity for our men to show theirs. When the Chief
Officer wanted a man to go down with him into the thick
smoke at No. 3 hatch they were all ready to follow him.
During those days in the boat I never heard a growl.
In the language of Davy of the *Aristomene*, they hadn't
the strength left in them to "pull a sodger off'n their
sister," but none of them hung back when a man was

wanted on an oar. One comes to look on them as one's protégés to a certain extent, and to understand their moods.

At noon that day they had been crouched on the bottom boards, exhausted and famished, not caring much what happened. As soon as the boat began to crash into the seas and to shoulder them out of her way one immediately sensed a change in them, a feeling of exhilaration. I watched them pull themselves on to their knees and gaze to windward and at the straining canvas. They were still exhausted and famished, water was still streaming over them, their unshaven faces were still white and haggard. The change was to be seen in the eyes, which have been called the "mirrors of the soul." The half-scared, half-despairing look of a beaten man had disappeared. It was replaced by hope, and by a readinsss to come back into the ring and to give and take some more.

A mistake was made that afternoon which put us out of the running for the month's pay and might well have lost the race for the men's lives.

During the two days we were struggling with the fire on the ship the Captain had done as much as any of us. In the boat he had his one biscuit and his half-tin of water, just as we did. He was about 65 years of age and was not a strong man. Besides that he had had to shoulder all the responsibility; and when he finally decided to make for the island he was worn out.

Since the start of the "race" at about 3 p.m. the previous day, therefore, I had been "coxing." During the night I was crouching, wet through and cold, on a wooden seat in the stern-sheets, clinging to the tiller and shouting directions to the men at the oars as the seas leaped out of the darkness at us.

About half-past one that afternoon I suddenly rolled off the seat into the bottom of the boat, my limbs so

14

cramped in that sitting position that I was unable to move them. I recollect feeling a pain as somebody pulled my legs straight, and then I must have dropped off to sleep.

I woke up towards three o'clock. For a few moments I lay there half asleep, wondering if it was " one bell," though I could not remember being called. I hoped the Third Officer had left plenty of sandwiches, for I was damned hungry. I stretched and yawned, and realised that my neck was stiff, and my pillow unusually hard. When I opened my eyes to see what was wrong with it I found that it was a cork lifebelt! I was lying in the bottom of a boat!

That discovery caused a small rift in the fog in my mind, and I remembered that we had abandoned the ship. Then I noticed that while I was sleeping the sail had been shifted round. We had been close-hauled on the port tack. As my mind cleared I saw that we were running free with the wind on the starboard quarter. That must mean an easterly wind! In that case we should make the land in a few hours. I looked aft. A sailor was at the tiller.

" What are you steering?" I asked.

" Nor'-west, sir," he answered. "Same as you was."

The sun sent me off on another tangent. I was lying on the port side, facing to starboard, and suddenly I saw it shine through a break in the clouds. That was strange: heading north-west—sun on the starboard side—and it was p.m.! If the man really was steering north-west, the sun was in the east in the afternoon—which was absurd!

That thought cleared my mind completely. I got up, took the tiller, and told him to get a rest. One glance at the compass explained the mystery. The helmsman on a ship stands behind it, looking forward as he keeps the

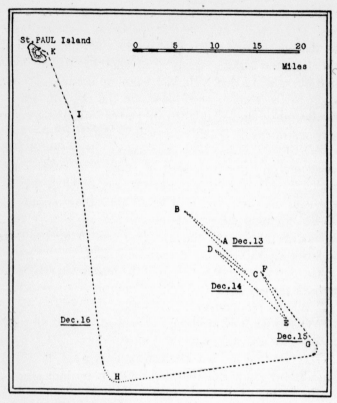

TRACK OF BOAT-VOYAGE TO ST. PAUL ISLAND.

A. Left ship 3.30 a.m., December 13.

A–B. Advancing under oars.

B–C. Laying to sea-anchor during gale, and drifting away from island.

C–D. Advancing under sail.

D–E. Running away from island under sail owing to mistake in steering.

E–F. Advancing under sail again when mistake was discovered.

F–G. Laying to sea-anchor during gale, and drifting away from island.

G–H. Under oars and sail on starboard tack, wind about N.W.

H. Wind hauling westerly, steering for island on port tack.

I. Sighted island 2 points on port bow 5 p.m., December 16.

K. Arrived about 10 a.m., December 17.

ship on her course.   There in the boat it was placed
right in the stern, and thus was behind the helmsman—
just the reverse!   At some time, probably in the confusion
as the boat yawed when I let go the tiller and rolled off
the seat, the sailor, exhausted in mind as well as body,
had not realised that.   He had therefore brought the boat
back to the course, north-west, on the opposite side of
the compass; and since then we had been running before
a strong fair wind directly away from the island!

It had, of course, been necessary to trim the sail for
what was apparently a shift of wind, and nobody had
realised what was happening.   It was to be hoped for
the sake of their peace of mind that they would not
notice anything strange about another apparent change
in its direction.   I put the tiller over and shouted to them
to lower the sail and dip it round the mast.

The difference in the motion of the boat when she began
to buck the sea again roused the Captain.

" What's the matter?" he asked.

" Only a shift of wind, sir," I replied.   " It's all right,
though, we can still make the course."

The fact that not one of them realised what the veriest
land-lubber could not but help notice is an indication of
their condition.

Supper was at five o'clock: one biscuit, a thin slice of
corned meat, and the usual half-tin of water.   The diary
remarks here: " Fortunately we had plenty of tobacco
and matches."

Were I ever to be placed in a similar plight, I should
be as careful about having a supply of tobacco as of food.
I admit it supplies no vitamins or calories and that
smoking on an empty stomach is not a good thing; but it
does help to soothe the terrible craving for food and the
sickly, sinking feeling that sap one's courage.   Both have
to be experienced to be appreciated.

Until 3 a.m., December 15th, similar weather conditions prevailed. Then the wind suddenly backed to the north-west and increased rapidly. At 8 a.m. we were again laying to the sea-anchor in a strong gale, very high sea, and dense rain, heavily engaged in another pitched battle with the prevailing westerly wind. It had brought up reinforcements and was attacking more strongly than ever.

Our defensive tactics were practically the same: the sea-anchor as a drag on the boat's bow and oars out on each side, though instead of using the rudder, we un-shipped it and put a long steering oar through a grummet in the stern. A sailor and I stood in the stern-sheets, and as each sea pushed the boat's bow to one side or the other we heaved on that oar to straighten her up, while the worn-out, desperate men dug theirs into the water to help us. Sometimes they only succeeded in digging them into the air and rolled backwards off the thwart. If they could get up again, well and good. If not, a bucket or tin was put in their hand and somebody else took their place.

We did not *live* through that day. We dreamed it away in the worst kind of nightmare, similar to that in which one is being chased. Struggle as one may to run away, one cannot move. In our case, pull and strain on the oars as we might to keep the boat head to wind and sea, we were never able to hold her up to it. Bail as we might, using every available bucket and tin, the water in the boat was never much less than knee-deep.

About ten o'clock in the morning the sea all but achieved the final victory. Three very high, steep ones raced towards us, their crests rearing up preparatory to breaking. I shouted: "Pull port!" and everybody heaved on his oar. We all tugged and strained, but the first sea knocked her head right off. Those bailing dropped their tins and buckets and put their weight on the oars; but the second one pushed her almost broadside on to it. The third one picked up the boat and threw it away, as a child throws its toy boat into the water!

I admit that that sounds like a "tall yarn." It is nevertheless true. Just as a bit of wood is tossed by a wave on to the beach, so were we literally hurtled through the air! We struck the sea again with a crash that threw us all down; but fortunately, though half full of water, the boat landed right side up.

Like other nightmares that one cannot remember when one wakes, I do not recollect much of the next hour or so of this one. In view of the fact that I am now "giving it to you in writing," we obviously managed to work the boat's head up to the sea again, and to bail out sufficient water to remain afloat. The diary says that we threw overboard all the lifebelts, canvas, rope, spare oars, etc., to lighten the boat as much as possible, and that a considerable quantity of biscuits was soaked in salt water.

As is often the case with a gale that springs up suddenly, it goes as quickly as it comes. By noon the rain had cleared away and the wind was moderating. We had won again!

During the afternoon I was able to "shoot the sun" and get an approximate position. The island still bore north-west, but it was then distant 46 miles. We had lost 16 miles since we started!

About three o'clock the sea had flattened out sufficiently for us to take in the sea-anchor and hoist the sail. The wind was then north-north-west, but had fallen so light that we made little headway against the heavy swell, and oars were brought into use once more. The men were getting so weak that regular reliefs could no longer be arranged. Each pulled until he drooped over his oar.

Then he was helped down on to the bottom boards and another took his place. As by that time we were shipping no water and it was not necessary to bail, they were able to rest between-whiles.

Thus we spent that night until 3 a.m., December 16th, when the wind freshened and we were able to proceed under sail alone. The food for that day consisted of one biscuit and the usual quantity of water, morning and evening.

The morning was fine and clear. The wind was hauling westerly and the swell flattening out. At 6 a.m. I managed to get quite good longitude "sights." At eight o'clock, as the wind was still veering, we dipped the sail and continued on the port track. During the forenoon it freshened to a strong breeze. At times we could hardly carry the whole sail and we had to resume bailing out the water that cascaded over the bow as the boat elbowed her way through the seas. We had tamed the "Westerlies" once more!

Noon observations together with the "A.M. Sights" made the island bear north-a-half-west, distant 31 miles— a gain of 15 miles. Shortly after noon the wind hauled due west, enabling us to "square away" a little and steer directly for the land. It moderated during the afternoon, but so did the sea, and we were reeling off four or five knots an hour.

As time passed and those 31 miles were eaten up we were afflicted with another ailment. It can be diagnosed: "Surfeit of look-out men."

With the exception of one or two men who were too ill to move, they all crawled forward to the bow and stared ahead over the gunwale for the first sign of land. About three o'clock there was a shout from one of them: "Land ahead!"

They struggled to their feet, jostling and almost fighting each other to get a view of it, and giving the boat a heavy list.

"Sit down!" I shouted. "Damn it, sit down! You'll capsize us!"

"It's land, Mr. Makin'!" they shouted. "Look at it! You're steering right for it!"

They were shaking each other's hands, patting each other on the back, and literally dancing in their excitement.

"How the hell can I see it? Get down!" I was beginning to be afraid they would lose their heads and do what the wind and sea could not do—capsize and sink us. "D'you hear me? Are you going to get down out of it or must I come along there to you?"

"God damn it! Let the Second Mate 'ave a 'dekko'!" said one kindly, thoughtful soul.

That had more effect than my shouting. Like a flock of excited sparrows round a piece of bread that one throws to them on the lawn, they sat down, all talking at once.

It did look something like land, but was obviously a small, hard bit of cloud, low on the horizon. I admit I was disappointed, though had it been land, my navigation would have been open to criticism. According to that, we should not sight it for a couple of hours.

"See it, sir?" one of them asked.

"I see what you mean," I replied, "but don't count on it yet. It's too far off to be certain."

"That's land all right," they assured me.

In a few minutes that bit of cloud had disappeared and they were silently straining their eyes once more. Suddenly a man pulled himself up and pointed to the port beam.

"There 't is!" he shouted. "That's land!"

They elbowed and pushed each other in their anxiety to get to the port side, and listed the boat right over.

"Listen to me!" I cried. "Sit down first!"

For a moment they looked at me. Then they sat down. "That's not land," I continued. "It's another cloud. We can't see land yet. We had 31 miles to go at noon. What are we doing?"

"Six or seven knots!" one of them answered.

"Say three or four," I said. "Well! We can't see land before six or seven o'clock. Keep quiet now and get some rest. You'll be on the oars again presently."

"One of us'll keep a look-out, sir!" a man exclaimed.

"All right then. The rest of you go to sleep!"

Science has yet to produce a soporific that could have put to sleep that boat's crew of excited, overgrown children. They crowded together in the bow, seeing land in all directions, arguing and almost quarrelling over it. I could hear their remarks.

"Say, that's land there!"

"Like hell it is! That looks more like it!"

"Betcher my supper biscuit!"

"Funniest-lookin' bloody clouds round 'ere I ever seen since I bin goin' to sea!"

About five o'clock there was a little smudge on the horizon, about two points on the port bow. It was very faint and they did not notice it. Most of the 31 miles were then behind us. That could be it. How much could one rely on observations taken from a boat, though? I began to feel sick. I was almost frightened to look at it in case it should prove to be another cloud. If it were one, its shape should alter, it should grow larger or disappear altogether. It did neither. It remained a faint, cone-shaped smudge.

I put the helm down a little. With that wind we could just lay up to it. For what seemed a long time I watched it develop, as a photographer does a negative. Then I felt sure. It was land!

"There it is, sir," I said to the Captain. "Right ahead."

That type of the genus *homo*, sometimes called "Jolly Jack, the sailor," is a strange animal, a mental chameleon whose changes have to be seen to be believed. That little cone-shaped smudge on the horizon was a magic wand which transformed the flock of excited, chattering sparrows into a boat's crew of grim determined men. The wind was dying out and we had little more than steerage-way. They heard the Captain say something about "oars" and "get as close as we could to the land before dark."

"C'mon, boys, shake 'er up!" one of them said.

Without waiting for an order, with no more noise or excitement, they dragged themselves on to the thwarts and helped each other get out the oars. They gave one more look over the bow. Their mouths were too dry to spit on their hands, but they went through the motion from force of habit, and then proceeded to give a feeble impersonation of men rowing.

It was pitiful to watch them. For a while the excitement of looking for land had livened them up; but when again it was a question of physical strength one realised the state they were in. They did not pull. They could merely dip the oars in the water and jerk them feebly, their unshaven faces ghastly white and haggard, gasping hiccoughs rather than breathing, their glassy eyes fixed on the man in front.

At 8 p.m. the land was plainly visible, and as there was still sufficient breeze to give the boat steerage-way, we stopped rowing. Rest and food were essential. Two firemen were unconscious. The Third Engineer was unable to move, and the Chief Engineer was occasionally delirious. Two biscuits, a slice of corned meat, and a full tin of water were served out, as well as a spoonful of brandy.

About half-past eight the wind fell to a flat calm, and everyone who was able continued rowing. The Captain's mind was beginning to wander, but nevertheless he steered, occasionally bursting into a wild laugh and shouting such remarks as: "Pull, my merry men!" or "Heave, mariners, one and all!"

In spite of that, the "sea-sense," instilled into him since going to sea at the age of 14 or 15, kept the boat steady on her course.

During that night of December 16th-17th I gained a practical working knowledge of the life of a galley slave. I also learned that average men with the normal amount of "guts" are never really beaten while any life remains in them. To all appearances they are "all in"; and yet, when one more effort is asked of them, they somehow manage to "force their heart and nerve and sinew . . . and so hold on when there is nothing in them except the Will which says to them: 'Hold on!'"

To this day I cannot understand how that boat's crew were able to remain on a thwart and put sufficient weight on an oar to move the boat. It was impossible to sit upright and pull, it caused such acute pains in the stomach. Bent almost double over the oar, one let the blade of it fall in the water. Then, holding one's breath, one tried to pull it. Each tug was productive of a hiccough. A certain number of hiccoughs resulted in an attempt to be sick which seemed to tear one to pieces inside. A short spell of that work apparently dissolved the stomach and backbone, for there was nothing left in the body to hold it up in a sitting position. Time after time a man slid off the thwart on to the bottom boards and lay there; but there was always someone to replace him. A short rest down there evidently solidified his spine and put his stomach back in place, for when before long there was a thud of another falling man he was able to get up again and carry on. During the dark, age-long hours of that night the boat never ceased to surge ahead.

At ten o'clock fog set in and we lost sight of the land. That caused another change in the chameleons, this time to defiance. To hell with the sea! To hell with the wind! To hell with the fog! They gasped and hiccoughed curses on that unholy trinity.

About midnight a light north-westerly breeze blew away the fog and we saw the island again. It also gave us a respite from the oars. We continued under sail on the port tack until 4 a.m., and then, when the island was abeam, went about and ran in towards it.

By that time the Captain was ill and light-headed, and the Third Engineer unconscious. The Chief Engineer was continually delirious and gave us technical details of some boilers he was building for a yacht.

Having the Sailing Directions with us, we had learned that the only landing-place was on the side towards which we were heading, and therefore had not to waste time looking for it. When about two miles from it we were again becalmed and had to continue rowing.

This last effort added one more affliction. For the first time we suffered thirst, compared with which hunger is a child's ailment. Until then the weather had been cold, and there had been so much rain that it had not troubled us greatly. During this last mile or two our tongues apparently increased in size until at last our mouths were too small to contain them.

A full tin of water and a spoonful of brandy were served out, to help us over that last lap. We struggled to within a mile, and then ran into a current that swept us along the coast and past the landing-place to where high cliffs rose sheer from the sea.

I cannot remember much of the last hour or two. A breeze must have sprung up, for the diary says: "We tacked and ran out from the shore to get clear of the current, and then worked up to windward of it."

Towards nine o'clock, finding that a counter-current was setting us towards the land, we went about once more and ran in.

About a quarter of a mile off-shore we saw a boat coming out towards us. We recognised it as the Chief Officer's, though it was manned by niggers and half-castes. When it got nearer we saw him in the stern-sheets, and according to the diary: "We tried to give him a cheer, but it was a very feeble effort."

They gave us a line and towed us in. The landing-place was a flat rock, and the crew of the other boat was standing on it, waving and cheering. I was at the tiller, and when the tow-line was let go about twenty yards from them I suddenly saw flat rocks and cheering boats' crews all round me. I suppose I put the helm hard over and steered alongside the wrong one. At all events, I ran her head on to the right one and rolled ingloriously off the seat into the bottom of the boat when she bumped!

STPAUL ISLAND

CAPE TOWN
←2800 miles

AUSTRALIA
1900 miles →

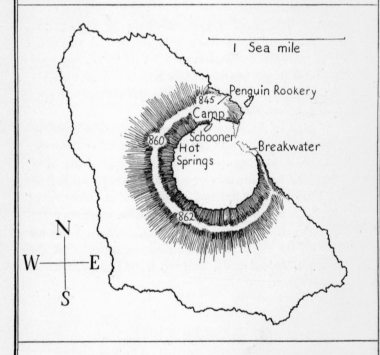

1 Sea mile

Penguin Rookery

845

Camp

Schooner

860

Hot
Springs

Breakwater

862

N
W   E
S

CHAPTER VI

ST. PAUL ISLAND

" Speak no harsh words of earth; she is our mother;

*   *   *   *   *

And there is coming for us all an hour
When we shall pray that she will ope her arms
And take us back again."

SMITH.

"WELL! D'you still think you'd be as well off in a boat as on St. Paul Island?"

Such was the Third Officer's greeting to me when at about ten o'clock that morning he and a sailor helped me out of the boat. There is no record of my reply. I probably made none. My tongue was still a few sizes too large for my mouth and I badly needed water. I evidently succeeded in making them understand that, for a boat's bailer full of it was held to my lips. I grabbed it with both hands and gulped it down.

My next impulse was to laugh heartily. Everything struck me as being so funny. The Third Officer, for example: I wondered if he realised that his dirty, salt-stained uniform and his week's growth of beard would scare all the birds off the island. I called him " Weary Willie," and the tall, thin sailor on the other side of me " Tired Tim." It was wasted on them, though. Neither of them laughed nor seemed to find any humour in it.

The island itself was a joke. I had never seen land like it. When I tried to walk it either rose up and kicked my foot or sank down out of sight, leaving me nothing to tread on. I stopped to discuss this extraordinary phenomenon with them, it wasn't mentioned in the Sailing

215

Directions.   Neither of them evinced the slightest interest
in it.

"Never mind that," said Weary Willie.   "Come on,
you'll be all right directly!"

All right directly? That wasn't funny!   Damn it all, it
was almost insulting!   I was as right as he was and I
tried to pull my arm away to prove it.

"Now you come and sit dahn wiv the rest of us, Mr.
Makin'," said Tired Tim soothingly.   "We got a nice
drop of 'ot cocoa all ready."

What? Cocoa? Neither was that funny.   That was
food, a very serious matter.   I signified my intention to
go quietly and they led me to a space of flat ground,
about thirty yards away.   All our people seemed to be
there, and there was a number of strangers, coloured
men, standing round, looking at them.

"What d'they want?" I asked.   "Island's s'posed
t'be un'nhab'ted. Sailin' D'rections says so."

"They're from the fishing schooner," replied Weary
Willie.   "We'll tell you about it by-and-by."

"Jest sit dahn 'ere, sir," said Tired Tim.   "We'll get
you some cocoa."

They placed me on a tuft of coarse grass.   It immediately began to roll like a ship with a moderate swell on
the quarter.

"'Ere y'are, sir," said a voice.   "This'll warm yer up
a bit. Got a drop o' brandy in it."

A hot cigarette tin was put in my hand. Steam, rising
from it, drifted up my nostrils and I sniffed its odour.
Cocoa and brandy? It was nectar and ambrosia, and it
magicked the little mound on which I was sitting into the
knee of one of the gods.

Sipping it was similar to turning steam into a central
heating plant. The first mouthful warmed up a radiator
in the pit of my stomach, and as others followed it the

heat spread down my legs to my feet and along my arms into my finger-tips. Then it slowly rose and my neck began to glow. Up and up it mounted, right into my eyes and brain, and as one focuses a pair of binoculars on a distant point of land, so did the world gradually become clear-cut and stable to me once more.

It became possible to distinguish the "Guardian and Giver of this Divine Drink." If he were Ganymede, he had taken the form of a very big and very red-haired Irishman, arrayed in what had once been a Chief Officer's uniform. A sock was tied round his neck, and he had a brilliant halo of red hair and whiskers. Standing over a fire of driftwood, he was dipping cocoa from a steaming tin pail with a boat's bailer. As I watched him and his acolytes caring for our sick men I saw that their lips were cracked and covered with sores. It was obviously painful even to talk or smile.

The surroundings began to interest me. I saw that we were in an enormous, circular, cup-shaped space, about three-quarters of a mile in diameter, the sides of it rising almost perpendicularly from the water contained in the "cup."

In some "High and Far-Off Time when the world was so new-and-all" the island had been a volcano, and we were actually inside the crater. Above us, the side of it rose to a height of about 800 feet. That decreased as one followed the rim round to the other side, where it was about 600 feet high. A small segment had been destroyed, making a gap through which the sea had flowed into it. There was a natural breakwater of rocks, 2 or 3 feet above sea-level, across this breach, with an opening, about 20 feet wide and, we discovered later, 6 feet deep at high water, in the middle of it. It was through this gap we had entered, and the landing-place, a natural wharf of huge rocks, was just inside it on the starboard, or right, hand.

15

For a radius of about 40 yards inland the ground, which was composed of rocks, and of earth covered with grass and rushes, was fairly flat. This became our "camping site" during our stay on the island. In fact, there was no other place to live. Everywhere else the sides of the crater rose sheer from the water. A small schooner was moored to the rocks at the landing-place, so the coloured men who were watching us were obviously part of her crew.

By then I was beginning to feel quite fit, and got up to give the others a hand. There was nothing to do, though. The Chief Officer and his men, having had a day to recuperate, had taken charge of everything, and apparently had put us all on the sick-list for that day.

I found the Captain and Chief Engineer lying on the grass. They were still weak, but Ganymede's potion had successfully recalled their wandering minds.

The Third Engineer remained unconscious for an hour after we arrived, but two firemen who had been carried ashore in that state were already showing signs of life.

There was obviously no need to worry about the others. The contents of that steaming pail had had the same effect on them as on me. They were already comparing notes with the other boat's crew, and the fact that they were beginning to lie profusely about what they did under sail was a sure indication of their return to normality.

"The Skipper reckoned we was doin' at least 10 knots!" said one of ours.

The boatswain had been superintending the distribution of the cocoa, and was then standing in the middle of them. He belonged to the Chief Officer's boat and his esprit de corps was touched.

"Ten knots!" he exclaimed scornfully. "The way that crazy, bloody Irish Mate was drivin' our boat he'd ha' sailed us right through this God damn rock and out the other side if we hadn't seen it in time!''

Meanwhile I heard their story from Weary Willie. They arrived on the evening of the 15th, thirty-six hours before us, and had escaped most of the gale we had experienced that day. The two hours during which we had steered the wrong course had made all that difference to our weather, and consequently to our '' time-on-passage.''

Almost immediately after they landed, the fireman who had been buried in the coal died. In his weak condition he had not been able to survive the exposure. They buried him the same day on the edge of the camp, as we came to call this flat piece of ground where we lived.

The Fourth Engineer, who was also in their boat, was very ill and continually delirious. Nothing they could do seemed to have any effect, and he was getting weaker. The others were all well except for the sores which had broken out on their lips.

'' You'll get 'em tomorrow,'' said Weary Willie cheerfully. '' It's the effect of the exposure in the boat.''

He explained the presence of the schooner. When they woke up the previous morning they saw her making for the entrance. It must have been a surprise to her captain and crew to see a crowd of ragged castaways waiting on the '' dock '' to take their lines and help them moor the ship.

The diary does not record her name; merely that she was French, of 60 tons, and came from the island of Réunion to fish. She was ballasted with salt in which they preserved their catch, and would probably remain until the middle of February.

My first thought was that we should be able to get away in her. She was so small, however, and carried so many men for fishing, that it would be impossible to take all of us. The Chief Officer had already made enquiries about it.   Most of us would have to remain on the island until the few she could accommodate reached Réunion and informed the authorities where we were.

Neither was she able to spare us much food.   She had very little more than was absolutely necessary for the needs of her crew.   The French captain had promised to give us a small quantity of rice each day, but beyond that we should have to fend for ourselves.   The amount of stores remaining in the boats was, of course, negligible, but fortunately the sea, both in the crater and round the island, abounded with fish, and we had plenty of fishing lines.   They had not yet located the provision depôt, but according to the Sailing Directions it should contain among other things a supply of biscuits and tinned meat.   There was therefore no prospect of starving.

Fresh water had been found.   It was brackish, but drinkable.   While he was telling me this the French captain came to us.

" I visite ze Capitaine," he said.   " 'E ees seeck, yes?"

"Nong!" replied Weary Willie.   "Venez, sivvooplay!"

" Mais, mon Dieu!   Vous parlez Français . . ."; and as Weary Willie winked at me and led him away on this official call a cascade of French sentences poured from his lips.

I got up and went to see the Fourth Engineer.   When I sat down beside him he looked at me.

" Making," he whispered.

" Yes," I answered.   " What d'you mean by behaving like this?"

He had recognised me, but that was all.   Instead of replying to me, he began to talk to himself, coughing frequently.   Suddenly he struggled to sit up, and cried: "Where are you?   I'm falling!"

I raised him to a sitting position and, placing an arm

round him, let him lean on me. He muttered a few sentences I could not understand. Then he raised his head and looked at me.

"I don't want to be left here," he said faintly.

"You won't be," I replied. "You'll go when we go."

"Promise me that, Making. Promise you won't leave me."

"Of course I promise," I assured him. "I'll see to it myself that you come with us."

His head fell back on my shoulder again and he was silent. There was a bad spell of coughing and choking. When it was over he began to talk about his home. The voice gradually grew fainter, and as it died away his head fell forward. With my free hand I tried to settle it comfortably for him; but when I lifted his face and looked in his eyes I realised that I was released from my promise. He had left us there. I laid him down and went to the Captain and Chief Officer to report it.

The time was then past noon and we "invalids" were ravenously hungry. There was a gap between our chests and hips, and we needed something solid inside it to help us stand upright.

While the cocoa and brandy had been doing their work, however, the other boat's crew had been busy. Some of them had collected more driftwood and built up a huge fire. The ship's cook had cleaned Ganymede's pail and placed it on the fire again, full of water. Others had caught and were cleaning a supply of fish, some of them twenty to thirty pounds in weight, large chunks of them being thrown into the pail to boil. As soon as the first batch was cooked the pieces were scooped out with a bailer and handed to our boat's crew.

Time after time those ragged, unshaven "Oliver Twists" held out flat bits of wood that served as plates for more, until eventually, for the first time in a week,

they were replete. Morpheus then superseded Ganymede. Their heads began to nod, and one by one they
lay back where they were and dropped off into a deep
sleep.

I found a highly desirable, semi-detached clump of
rushes, and knew no more until I woke up about half-
past four.

"Want a hot bath, Making?"

It was the voice of Ganymede, the Chief Officer. I
rolled over and looked at him.

"Wha's 'at?" I asked, halfway through a yawn.

"Care for a hot bath?" he repeated.

"Hot bath? On a desert island? All right, I'll bite.
What's the answer?" I thought he was trying to be
funny.

"Come along and I'll show you," he said. "I'm going to have one."

I got up and went with him. We left the camp and
scrambled over some rocks until we came to a large hole
that had been dug in the earth. It was full of water, and
was only a few feet from the sea.

"Hop in!" he said.

Not knowing whether he was serious or not, I stooped
and dipped my hand in it.

"Ow!" I cried in surprise.

It *was* hot. It almost burned my hand.

"Soak yourself in it," he said. "It'll do you good."

I stripped quickly and climbed gingerly down into it.
It did do me good. I could almost feel the salt in my
skin dissolving and being boiled out of me.

"D'you provide soap, too?" I asked, grinning up at
him as he was undressing above me.

He picked up a handful of sand and threw it at me.
"That's what we've had to use so far," he answered,
laughing.

Beggars can't be choosers, so I rubbed myself all over with sand. I probably did not look much cleaner, but at all events I felt less like an "untouchable."

"Where did that hot water come from?" I asked while we were dressing.

"It just growed," he replied. "It comes up hot every-where. We started digging for water yesterday and found it all along here. Haven't found any cold yet. This old volcano can't be so extinct as they say. It must be damn hot underneath. Look here!"

He picked up a piece of wood and scratched a hole in the ground, a few inches deep.

"Feel it!" he said.

I put my hand into it. The earth was warm, and hot water was welling up, though we were not more than six feet from the sea.

"We have to let the water cool off before we drink it," he explained. "It's all brackish, though. Too close to the sea, I suppose. The cliffs are so steep we can't get far enough away from it."

When we returned to the camp it was practically deserted. The meal and the afternoon's sleep had been just what the doctor would have ordered for our boat's crew, and they were out in the middle of the crater, fishing. The chameleons had changed once more: this time they were children, enjoying a holiday. We could hear their shouts and laughter echoing from one side of the "cup" to the other as they hauled in the fish.

We sat down by the fire with the Captain and engineers. It was arranged that the Fourth Engineer should be buried that evening, and when the boats returned some men were told off to dig a grave. The only shovels avail-able were pieces of wood that had been found on the rocks and hacked into shape with a boat's axe. A coffin was made with some bottom boards and canvas. When it was ready he was placed in it, and an ensign we had brought with us was spread over it.

Supper was merely a repetition of dinner. More pailfuls of boiled fish were stowed away in our midship sections, which were again empty and clamouring for a refill.

There were no jokes or laughter at this meal, though. The death of the Fourth Engineer and his funeral that was to take place shortly had cast a gloom over them. They probably realised that it might have been any one of them.

When everyone had finished the Captain led us to the Red Ensign. All hands fell in behind the coffin as it was carried to the grave. While a few men lowered it down the remainder of us gathered round. Suddenly the Captain looked at the Chief Officer with an undecided expression on his face. He had obviously just remembered that we had no Prayer-Book. For a few moments there was a dead silence. The Chief Officer broke it. He cleared his throat, looked round, and then began to recite:

" Our Father, which art in Heaven,
    Hallowed be Thy Name . . ."

Most of them knew it, and they repeated it after him:

" . . . For Thine is the Kingdom,
    The Power, and the Glory,
    For ever and ever. Amen."

The Captain motioned to two of them. They picked up the makeshift shovels and gently laid earth on the coffin.

The sun had set when we came back to the camp, and as we had no lights, that meant it was nearly bed-time for us. The Captain and Chief Officer had been invited to sleep in the schooner's cabin. Her main hatch was to serve as one large bed for the three engineers, Weary

Willie, and myself. At the edge of the camp were two stone huts in which the fishermen salted down their fish. Neither had roofs, and the walls of both were crumbling. Our men had taken possession of one, cleaned it out, and spread a boat's sail over the top. By imitating sardines, there was just sufficient room for them to sleep in it. One of them had scratched on a stone at the entrance: "God bless our home!"

No one was in a hurry to go to bed that night. The fire was burning and we all sat round it in the growing darkness. Occasionally a man got up and threw on some more wood. The Captain was with us. There had been quite a long silence when suddenly he began to talk to them. It was not a speech; he merely spoke to them as man to man. He reminded them of what they had been through, and pointed out that, although they were safe, it would not always be a holiday. They were sure of being taken off the island eventually, but it would not be for some considerable time. There would be spells of cold, wet weather and they had practically no shelter. They would have more discomforts, perhaps even hardships, to endure.

"We must be patient," he concluded, "help each other, work together and stand by each other as we have done during the past week; and in a few months we shall be home."

That circle of men listened intently. In the light thrown on their faces by the fire one could see them drinking in every word. When he finished there was a unanimous "Aye, aye, sir!" and the boatswain jumped to his feet.

"Three cheers for the Old Man!" he shouted.

They all stood up and waved their caps. Their cheers echoed to and fro across the crater.

"Three more for the Chief Officer!" said somebody

else; and the response brought the crew of the schooner out on deck to see what was the matter.

The Old Man and Ganymede got up and gazed round the circle, a smile on their faces.

"Good-night, lads!" said the former.

"Don't get nightmares and kick each other out of that hut!" added the latter.

"Goo'-night, Cap'en!" — "Goo'-night, sir!" — A chorus of "good-nights" followed them to the schooner.

So ended our first day on the island of St. Paul. The men gradually drifted along to their hut, and we to the schooner's main hatch. We stretched out on it and pulled a boat's sail over us. Weary Willie was next to me. For a while he turned over and over and round and round, trying to find a soft bit of plank.

"Golly! What a bed!" he growled at last.

"Isn't it?" I said sleepily. "One would be almost as well off in a boat. Yes? No?"

CHAPTER VII

CASTAWAY

" La société n'est autre chose qu'un cercle de besoins et qu'un échange de secours."—MARMONTEL.

"DEC. 18TH: We turned out at 6 a.m.," says the diary, "and had a most welcome bath in the hot spring the others had found along the rocks."

Verily I say unto You-Who-Live-Ashore: "Truth is stranger than fiction!"

As a boy I had eagerly devoured such books as "Robinson Crusoe" and "Swiss Family Robinson"; but the imagination of their authors which provided a Man Friday for the former and ostriches for the latter to saddle and ride never succeeded in conjuring up natural hot baths for them.

This day was spent in eating, sleeping, and organising some sort of routine. All our food had to be caught in the sea, our fuel gathered on the rocks and brought to the camp, the fire kept burning and meals cooked.

We sorted ourselves out without any difficulty. A number of men who liked fishing were given one of the boats, and their duty was to see that a supply of fish was always on hand. Others, who did not care for that, became the hewers of wood and drawers of water. Their mission was to collect the driftwood that was washed up on the rocks and chop it up. They also had to bring water from the spring for drinking and cooking. When the fishing party did not want the boat they were entitled to use it to bring wood from distant parts of the crater. The responsibility for the fire and cooking naturally fell to the steward and cook. They had as assistants the cabin boy, mess-room boy, and the cook's boy—youngsters of about 15 or 16 years of age.

Weary Willie, the Second Engineer—a Scotch-Canadian whom we called Mac—and myself were given a roving commission. We had to be out and about, exploring the island and finding what we could, food, fuel, and the necessities of life being, of course, the principal object in view.

The dog nominated himself our scout and usually accompanied us. He and the cat had stood the boat trip better than any of us; but the latter was not built of the stuff from which pioneers and colonists are made. She became a mere beachcomber and spent most of her time cadging meals in the schooner's galley, or hanging round the men who were cleaning fish.

One of the first things organised by the officers and engineers was a new dormitory. It was impossible to spend another night on the schooner's main hatch. Not only were we sore next morning after sleeping on the rough wood, but for years cargoes of fish had been carried in the hold and a stale smell of it drifted up to us between the planks. During that morning we found a nicely-situated clump of rushes, large enough to make a bed for the five of us. We rigged a tent over this with a boat's sail, rolled grass in bits of canvas for pillows, and moved in that evening.

Arrangements were also completed for a supply of rice from the schooner, and we received a little each day. It only amounted to about a couple of teaspoonfuls per man; but as there were then thirty-two of us and we might be there a long time, the aggregate would be a considerable portion of their scanty stock. Our food each day while we were on the island consisted of that and boiled fish.

During the whole of this first day we were hungry.

After completing a job, or when we awoke from an hour's sleep, we cut off a chunk of fish, boiled it in an empty meat tin on the fire, and ate it as soon as it was cooked.

By bed-time that night our lives were ordered and arranged in readiness for the following day. We were well fed and all was as well as it could be with our world, except that Weary Willie's prophecy had been fulfilled: our lips were cracking and sores were breaking out all over them. For some days they were extremely painful, and, of course, we had no vaseline or medical stores of any kind.

December 19th: Our day commenced about 5 a.m., and by six o'clock we were sitting on the grass round the fire, consuming enormous quantities of boiled fish.

After breakfast Weary Willie, Mac, myself and dog set out on our first exploration. We started up the hill between the camp and the breakwater. It was fairly easy going for a while and soon we saw the remains of what had once been a hut. It had no roof, and the sides were in ruins. It was the provision depôt! Among the débris we found two barrels of biscuits. The heads of both were out, and one had been overturned. Rotting biscuits were scattered over the ground. The year of their manufacture had been baked in them: 1892!

There were also three casks, containing tins of meat. These bore the same date but, though rusty, were in a fairly good state of preservation. Other barrels, which presumably had once been filled with blankets, matches, and other stores, were lying on their sides, empty!

From there we continued on up the "Peak," as we called this side of the gap in the crater rim, to investigate some strange noises we had heard during the night. According to the diary: "It was like a million rooks, all cawing at once."

After climbing over a ledge of rock about 300 feet above the camp the mystery was solved. We were then on the edge of the gap, overlooking the open sea on one side and the interior of the crater on the other. Above us was a large expanse of ground, rising steeply, but smooth and free from rocks. On it were thousands of penguins. The ground was literally carpeted with them.

"Eggs!" shouted Mac; and he walked in among them, pushing them out of the way with his foot.

"Ow!" he exclaimed almost immediately, and came hurriedly back to us.

Apparently they had not seen enough of man to be frightened of him, and they showed their resentment for this disturber of their peace by viciously pecking his knees and calves.

Keeping out of reach of a serried line of beaks that cawed and honked at us, we walked round the edge of their territory and climbed on to a rock from where we could overlook them. From their "rookery" the ground dropped steeply to the sea below. It was covered with large stones and boulders, and winding in and out among them were two paths. These were about a foot wide and were miniatures of such roads as one sees on the mountains between Naples and Amalfi. There were similar hairpin bends, complete with precipice on one side and steep cliff on the other. Used by these thousands of birds during hundreds of years, they were worn perfectly smooth—much smoother than the Naples-Amalfi road when I went over it in a rattle-trap Fiat with an Italian chauffeur.

Both paths were filled with these quaint little pedestrians, who were probably the first to use the "one-way" traffic regulations. On the one close under us they were walking in Indian file down to the sea, almost treading on each other's heels. At the bottom they dived in and dis-

appeared. There was no jostling or bad temper. They
"queued up" at the edge of the rookery and one by one
stepped on to the path. A few yards away was the "up"
road, filled with those who were wending their way homeward.

"Let's go down and watch them diving," I suggested.

"You go first," replied Mac, rubbing his legs.
"They've got a mighty mean beak on them."

We scrambled off the rock and stood by the side of the
"down" road. They continued to walk solemnly past.
A few of them looked up, but otherwise they took no
notice of us.

"Shoo!" I cried suddenly, waving my hand.

That dislocated the traffic. Those already past me continued on their way. The others, above me, halted,
cawing and croaking at me. I stepped into the gap that
this made and began to walk down. Apparently, provided we did not molest them, they had no objection to
us using their road, for I could feel them following close
on my heels.

"Shoo-oo-oo!" shouted Weary Willie.

I looked round. He was holding out one arm like a
traffic policeman. Those above him stopped and
"honked," and he stepped on to the road about twelve
penguins behind me.

There was a loud "Shoo-oo-oosh!" from Mac that was
followed by another chorus of caws and hoots, and he
joined the procession.

The dog was jumping over stones and rocks by the side
of the path. I slowed down to leave a gap for him between myself and the bird ahead.

"Come on!" I said to him.

"Not bloody likely!" his expression seemed to say.

I called and whistled to him, and eventually he sidled
very cautiously and circumspectly into line.

So we ambled slowly and easily down to the sea. Occasionally those walking up the hill looked at us and gave a surprised croak, as much as to say: "Who hatched you?"

Otherwise their attitude gave us clearly to understand that they considered us social outcasts. Personally I felt like one. In their black jackets and white shirt-fronts they looked so immaculate and well-groomed. We resembled three ragged, unshaven Gullivers, trying to gate-crash into the Lilliputian Smart Set.

Arrived at the bottom, we sat down and watched them. The procession never thinned nor ceased. In fact, during our stay on the island we visited them frequently and at different times of the day, but those two roads were always filled.

When we were tired of looking at them we scrambled along to a flat rock that was the terminus of the other path. We had no trouble in joining them for the walk home. When there was a space one of us stepped in it, and the next penguin followed. They were perfectly courteous and friendly, so naturally we showed them how well-mannered human beings are when they line up at a bus stop during the rush-hour.

We branched off from the road shortly before reaching the rookery, obviously much to the dog's relief. Both going and coming he had walked between me and the penguin ahead, looking very apprehensive. Occasionally he gazed round with an expression that said: "I hope you know what you're doing."

When we left them he lifted his head and tail again. Keeping well out of reach of the fence of beaks, he ran along in front of them, barking furiously—a canine "Fuzzy-Wuzzy," not daring to attempt to break the penguin square.

We worked our way round them and continued up to

within about a hundred feet of the summit, where we were stopped by an unscalable cliff. By then our abdominal timepieces were indicating the food hour, and we began to climb down the other side of the rookery to the camp. This led us back into the rushes and coarse grass with which the island seemed to be covered. There were no trees, and so far as we had seen, no other vegetation. There we saw the first signs of animal life: rabbits. The grass was full of them. We bombarded them with stones, but registered no hits. The dog was of no assistance to us. They did not even interest him. His shipboard education had not made of him a "go-getter." He still looked upon himself as one of the idle rich who should have his food brought to him.

The Captain would want to know what was in the provision depôt, and we called there once more to take back some biscuits and a tin of meat to show him. Mac picked up a sample of the former.

"1892!" he growled. "I'll have to be mighty hungry before I eat that mouldy relic of the gay nineties."

"You engineers ought to be made to serve your time in sail," said Weary Willie. "They're all right for cracker-hash."

Our return to camp resembled the California gold-rush. We were the "forty-niners," coming in with a "strike" of nuggets and dust. From a distance we could be seen carrying something, and everyone streamed out to meet us. Biscuits were passed from hand to hand and carefully appraised.

"'Ere! Let me see 'em!" exclaimed the steward.

Realising that he was the authority on the subject, they made way for him. He took one, tested its weight, broke off two pieces and gave one to the cook. They both nibbled and tasted it.

"Bit mouldy!" remarked the cook.

16

"Middle seems all right!" observed the steward. "We can use that!"

"Break 'em up and soak 'em, and then we can . . ." and the two experts walked away, deeply engrossed in the potential culinary value of those dirty, weatherbeaten, eighteen-year-old biscuits.

"What's in the tin, sir?" asked a man.

"Meat!" answered Mac.

"Blimey!" and "Bit of awright!" were some of the exclamations as the tin was handed round for inspection.

"What's it all about?" shouted Ganymede.

He and the Captain were standing by the fire. An escort was formed round the "strike," and it was borne in triumph to them.

"It's from the provision depôt, sir," I said. "That's all there is. There are no blankets or matches."

Each of them broke off a piece, looked at it and placed it in his mouth.

"What d'you think of it?" asked the Captain.

"Hard to say," replied Ganymede. "There's plenty of fish, anyhow."

"I'll open the tin of meat, sir, shall I?" suggested the carpenter eagerly.

"Yes, might as well see what's in it," the Captain answered.

While "Chippy" hacked at it with an axe the men crowded round, like children watching Christmas presents being unpacked. When it was opened he dug out a piece of stringy meat and offered it to the Captain. At the same time twenty or more dirty fingers were surreptitiously poked into the tin and licked clean.

"Not much taste to it," remarked Ganymede.

"Beggars can't be choosers," observed the Captain. "Steward!"

"Yes, sir!"

"What can you do with this?"

Gangway was again made for him and the cook, and they were given a sample of the meat.

"Make a stoo!" suggested the cook.

"Put today's rice in it!" added the steward.

"Wash them biscuits and break 'em up. They'll be all right in a stoo!" continued the cook.

"There won't be much each. We'll serve it after the fish!" The taste of meat was giving the steward big ideas.

"All right! See what you can do!" said the Captain as they carried it away.

We then had to give an account of where we had been and what we had seen. We described the rookery.

"Why didn't you wring a few of their necks and bring them back?" exclaimed the Chief Engineer. "They may be fit to eat."

Weary Willie, Mac, and I gazed blankly at each other. That thought had not entered our minds. I don't think any of us could possibly have twisted the necks of those well-dressed, courteous little people who let us walk with them. They were too human.

While we were away, they told us, a seal had appeared on the breakwater. The schooner's crew stopped their work to go after it. They surrounded it and clubbed it to death with stones. The blubber had been stripped off to be boiled down for oil.

After dinner we went to look at the remains. It was an enormous animal, 10 feet from nose to tip of tail. After extracting the oil the Frenchmen had fried some of the blubber, and they gave us a bit to eat. According to the diary: "It tasted all right, but was too oily to eat much."

During the afternoon we and a couple of men returned to the "Peak," taking with us a boat's mast. This was placed upright in a conspicuous position, and an ensign was hoisted on it, upside down: the signal of distress. A look-out post was established there that evening, and during the remainder of our stay two men were stationed by it day and night to watch for ships. Another fire was lighted on the breakwater to attract the attention of passing vessels.

All the "stoo" had been eaten at dinner-time, and as usual our supper consisted of boiled fish. Two penguins, killed by the men during the afternoon, had been cooked, but to the relief of Weary Willie, Mac, and myself, they were too tough and tasted too fishy to eat.

When we had cleaned our tin and wooden "plates" after that evening meal the fire was built up and we all collected round it. This became a nightly routine. The head of the Tribe, the Captain, took a seat on a pile of rushes. His Councillors, the officers and engineers, made themselves comfortable on the grass near him. The remainder of the ship's company, the Tribesmen, sat in a circle round the blazing driftwood.

By Tribal Law any man could speak on any subject, and those nightly "pow-wows" on St. Paul rivalled the Arabian Nights Entertainments. We listened to stories of the sea and of adventure by a British captain and a Scandinavian seaman. Folk-lore was taught us by a Greek fireman and a Cockney sailor. Tales, such as will never be published in a book, were told us of ships and men by an Irish chief officer and a Scotch chief engineer. We learned all there is to know about gaols and the police from Poplar to Callao. A wizened old seaman who had sailed in every imaginable type of ship for the past fifty years instructed us in the art of "crimping" and "shanghai-ing" as it had been practised on him in 'Frisco before most of us were born. He spun us yarns of "hard-case packets" where the Mates laid out men with belaying-pins.

"Them wuz real ships!" he told us one night.

Had a record of those conversations and discussions been kept, and were it possible to write them down in the "English as she was spoken," a large and interesting book could be written.

Occasionally a wisp of smoke from the fire blew in one's face, and now when I smell the smoke of burning wood in the country I can always see in my mind a picture of that circle of men. Sometimes they are leaning forward, listening intently to a story by the Captain about a disabled ship he had picked up and towed into port. From time to time they interrupt him.

"Ow didger get yer 'awser aboard 'er, sir?"

"Did all the crew get selvidge money, sir?"

Another favourite memory is of them all lying back, roaring with laughter, while the boatswain tells them of a fight he once had with three Chileno policemen before they managed to chuck him into the calaboose in Valparaiso.

"Gawd's troof, Bose! You must 'ave 'ad a skinful!" they said.

There was an established ritual to end the palaver. The Captain and Ganymede were the first to leave, and all hands stood up when they rose.

"Good-night, men!" were their parting words.

"Goo'-night, sir!" was the response from the Tribe.

December 20th: After breakfast four of us took a boat. Outside the breakwater was a high rock, called Nine-pin Rock. The previous day we had noticed a lot of sea-birds on it and we went in search of eggs. A flat ledge at the foot of it made a convenient landing-place, but owing to the heavy swell it was impossible to get alongside.

As we were pulling back a large seal could be seen asleep on the breakwater. We secured the boat to a rock and crept up close to it. It was about 12 feet long, and the head, something like that of a terrier, was ridiculously small on such a huge body, the girth of which was enormous.

Having my revolver with me, I crawled to within a yard of it and put three ·38 bullets in its head and neck. That merely awakened it. It looked at me, opened its mouth and lurched towards me. I moved rapidly in the direction indicated by the words: "He who fights and runs away . . ."

We tried throwing stones at its head as the Frenchmen had done. It showed its contempt for that method of attack by picking up a large pebble and cracking it with its teeth. Then it floundered towards us and we carried out another strategic retreat, whereupon it gave a derisive bark and slid off the rocks into the sea.

Dinner, of course, was boiled fish and a little rice. During the afternoon Mac and I walked, or rather scrambled, part of the way round the crater, rabbit hunting. The place was overrun with them. One went to earth about a yard from us. Mac immediately rammed in his stick and hit it. When we pulled it out we found that the hole was only a foot deep. Apparently many of these were only temporary hiding-places, not actual burrows, and we caught two more in the same way. For supper, rabbit and '92 vintage biscuit "stoo" was served after the fish.

While we were out we saw some goats near the top of the crater and reported them when we returned to camp. The French Captain heard us talking about them.

"Goats? What ees?" he enquired.

We described them by gently butting him in the solar plexus.

"Ah! Mais oui! Les boucs!" he exclaimed. "I chasse wiz fusil!"

He rushed on board the schooner, returning in a few minutes with a gun.

"Allons!" he shouted excitedly.

Half the schooner's crew, most of us, and the dog followed him. We tore up and round the crater, falling over rocks and tripping in rabbit holes. Eventually, out of breath, we saw the goats.

"Attention!" he whispered. "A plat ventre!"

The thirty or more of us lay down in the grass. Spread out like skirmishers, with him a few yards in advance, we began to stalk our prey. Arrived within easy range, he motioned to us to stop and drew a bead on one of the "boucs." We held our breath in suspense. Goat's meat should be good. For an interminable time he sighted, and then—the dog rushed from behind a rock towards them, barking furiously.

They scattered and ran. The French Captain leaped to his feet, gesticulating frantically and inadvertently firing a shot across our bow. We distinctly heard the "ping" of the bullet.

"'Cré nom de sacré nom!" he shouted furiously. "Quelle idée d'amener un chien!"

"Sacré chien!" and "Bloody dog!" were the mildest of the invectives that were poured on its head by the schooner's crew and our men.

In the middle of the excitement the animal in question trotted towards us, proudly wagging its tail.

"I've driven 'em away," he seemed to be trying to say. "The danger's over. You can stand up again."

"Mon Dieu!" said the Frenchmen.

"My Gawd!" said our men.

Other than that, words failed us as we started back to the camp.

That evening was cold, and we huddled closely together round the fire. A mist that had formed round the rim of the crater was, according to the Frenchmen, a sure sign of bad weather.

December 21st: "We shall have more discomforts, perhaps even hardships, to endure. We must be patient. . . ."

The Captain's words, spoken on the night of our arrival, were brought home to us this day. We were awakened soon after midnight by heavy rain. Streams dripped through the boat's sail that covered us, wetting us and the rushes on which we lay. It was impossible to sleep. We therefore got up and went out into the darkness. There was a gale of wind, and as we had no oilskins or rain-coats of any kind, in a few minutes we were soaked to the skin. There was nothing to do but crawl back under the sail and sit shivering on the wet rushes until daylight.

All hands were in the same plight, and the rain lasted all day. We did not trouble to catch any fish. There was no fire to cook it, all our wood was wet. Standing or walking about in the rain, we ate biscuits from the pro-vision depôt. At all events they were clean. The rain washed them while we munched them.

During the morning the Captain, two men, and I went to the provision depôt to see if there was any possibility of covering and protecting the stores from the weather. About all the good we did was to occupy our minds for an hour or two. There were only wet rushes to pile on them.

Some of the men passed away their time helping the Frenchmen grind salt. The latter began fishing this day. They went out at 4 a.m. and returned at about nine o'clock with 526 fish, some of them over thirty pounds in weight. They caught them all round the island about a quarter of a mile off-shore in twelve fathoms of water, using crayfish as bait. Later in the day one gang gutted and scrubbed them and another salted them down.

When darkness came we crawled under the sail once
more and sat on the wet rushes until daylight, rain dripping over us, a cold wind seemingly blowing right through
our chilled bodies, our teeth chattering. The rain began
to clear away soon after midnight.

December 22nd: Even under those conditions we dozed
from time to time during the early hours. At last, when
we pulled aside the sail and looked out, we could dimly
see the rim of the crater against the sky. It was the first
sign of the dawn and we came out, so stiff with the cold
that we could hardly walk. By that time there was no
wind and all the stars were shining. In the semi-darkness
we found our way among the rocks to the "bath" and
stripped. After wringing out our wet clothes and spreading them on the ground we lay in the hot water and
watched the birth of another day.

Gradually the crater rim hardened. The schooner's
mast and rigging began to stand out distinctly from the
dark background of rock. The night-watchman in the
Heavens went his rounds, snuffing one by one the night-
lights. Some long narrow clouds near the horizon, seen
through the broken side of the "cup," became edged with
colour. As we lay in that pool of hot water we watched
the greatest of all artists mix colours on His palette until
at last in a blaze of gold the sun appeared.

The only difference between our standard of living and
that of our ancestors some thousands of years ago was
that they had a dry cave in which to sleep and we had not.
As we watched that sunrise there was probably still less
difference between their idea of a Supreme Being and
ours. Like them, our sole concern was to live; and that
was only possible if we had food and warmth. Without
the blazing disc which had just risen from the sea we could
have neither.

We climbed out of the pool and stood on a rock, looking at it and feeling its warm rays on our naked bodies. The men came out of their hut and threw off all their cold, wet clothes. Standing there completely nude among the rushes and on the rocks, gazing intently at it, they seemed literally to be worshipping it. I think that for the time being our minds, like those of our forbears, were incapable of conceiving a greater Deity than He at whom we were looking, call Him the Sun, Ra, Savitri, or what you will. There was no other God but He who could warm our chilled bodies after the cold and misery of the past twenty-four hours; it was He who would dry our firewood in order that we might have fire to cook the fish we caught; only He could drive away the blackness and loneliness of the night and bring us light and cheer.

Before noon our clothes were dry, the fire was burning, and we were eating huge slabs of boiled fish.

After dinner Mac and I crossed the breakwater and climbed round the cliffs outside it. While clambering over some rocks our hands became covered with a greasy-clay substance. Apparently it contained some cleansing property, for when we rinsed it off they were fairly clean. I have no idea what it was, but, though rather gritty for the face, as a substitute for soap it was preferable to sand.

Later that afternoon we explored some more of the crater and found a lot of dry turf, resembling peat, that made good fuel. This was beginning to become a problem. We used a lot of wood for the fire on the breakwater as well as for cooking, and were already obliged to go far afield for it.

The fishermen caught 1,236 fish, and were working late. That night while we sat round the fire, talking, they were busy close by, cleaning them by the light of the flames. We consequently had to walk "home" to bed, in boots

through which our toes were protruding, over a carpet of
fish-heads and entrails.

December 23rd: The diary begins: "This is the day
we were due at Melbourne. Instead of picking up the
pilot at 6 a.m., we were picking lumps of boiled fish out
of a bucket!"

The piscivorous diet was beginning to pall on us. With
such appetites as ours, fresh fish, eaten only a few
minutes after it was caught, was delicious—but one can
have too much of a good thing. When at 6 a.m. the cook
slapped a chunk of boiled fish into my tin a vision of
ham-and-eggs, toast, and coffee came between me and it
like love's first disillusion: "She's not the kind of girl I
thought she was!"

Living under those conditions, one does not miss such
things as theatres and umpteen-course dinners. During
those weeks of discomfort, hunger, cold, and dirt I never
hankered after luxuries; but I craved the simple things
that one takes for granted at home and never notices: some
vegetables and meat, bread and butter, a glass of water
that tasted fresh, not brackish. I would have given anything for some tooth-paste, a few cakes of soap, clean
underwear, a bed with sheets. We soaked ourselves in
the hot water, and rubbed our bodies with sand and the
greasy clay; but, like the leper, one still felt "unclean."
When one looks day after day at dirt engrained in the
hands and body one comes to hate the sight of them.
The filth and the monotony of the food, like the cold, wet
weather, tried our patience more, and made it harder to
live up to what the Captain had asked of us, than all the
danger we had been in.

After breakfast a party of us made the first serious
attempt to climb out of the crater and have a look at the
top of our world. The French Captain lent us his gun in

case we saw the goats. We worked our way up and round
the side to a height of about 500 feet. Then we crawled
up a very steep incline of grass and stones, at the top of
which was an almost perpendicular wall of rock.

Clinging on by the "skin of our teeth," we were
scrambling along the foot of it, hoping to find an opening
in it up which we could climb, when Mac dislodged a
stone. It struck the dog. He rolled down the slope and
fell over another "wall," dropping about 40 feet. We
hurriedly slid down to the edge of it and looked over.
He must have borrowed one of the cat's nine lives, for he
was on his feet again, shaking himself and looking round
for us. When he gazed up and saw our faces peering at
him from above he began to walk downhill, barking as
much as to say: "That's enough of this damfool business.
I'm on my way!"

We followed his example, "preferring," the diary
says, "not to descend in such a hurry."

After dinner there was another seal on the breakwater,
but, instead of going after it, we slept all the afternoon.

December 24th: During the morning we had a swim.
Later in the day several of us took a boat and pulled all
round the crater close to the rocks. In a number of
places we saw steam issuing from the grass and between
the rocks. When we landed and dug holes we found
more hot springs. One large rock was rolled over, and
underneath it was a swarm of creatures, resembling huge
beetles, that apparently lived in that hot, steaming earth.
All the fresh water seemed to be on our side of the crater.
We found none on the other side.

There was a lot of drift-wood there, and we loaded the
boat with it. We also saw the seal I shot on the 21st
lying dead on the rocks.

Having noticed the fishermen catching crayfish to use

as bait, we made the boat fast to a rock to try for some ourselves. A dead fish was tied on a line and lowered to the bottom. After a while we cautiously hauled it up. Several large crayfish, resembling lobsters without claws, were clinging to it, and we lifted them into the boat. We caught thirty-eight, some of them 18 inches long.

December 25th: Today's entry in the diary begins as follows:

"CHRISTMAS DAY
MENU

Breakfast	...	...	Crayfish and Rice
Dinner	...	...	Fish and Rice
Supper	...	...	Rice and Fish

If we are here much longer we shall grow scales!"

After breakfast Christmas calls were paid. We came off best. All we could offer the French Captain was: "Merry Christmas, Capitaine."

To his "Joyeux Noël, mes amis," he added a drink of cognac to his and to our men. We were invited on board the schooner for punch.

The conversation as we sat round a basinful of that Christmas cheer in his microscopic cabin is difficult to record. He knew a few English words. Between us we remembered an equal number of French ones. He passed round the punch and we lifted our glasses.

"Good 'elt!" he said.

"Songtay!" we replied; and there followed a somewhat embarrassing pause.

"You catch plenty fish this year, Capitaine?" somebody asked him.

"What ees?" he enquired.

"Pwahsong! Beaucoup?" another added helpfully.

"Ah! Poissons—ze feesh!" he exclaimed. "Mais oui. Ça va. I t'ink so."

There was another long pause during which we sipped our punch, hoping that somebody would find something to say. The Capitaine cut in that time.

"Englis vair difficile," he remarked.

"Vous parlez bien," we assured him. "Français difficile."

"You spik good," he replied.

After that exchange of mendacious compliments the conversation gradually languished, and I can remember no more of it.

During the afternoon some of us rowed to the other side of the crater and caught sixty crayfish and six rock-cod.

That Christmas proved to be a wet one in every sense of the word. It began with punch and ended with heavy rain. The night was a repetition of the previous wet one: sitting under a dripping boat's sail, waiting for daybreak, soaked to the skin and bitterly cold.

December 26th: Breakfast consisted of watery '92 biscuits, and we spent the morning walking or running about in the rain to keep warm. About noon it cleared, and we were able to dry ourselves and our clothes. Later we got the fire going, had some boiled fish, and slept for the remainder of the afternoon.

During the evening Ganymede and Mac went along the rocks and had a swim. While they were in the water one of them trod on something soft that clung to his leg. He pulled himself out, dragging it with him. It was a small octopus!

"No more swimming here!" is the last entry in the diary for that day.

December 27th: After breakfast Mac and I made another attempt to find a way out of the crater. This time we went via the penguin rookery. It was fairly easy going until one was above them, and we hoped to discover a break in the rock to get over the last hundred feet, which was always the difficulty.

For a little distance we had to walk through the penguins, and we made ourselves thoroughly unpopular with them. They refused point-blank to allow us over the frontier. We tried coaxing them, and were met with very decided "nothing-doing" honks. Waving our arms at them merely seemed to give them the impression that we were a pair of slap-stick comedians, specially engaged for their entertainment. They flapped their small wings in imitation of us and croaked their applause. When we shouted at them they lined up shoulder to shoulder and literally hooted us. Finally we walked round them, and when we found a space where the ground was not so densely populated we hurried through. Some had to be moved out of the way by placing a foot on their breasts and gently toppling them over. There they lay, kicking their legs in the air and shouting for help, all their dignity gone from them, while their pals ran after us, cawing and pecking our legs.

After we were above them we worked up and round the Peak, outside the crater. Eventually we found a cleft in the rock and crawled up it on our hands and knees to the top.

This point, the Peak as we called it, was about the highest part of the island, over 800 feet above sea-level, and the ground sloped downward in all directions. We walked along the eastern side to the northern end where the cliffs rose sheer from the sea to a height of about 200 feet.

To us, knowing nothing of botany or geology, the

formation and vegetation up there seemed very much the same as that inside the crater: rocks, and earth covered with grass and rushes. There were many huge piles of lava, 15 to 20 feet high, and in some places we came upon fissures, about a foot wide and 40 to 50 feet long. We lay on the edge of them, but could see no bottom. Stones that we threw in rattled from side to side until they were so far down we could no longer hear them.

While jumping and scrambling over boulders we saw a large expanse of moss or fine grass. It was very smooth and green, like a well-kept lawn. We left our rocky road to walk on it, but immediately began to sink in. In a moment we were knee-deep in soft, warm mud—we had considerable difficulty in dragging ourselves out. When eventually we were again on solid ground we sat down and looked at each other's scared faces.

" Say!" exclaimed Mac. " This is one hell of an island to dump a white man on!"

We each had a stick, about 5 feet long, and after scraping most of the mud off our legs we pushed them into the moss. They went in quite easily, and at that depth, 5 feet, touched nothing solid. The lower part of them was steaming when we pulled them out.

" And the moral of that, dearly beloved brother," I remarked, " is that on this one hell of an island at all events the hard road is sometimes the wisest and safest."

" Right now," answered Mac, wiping more mud from his legs with some grass, " I'm not feeling in the mood to listen to sermons."

There was only one thing to be seen at the northern end of the island: the sea—an unlimited expanse of green carpet all round us. Sitting up there, one had a deeper sense of our isolation from the world. I doubt if either Mac or I enjoyed that morning, fond as we both were of wandering about and exploring. Everything we saw tended to impress upon us that nature itself was our bitterest enemy, and that compared with it the *homo sapiens* is a very feeble and insignificant atom.

Not only that, it would not even fight fair. It was continually "laying for us" and trying to "get" us by some underhand trick. It tempted us off a difficult, rocky track on to a smooth lawn, only to engulf and smother us in hot mud. It placed bottomless fissures in such a position that after climbing over a rock we should jump into them before realising they were there.

The green carpet all round us, that looked so smooth and finely woven from that height of 200 feet, was its ally. The pounding of the surf on the rocks below was a warning to us not to be too cocksure because we had won the "Battle of the Prevailing Westerly Winds." That was only a rearguard action during our retreat from one position to another. There on the island we were still no better off than a beleaguered army that it was trying to starve into submission. Given time it would probably succeed. Those of us who did not get away in the schooner would have to remain there until nearly mid-winter, when the climatic conditions down in that latitude, together with the lack of shelter, clothing and food, would make life almost impossible.

We looked out over it, our thoughts probably resembling those of an animal in the zoo that snarls at the people on the other side of the bars. Like John, we were in Patmos; unlike him, temporarily at all events, we were not in the Spirit, and as I sat there my inclination was to snarl at each point of the compass.

While we were enjoying that "gloom" another surprise was sprung on us. We suddenly noticed mist gathering on the Peak a mile away.

"Come on!" I said, "before it gets too thick to see."

We did the mile up an incline that took us from an altitude of 200 to 800 feet in almost record time. There was not enough of the pioneer and explorer in our make-up to enjoy finding our way back in dense fog between fissures, patches of hot moss and the edge of the cliff.

We could barely see a stone's throw when we reached the Peak, and we literally tobogganed down the cleft in the wall of rock. A portion of the seat of Mac's trousers is probably still there. It was ripped out by a sharp stone he slithered over to an accompaniment of lurid Canadian oaths.

When we arrived at the edge of the rookery out of the fog we were winded, and we sat on the grass to rest and to seek permission "to pass freely without let or hindrance" through it. The penguins seemed to be beginning to recognise us and to realise that we meant them no harm, that we merely wanted a "transit visa" through their territory, for when we got up to continue our journey they made way for us. A strong escort of them formed up all round us, however, and accompanied us to the lower frontier, their honks clearly warning us: "Don't try any monkey business!"

Mac and I spent the afternoon collecting large stones with which to build a cairn over the graves of the Fourth Engineer and the fireman.

A heavy mist lay over the top of the crater all night.

December 28th: At daylight there was a dense fog over the hills and drizzling rain in the camp, but it cleared away before breakfast.

Mac and I finished the cairns, and then made two crosses from drift-wood which we placed at the head of the graves. Later I began to teach him semaphore signalling to pass away the time.

During the afternoon he and I caught a small octopus among the rocks. The body was roughly the size, shape, and colour of a football. Its arms were about 18 inches long. We brought it back to the camp and gave it to the Frenchmen, who cooked and ate it. They offered us some, but much as we should have enjoyed a change from the fish diet, our stomachs turned against octopus.

While we were eating supper the goats were sighted, quite low down on the Peak. They were reported to the French Captain, and he and some of his men went "gunning" for them. We did not join the party, but could see them quite distinctly. They manœuvred the goats between themselves and a wall of rock; but then something went wrong again. We saw the "boucs" execute a miniature "Charge of the Light Brigade," break through the cordon and escape. In the words of the diary: "The Frenchmen cornered them, and then, as usual, lost their heads and the goats as well!"

December 29th: A fine hot day. After breakfast a seal was reported on the breakwater. The French Captain and his men shot and clubbed it to death. Our Captain and I rowed over to watch them strip off the blubber. It was a filthy, messy job, though, so we went fishing instead and caught twelve crayfish and an octopus.

I felt sick all day, and slept throughout the afternoon. In the evening I walked along the breakwater to the dead seal and cut off a bit of its flesh. Like everyone else, I was beginning to loathe the sight and smell of fish. I fried this seal meat for my supper. It was impossible to eat it, however. I have never chewed oily, fishy leather, but that is what I seemed to be trying to eat.

This was a bad day for everyone. All hands apparently "got out of bed on the wrong side" and were irritable and bad-tempered. After doing the routine community work they wandered off by themselves.

Two of the men began fighting and had to be separated. I forget the apparent reason for the quarrel. The diary, I think, gives the actual cause: " We badly need a big dinner of roast beef and vegetables.''

December 30th: A strong westerly gale with rain squalls was blowing all day, though we managed to keep sufficient fire going to cook the fish. When gales are from this direction the hills cause the wind to blow round the inside of the crater. This forms a small circular storm of almost hurricane force. In the centre of it the water is churned up and rises like steam.

During the morning I went to the breakwater with the French Captain and we killed a seal, the largest we had seen. It was 14 feet long, and the circumference of its body measured 8 feet. The blubber was 5 inches thick. Another was killed later in the day.

I borrowed a thermometer from him to take the temperature of one of our hot " baths.'' In spite of being exposed to a gale of wind and to squalls of rain, it registered 130° Fahrenheit.

December 31st: New Year's Eve and a fortnight on the island. Our men spent the morning stripping blubber off a seal for the French Captain. They cut out the heart and liver for their own New Year's Eve supper.

After dinner I borrowed a boat from the schooner and took their boy with me, fishing. We caught twenty-four crayfish and thirty-four other fish, some of them over ten pounds in weight.

During the evening we had another " shoot,'' this time for rabbits. Mac and I accompanied the French Captain, some of our men coming with us as " beaters.''

We climbed some distance up the side of the crater and took up a strategic position. Before long we saw one loping towards us within easy range.

"Allez! Shoot!" said Mac.

"Sh-sh-sh," whispered the Capitaine. "Silence! 'ttendez un peu!"

Brer Rabbit halted, settled himself comfortably on his haunches, perked up his ears, and proceeded to admire the scenery. The Capitaine took careful aim, gave it one barrel, and killed it. He immediately jumped to his feet and rushed to pick it up. Halfway he tripped, "bang" went the other barrel, and one of our men dropped with a scream.

"Oh, my Lord!" exclaimed Mac. "What's he done now?"

We both ran towards the man. The others were already crowding round him.

"Mr. Makin'!" shouted one of them. "Come 'ere, sir. Williams is shot!"

We barged through them. The man was lying on his back. I heaved a sigh of relief to see that his eyes were open and to hear him cursing.

"Where are you hit?" I asked.

Instead of answering my question, he said angrily, "Don't that sportin' capitano know the difference between me and a bloody rabbit?"

"You can tell him what it is presently," I replied. "Let's see what's the matter first."

"It's me leg, sir," he said. "This one."

Then I saw blood soaking through his trousers. Mac and I ripped off part of them. He was shot in the calf. We were wiping it with the torn bit of trouser leg when we heard the Capitaine's voice.

"Nom de Dieu!" he shouted furiously, gesticulating with the dead rabbit. "Qu'est-ce que vous faites?"

He elbowed his way through the men, saying something to the effect that we should chase all the "lapins" off the island. Suddenly he caught sight of Mac and myself wiping blood off the man's leg.

"Tiens! Tiens! Tiens!" he exclaimed. "What ees?"

"That's your fusil!" answered a man.

"Comment? Fusil?" he said; and turning to me, added, "You spik, Mistaire Makkin."

"C'est un accident avec votre fusil," I replied, doing my best to explain. "Matelot—er—wounded."

"Moi? C'est moi?" Then he dropped on his knees beside us, exclaiming, "Mon Dieu! Mon Dieu! Mon Dieu! Mon Dieu!"

"That's all right, Capitaine," said Mac. "Pas beaucoup."

The wound was only in the calf and not serious. It looked worse than it was. It ended the day's sport, however. Two men joined hands, the casualty sat on them and was carried back to camp.

We made him comfortable in our tent, and while we were bandaging the leg properly with a piece of an old shirt the Capitaine hurried to the schooner. In a few minutes he returned with a bottle of cognac. He gave the man a big "three-fingers." Then he turned round and began to ask "mille pardons" of our Captain. While he was doing that the wounded man, after winking at Mac and me, reached for the bottle and swallowed another stiff dose.

Suddenly he flew off on another tangent. He shouted for a boat, and while it was being brought alongside went on board the schooner. He returned with his gun and a bag of cartridges. Placing them in the stern-sheets, he stepped in, ordered his man out, and rowed himself to the middle of the crater. We saw him pick up his gun,

look at it for a moment, and then throw it and the cartridges overboard. He pulled slowly back, jumped ashore,
and came to our Captain.

"Voilà!" he exclaimed, with tears in his eyes.

Having made that *amende honorable*, he walked slowly
back on board the schooner.

When out with a gun he was "Public Enemy No. 1,"
but he was so genuinely upset over this "shooting," and
so anxious to do all he could to make amends, that we
were sorry for him. As a matter of fact, we liked him,
though at times it was difficult to take him seriously.

After supper preparations were made to celebrate New
Year's Eve. A lot of fish were cleaned, a huge fire was
built up, and the Tribe held a pow-wow until 11 p.m.
Then the fish was boiled, the seal's heart and liver were
fried on the lid of a meat tin, and we made another meal.

It is the custom on shipboard to welcome in the New
Year by ringing the bell and, on a steamer, blowing the
whistle. Having no ship of our own, at midnight we went
on board the schooner and rang theirs. At the same time
we stood round her main hatch, burning "blue lights"
that we had brought in the boats to attract the attention
of ships, and singing "Auld Lang Syne."

The Capitaine and his men came out and joined us, the
former bringing a large bowl of punch. Until 2 a.m. we
held a sing-song on the hatch. He sat there with us, while
his men squatted round on the deck, listening and applaud-
ing. Ganymede finished the concert with "Father
O'Flynn."

"Your turn now, Capitaine!" he said when the
applause had died away.

The Capitaine ran to his cabin. In a few moments he
came back with a mandoline and sang two songs in which
the word "amour" was frequently repeated. Then
Ganymede stood up.

"How many sailing-ship men here?" he asked.

"Me, sir," answered most of our "deck crowd."

"Capitaine," he continued, "you like to see how English ship set sail?"

"No compris vair good," was the reply, accompanied by a puzzled look.

"You regardez," said Ganymede; and turning to us, he gave a Cape-Horn bellow: "Loose the mains'l!"

For a moment we did not realise what he meant, and merely looked at him.

"Jump to it, you no-sailors!" he shouted. "Get that mains'l loose!"

Suddenly we grasped the idea, jumped for the schooner's boom and cast adrift the sail.

"Stretch the halliards along!" he continued. "Tail on, you 'black squad,' we'll make sailors of you."

Officers, engineers, sailors, and firemen passed the halliards along the deck and "tailed on."

"Allez, Capitaine!" he shouted again, motioning with his arm.

All the Frenchmen, grinning and laughing, got up and "froze on" to the rope with us. Then he beckoned to the wizened old seaman who had told us about "crimping" and the old "hard-case packets."

"You're the man for this,' he said. "Show these steamboat wallahs how sailormen do a job."

The "Ancient Mariner" rolled along the deck and "hung on beforehand" with him. There was a pause.

"Well! Let's hear from you!" said Ganymede.

A grin spread all over the old man's face. He spat on his hands, and in a cracked, high-pitched voice began to sing a chantey as it was only sung in the "Iron Man Age"—no imitation resembles the real thing:

"Blow the man down, bullies, blow 'im right down."

As we lay back on it the first time only our " deck crowd " were able to " give it lip ": " Wey, hey, blow the man down."

He sang the second verse: " As I was a-walkin' down Paradise Street."

That time the response was twice as loud. All the " black squad " had got it.

Then came the third verse: " A pretty young maiden I chanced for to meet."

The Frenchmen could not understand the words, but by that time they had picked up the tune. The roar of that and the succeeding choruses, together with the rattling of the patent sheaves, must have roused the inhabitants of the rookery from their beauty sleep.

Our Captain stood on the main hatch, watching the sail. When it was " two-blocks " he shouted: " Belay-ay-ay!"

The schooner's mainsail was set. The lowering and furling of it ended our " first-footing."

" Capitaine," shouted Ganymede when it was secured, " the Marseillaise!"

The Capitaine jumped on the main hatch. His men crowded round him, singing the song that immortalised Rouget de Lisle:

> " Allons, enfants de la Patrie,
> Le jour de gloire est arrivé."

At the end of it he looked at Ganymede, waved his cap and cried: " Vive le Roi! God sav' Keeng!"

Ganymede led us, and our chorus must have awakened the penguins once more:

> " God save our Gracious King,
>
> . . . . .
>
> Long to reign over us;
> God Save the King."

So we ushered in the year of our Lord 1911.

January 1st: The Capitaine carried on with the celebrations immediately after breakfast. He served out cognac to his crew, sent a bottle ashore for our men, and invited us to sit round another bowl of punch.

Those of our men who had eaten seal's heart and liver at midnight were sick. Some of them did not even turn out for their share of the bottle, " and that," remarks the diary, " is saying something! "

During the morning the Frenchmen held what they called a masquerade. Some of them left the camp and hid behind the rocks. Presently they reappeared, wearing a cloth round their waists and head-dresses and tails made of rushes. Their bodies were covered with clay, and their faces with some red concoction. Others ran towards them, put chains on them, and led them through the camp to the schooner. There they performed what the diary calls a " war dance or something," after which they came ashore and repeated it for us. Then they returned on board, and having given one more dance, jumped overboard and swam away out of sight behind the rocks.

For our New Year's dinner the Capitaine gave the Captain, officers, and engineers a bottle of wine and a tin of sardines between them, and one sausage each. We slept all the afternoon and then caught and cleaned fish for supper.

" Not a bad New Year," concludes today's entry in the diary, " considering what we had to celebrate with."

January 2nd: During the past day or two I had been watching Mac. Something apparently was wrong. He had seemingly been having fits of aberration during which he wandered aimlessly about the camp. Occasionally he stopped and gazed intently at rocks. One seemed to have a particular fascination for him. The previous evening I noticed him scratching hieroglyphics on it with a rusty nail.

"Going to engrave 'R.I.P.' on it for all the fish buried in you?" I asked.

"Am I supposed to laugh at that?" was all he replied as he walked away.

That was unlike him. He had always been one of the cheeriest of us, and during our wanderings he and I had become very pally. When one of us had a new idea it was invariably shared with the other. I began to wonder whether the conditions under which we were living were affecting him.

That morning he turned out all our stores until he found a marline-spike. He took it to the rock which had attracted him. With the spike and a heavy stone he began to chisel marks on the rock. Gradually the method in his madness became clear to me. About noon he stood up and admired his work.

"Say! What d'you know about that?" he asked me proudly.

My mind was eased. He was still sane. He had merely been preparing a surprise for us. On the rock was this inscription:

"S.S. *Parisiana*.
Burned at sea
December 12th, 1910."

The boatswain supplies the only other pre-dinner front-page news.

We suddenly saw him running down the hill, waving a handful of greenstuff.

"Dandelions!" he shouted excitedly. "We'll make some tea!"

We had heard of dandelion tea and gathered round him and the fire. He boiled some water in a meat tin, chopped up the greenstuff and dropped it in. After letting it boil

furiously for about half an hour he poured the liquid off
into another tin.   When it was cool enough to drink it was
passed round to be sampled.   Never having drunk that
kind of tea, I am unable to say whether he had succeeded
or not.   If he had, I cannot conscientiously recommend
it either as a pleasant or a refreshing beverage.

" The brackish water's spoiled it," remarked Mac, noticing the look of disappointment on his face.

"Must have sugar, too," added Weary Willie; and
that was the end of the dandelion-tea experiment.

After dinner Weary Willie, Mac, and I accompanied a
party from the schooner on what Mac called a " Jack-and-
Jill " expedition.   The Frenchmen, loaded with bottles,
were going somewhere up the hill for fresh water.   They
followed a track discovered on previous years that led
us up and round the crater until we were almost opposite
the camp.   We climbed over the rim and walked a few
hundred yards along the " roof of the world " to our
destination where we were about 400 feet above sea-
level.

There they showed us an enormous cave, and inside it,
about thirty or forty feet from the entrance, was a pool
of water, icy-cold and perfectly fresh—the first good drinking water we had found.   Round the sides of the cave
were masses of moss and fern.   Several narrow tunnels led
downward from it towards the centre of the island.   We
crawled a considerable distance along one of them, but
presently, owing to the impurity of the air, we had difficulty in breathing, and a candle, given us by the Frenchmen, flickered and went out.   There being then no room
to turn, we had to back out hurriedly, stern first.

Unfortunately the water was not of much use to us.
A whole afternoon was spent in fetching it, and owing to
the difficulty of the climb, we could only bring back a
few bottles of it.

On the south side of the island we saw three small extinct volcanoes, covered with the usual grass and rushes. By this time we had covered most of the ground, but apart from the patches of hot moss, had found no other vegetation.

On the way back we killed a rabbit with a stone—the first for a long time. Our first success, when we had chased them into shallow holes, had never been repeated.

January 3rd: A north-west wind, and mist over the hills, but we had no rain. Mac and I mixed up a sort of putty with oil from seal's blubber and clay. With it we filled in the letters he had cut in the rock.

After dinner two seals climbed on the breakwater and went to sleep. I went with the Capitaine and some of his men to kill them. Having thrown away his gun, he had taken a revolver, and he put twelve bullets into one of them. That only seemed to tickle it and wake it up, for it barked at us and slid back into the water. The other was killed with bullets and stones.

During the evening Weary Willie, Mac, and I unravelled a piece of rope until we had a bundle of rope-yarns. We chopped a lot of wooden pegs from driftwood and then proceeded to set rabbit snares on our side of the crater.

A peg was driven into the ground by the side of the burrow, and one end of a rope yarn was hitched to it. A noose was made in the other end and placed in such a position, we hoped, that the rabbits would put their heads through them and be strangled.

January 4th: The Captain, Weary Willie, and I spent the morning gathering limpets off the rocks on the other side of the crater. We collected a bucketful of them and ate them for dinner. They were not very nice. The best

that can be said for them is that they were a change from
fish. We were so heartily sick of the latter that unless we
were very hungry our stomachs turned against them. The
provision depôt meat was no help to us, even fish was
preferable.

The seal which had received twelve bullets the previous
day was asleep on the rocks, near to where we were
looking for limpets. The Captain had his revolver with
him and gave it a few more. It didn't seem to mind very
much, and merely splashed back into the water again.

Later Mac and I went round our rabbit snares, but
had no success. The manilla rope yarns we used were
probably too stiff. We sat down by the side of the last
burrow and slept until supper-time.

January 5th: In the morning the boatswain found a
large flag-staff on the rocks and brought it back to camp.
On it was a brass plate with this inscription:

" Planté le 24 Oct., 1892, par le *Labourdonnais*."

We assumed from this that the *Labourdonnais* had
" planted " our '92 vintage biscuits at the same time as
the flag-staff.

No fish could be caught for breakfast and we had to
get cray-fish from the other side of the crater.

The daily entries in the diary become shorter as time
goes on. This was partly due to the fact that we had
settled down into a groove and that there was nothing
more of interest to be found on the island.

Reading between the lines, however, one can sense a
growing anxiety about the future. Conditions were becoming worse as the weeks went by. We were beginning
to experience a difficulty in catching sufficient fish for
our needs. Every day the Frenchmen caught about a
thousand, many of them twenty to thirty pounds in

weight. After they had cleaned them they threw the refuse back into the sea. The result was that the survivors inside the crater were too well fed to be attracted by our bait.

The question of clothes was an even more serious problem. It was only a matter of time before we should have none to wear. For five consecutive days in the boat they had been continually wet and sodden with salt water. Since our arrival on the island they had been soaked a few more times in the rain, and for three weeks we had been walking and climbing over stones and rocks. Boots were falling to pieces. The sole of one of mine was almost completely divorced from the upper. In order to wear it, I had to tie it on my foot with rope yarns. Some of the men had to lash bits of canvas or sacking round theirs to prevent them falling off.

Trousers and coats were in no better condition. The knees of both of mine were gone, and I had sewn a piece of an old sack in their place with sail twine and palm and needle. The seat of Mac's, which was left on the Peak, was replaced by a bit of stiff canvas.

"I guess it's solid," he remarked, "but it's mighty uncomfortable to sit down in."

The cloth was becoming so rotten that it was almost impossible to do any more repairing. In a very few weeks we should have nothing to wear, unless we could find enough sacks for all of us.

On the following day, January 6th, we had a sample of what we must expect later on, with the approach of winter. There was a very heavy north-west gale and dense rain— the worst we had had. Small circular storms of hurricane force whirled round the interior of the crater. It was impossible to stand up in the wind, and our boat-sail tent was useless as a shelter. We could merely sit or stand on the lee side of a rock, completely soaked and bitterly cold.

During the morning we had nothing to eat, but later on were so famished that we opened a tin of provision-depôt meat and, standing in the wind and rain, ate it just as it was.

The gale began to take off about 3 p.m. and the rain ceased. It was not possible to dry our clothes, and we had to spend the night in them as they were.

January 7th: The gale had blown itself out and the weather was fine. Again we had difficulty in catching fish, the total for the day for thirty-two men being twenty-four of various kinds. Two seals were seen on the break-water, but both escaped in spite of bullets in them.

" One went minus his tail," adds the diary.

The flag-staff of the *Labourdonnais* was set up on the breakwater, and another ensign hoisted on it, upside down. Except during the gales, that on the Peak had been flying all the time. The two look-out men still kept watch by the latter.

The entry for January 8th is very brief and contains nothing of interest. I quote that of the 9th, it being typical of those days:

" January 9th: Fresh north-west breeze and sky over-cast. Just the same old routine: catch and clean the day's fish, and pull a boat round the crater. The only place for a walk is up the hill. Too much of that gives one an appetite that fish alone won't satisfy, and it's a job to keep one's boots on. Heavy rain all the after-noon, clearing about 4 p.m., the wind hauling south-west."

January 10th was a better day. The weather was fine, and fish bit well. During the morning Weary Willie, Mac, and I rowed round the crater. We found more steam rising from the earth, and in one or two places rolled large rocks away from it. The ground underneath was clay and too hot to touch. When we dug a hole the steam became thicker, but we saw no water.

After dinner we three went over the top of the island again by way of the Peak and the rookery. We walked to the water cave and came down that way.

The outstanding incident of the afternoon was that the dog caught a rabbit, the first since we landed. "The cat," the diary states, "catches one or two small ones every night—but she eats them herself!"

January 11th: About 5.30 a.m. the whole population of the island, British and French, was busy in the vicinity of the camp with its various early-morning occupations. The Captain and Ganymede were strolling along the landing-place towards the boat, which had just returned with the breakfast fish. Clad in my trousers only, I was sitting on a stone close by, trying to wash the remains of my shirt with our clay substitute for soap in a bucket of hot brackish water.

Wood was being chopped, and water brought to the fire, where the steward, cook, and three boys were making preparations for the meal.

The Capitaine was watching his men operate a machine they had rigged to press salt out of their fish before drying them in readiness to ship on the schooner.

"Been lucky this morning," remarked the Captain, looking down into the boat as the men began passing out the fish.

"Yes, sir! They're bitin' good-oh today. Look at this one," replied a man, holding one up by the gills.

While it was being passed round and commented on faint shouts could be heard above us. Nobody paid any attention. An argument had started between our two

18

schools of thought: the respective merits of cray-fish and octopus as bait.

"Beaucoup feesh?" shouted the Capitaine to them from his press.

"Oui! Plenty bon!" somebody replied.

As I was cautiously wringing out my shirt, terrified lest it might come to pieces in my hand, the cat jumped down into the boat. Seizing a small rock-cod, she furtively carried it into the locker in the stern-sheets.

"Cleaned that fish yet?" called the steward. "Water's boilin'."

The dog sauntered up, caught sight of the cat in the boat's locker, and leaped down after it. There followed some barking, hissing and scuffling, and the cat fled to the schooner, leaving behind a partly eaten rock-cod. The dog jumped back among the men, wearing the expression of a boy-scout who has done his daily good deed.

While they were passing the fish out of the boat the shouts from above could be heard again, more clearly this time.

"That's the look-out men!" exclaimed a man suddenly.

All hands gazed up towards the Peak. The two men who were on duty at the flag-staff were running down the hill, shouting and waving their arms.

"They've seen something!" said the Captain.

Without a word, Ganymede, the Chief Officer, dashed up towards them. The dog, sensing the excitement, rushed ahead of him, barking furiously, the remainder of us following behind as though beagling with one dog.

The look-out men were winded when we met them and could only point seawards.

"What is it?" the Chief Officer barked at them. "A ship?"

"Yes! Steamer!" they both replied.

"Tell the Captain!" he shouted to me.

While he continued on up the hill to the flag-staff with the look-out men the remainder ran back to the camp with me.

"Steamer reported, sir," I told the Captain. "Chief Officer's gone to see what it is."

"Collect up all our gear," he ordered. "Get it into the boats as quick as you can."

The men stampeded in all directions. In a few minutes our boat-sail tent was pulled down, and bottom boards, oars, breakers, buckets, and the rest of our household goods were on the landing-place and being stowed in the boats.

"What shall we do with this morning's fish, sir?" asked the boatswain.

"Put it back in the boat. They'll be glad of some fresh fish," replied the Captain; and, turning to me, he added, "Run out to the breakwater and see if you can see anything."

A few men and I made a record sprint there and hurried along it until we could see round the point. I suddenly felt somebody slapping my back. It was the donkeyman.

"There she is, sir!" he shouted in my ear. "Look at 'er! It's a steamer! She's comin' in! We'll get away from 'ere now!"

He stopped thumping my back and continued to his mates, "See 'er, boys? We're all right now! She'll take us off!"

In his excitement he was almost incoherent. The others were no better. The sight of the ship had gone to their heads like strong drink. They were singing, shouting, and dancing, pounding each other's backs and shaking hands.

Actually the ship was a long way off, too far yet for us

to see in what direction she was heading, or for her to make out our signals.

"Come on, men," I said. "Let's get back to the boats."

On the way back we met others, who were hurrying out with armfuls of damp driftwood. They piled it on the fire and clouds of black smoke began to rise from it.

"It's a steamer," I told the Captain, "but too far off to see how she's heading."

"Probably made the island to check her chronometers," he remarked, adding to Weary Willie, "Go up to the Chief Officer and tell him to come down at once. I'm going out to try to intercept her."

Weary Willie, the Third Officer, hurried up the hill. The Captain walked over to the Capitaine, and they both went on board the schooner.

The excitement had spread to the Frenchmen. They had stopped work on their press and joined our men in a back-thumping, hand-shaking dance contest. The camp had become a mad-house.

The two Captains returned as the Chief Officer came running down the hill.

"She's making for the entrance, I think," he said.

"Man the boats!" ordered the Captain.

The lunatics regained a little sanity and jumped in, spitting lavishly on their hands as they sorted out the oars. Captain and Capitaine shook hands.

"Au revoir," said the former. "Merci beaucoup."

"Bon voyage, mon ami," replied the latter. "You come 'nuzzer time, yes?"

The Captain laughed. "More better see you in Angleterre or France, not St. Paul," were his last words.

We all shook hands with the "Public Enemy No. 1." "Au revoir" and "Merci beaucoup" were all we could say to him in French.

"Bonne chance, mes amis!" he shouted as we shoved off.

He and his crew ran to the opening in the breakwater and cheered us as we pulled through it. We stopped rowing to give them three cheers, and then all hands, double-banked on the oars, lay back on it.

By that time the ship could be seen distinctly, and she was heading towards us. When we were about a mile off-shore a thin wisp of steam at the top of her funnel was noticed.

"I believe that's her whistle!" yelled Ganymede whose boat was neck-and-neck with ours. "She may have seen us!"

If it was, we were too far off to hear it. She may have been merely blowing off steam.

Half a mile further. She was still heading towards us, and we caught sight of another white patch against her funnel. A second later there was a faint sound that everybody recognised. It was the cough and gurgle of a cargo boat's whistle clearing its throat, followed by its plaintive wail. She had sighted us!

At 7.30 a.m. her crew were throwing us lines as we ran alongside. A minute later we were climbing up the side-ladder. A derrick had been rigged in readiness. The boats were slung, hooked on, and hoisted aboard. We saw the fish we had brought with us passed out and carried to the galley.

As we stood there, watching them, our feet were literally caressing the deck planks. Men were patting and stroking the stokehold fiddley. The dog walked a few yards along the scupper, sniffing loudly. Then he turned his head towards us and barked as much as to say: "Get a noseful of this. You can't beat it!"

A clanging of engine-room telegraph gongs was followed by a shiver of the deck planks and a rumble down below.

We were on a ship and under weigh. We felt as a fish must do when it is thrown back into the water.

"Come along to my room," said the Second Officer of the ship to me. "We'll rake out some clothes for you. As you are now, you're liable to scare the sea-gulls."

"Mr. Makin'!" exclaimed a voice behind us as we were walking forward.

I turned round. It was the boatswain. He had a worried look on his face.

"What's the matter?" I asked.

"Did you 'ave the cat in your boat, sir?"

I shook my head. The rock-cod snatcher had been left behind!

CHAPTER VIII

"D.B.S."
(Distressed British Seamen)

" For this my son was dead, and is alive again ; he was lost, and is found."—*St. Luke* xv. 24.

THE Second Officer's cabin was similar to most cargo boats' rooms—a mere box in which was a bunk with a couple of drawers underneath, a settee, and a wash-basin. Bare and uncomfortable as it would appear to You-Who-Live-Ashore, to me it was home, and I gazed all round me, taking in all the details.

Suddenly I noticed a man staring at me. Something about him seemed vaguely familiar. He was the same height and build as myself. His hair would have been fair had it been clean, but it was long, tangled, and dirty. Perhaps it was the beard that made it difficult to "place him." That was reddish in colour, from an inch to 2 inches long, untrimmed, and, like the hair, dirty. Dirt was engrained in his neck and round his ears. He wore no collar. A small piece of unclean and buttonless shirt was visible. Altogether, quite an unpleasant-looking person. Where on earth had I met him?

" Hardly recognise yourself," said the Second Officer.
" Good Lord! It's me!" I exclaimed.

The realisation that that revolting caricature of a down-and-out beachcomber was my own reflection in a mirror was sufficient shock to ruin my grammar. For a moment, in the excitement of finding myself in a ship's cabin once more, that possibility had not dawned on me.

I then became thoroughly interested in myself and con-

tinued the inspection downward. In that direction I was
no more pleasing to the eye than from the neck up. What
had once been a double-breasted uniform coat with brass
buttons and two gold stripes was merely a dirty, ragged
piece of cloth of uncertain colour. The buttons were replaced by bits of sail-twine. There were no elbows in
the sleeves, and the wrists were frayed to ribbons. A
piece of an old and dirty sack was roughly stitched with
twine over both knees of the trousers, and the bottom ends
of the legs were in the same condition as the wrists of the
coat. They were considerably shrunk by the immersings
in salt water and the greater part of two dirty calves was
exposed.

There were no socks. The feet were partially encased
in rotten leather that was lashed on them with ropeyarns.
Toes wiggled through the ends of both.

While I was taking in those details the Second Officer
had filled the basin with hot water and laid out his shav-
ing gear.

"See what you can do with that," he said.

For the next ten minutes I went through the tortures of
the damned. During them, however, I advanced through
centuries of evolution as it is expounded by Darwin. I was
admiring my handiwork when one of the ship's sailors
appeared at the door with a pair of scissors and a comb.

"Like an 'air-cut, sir?" he asked.

"Yes! Rather! Can you do it?" I replied.

"Oh! I cuts all the 'air on this packet on long trips.
I just done your Cap'en's. Sit dahn 'ere, sir, I'll soon
'ave it off."

I sat on the edge of the settee. He wrapped the Second
Officer's towel round my neck and began to shear it off
by the handful. When he had finished the room was
nearly carpeted with it. The Second Officer returned
while he was sweeping it up.

"Bath's empty," he said. "What about it?"

"Can absolutely do," I answered. "Lead me to it."

In a quarter of an hour I had scrubbed myself with real soap, dried myself on a real towel, and was experiencing the sensuous feeling of real clean underwear against my skin. Clean body! Clean clothes! Only one thing remained: ham and eggs and coffee!

I heard the voices of Ganymede and Weary Willie outside and went out to them. They were hardly recognisable after their reconditioning.

"What time's breakfast on this man's ship?" asked Weary Willie.

"Heaven help their ham and eggs," replied Ganymede. "I've dreamed of nothing else for three weeks."

The ship's steward came to us. "Breakfast is ready, sir," he said. "I guess you can do with a bit."

We followed him into the small dining saloon. Their Third Officer was on the bridge, and there was just room for the two Captains, two Chief Officers, two Seconds and our Third to squeeze in round the table.

A plate, loaded down to the scuppers with bread and butter, was close to Weary Willie. He looked round furtively, edged a slice off it, broke off a large piece and slipped it into his mouth. My eyes were riveted on a pot of marmalade. Ganymede was literally licking his lips in his impatience to get on with the good work.

Suddenly the steward appeared at the door. He was carrying a large steaming dish. Instinctively we all straightened ourselves up and stared at it. We watched him place it on the table and . . .

We slowly deflated and slumped back in our chairs. I heard Ganymede, who was next to me, mutter two words that cannot be repeated here. Weary Willie looked as though he were about to burst into tears. Our Captain had already suffered so much that he was only capable of registering patient resignation. I felt an almost uncontrollable urge to behave like a child who is being scolded by its nurse: stamp my feet and scream. That dish was heaped up with FISH!!!—the fish we had brought with us in the boats.

"Good of you to think of bringing it," remarked their Captain. "Fresh fish is a nice change!"

"Yes—er—yes, isn't it?" replied our Old Man. "Ship's food—um—isn't very attractive—as a rule."

We were nine days on that ship. Our "opposite numbers" gave us such things as a suit of underwear, shirt, socks, etc., and we passed away the time improving the appearance of our other clothes. The patches of sacking and canvas were removed and carefully replaced by pieces of cloth they gave us, sewn on with cotton instead of sail-twine. Buttons of various shapes and colours were collected and stitched on in lieu of the string fastenings.

On January 20th we were landed in Albany, West Australia, wearing those clothes and the remnants of our boots, the latter having been carefully blackened and neatly lashed on our feet with black spunyarn instead of yellow manilla ropeyarns.

A letter I posted from Naples on the way home gives an idea of the kindness shown us there:

"The people in Albany were very good to us. We were in a very ragged condition when we landed. The Mayor and some Town Councillors took us straight to the tailor and boot-maker shops and gave us a complete rig-out: suit of clothes, underwear, shirt, collars, socks, boots, etc., and a dinner at the hotel."

That same night we were sent on by rail to Fremantle. After staying ten days in the P. and O. Hotel we came

home D.B.S. (Distressed British Seamen) in the Orient
Line S.S. *Osterley*.

During the trip we were shown more kindness. The
Board of Trade provided us with second-class accommodation, and most of the passengers were Australian.
For an evening or two they asked us into the smoke-room.
We had practically no money, and usually made some
excuse to avoid accepting their invitations. They
promptly guessed the real reason, however, for one day
when Ganymede went to his cabin he found a handful of
sovereigns lying on his bunk. He never discovered who
put them there.

When we arrived in Plymouth on March 3rd we received
our first letters from home. The words at the head of
this chapter are taken from the one I received from my
mother.

The family had had an anxious time. When the ship
was overdue they watched the reinsurance rates slowly
mounting, until eventually we were posted "missing."
A cable I sent them as soon as we landed in Albany
reached them shortly after a friend at Lloyds had tele-
phoned to say we were safe.

There was a Board of Trade enquiry into the loss of the
ship, and we were kept at home some months in order to
attend it. Mac, the Scotch-Canadian, who had no friends
or relatives in England, stayed with us the whole time, and
during that long holiday he and I continued our explora-
tions in and around London.

One of them took us to Epsom to see the crowds on
Derby day. After investing several sixpences with
shabby-genteel persons who slipped us an envelope containing the name of the winner we finally entrusted a
sum of money to a bookmaker to be placed on Sunstar
for the Derby. When we heard that our horse had won
we jubilantly returned to collect. The bookie, however,

had not waited to hear the result of the race, and we arrived just in time to watch the crowd break up and set fire to his stand and landau.

We all had to be in London while the enquiry was taking place. Ganymede and his wife spent a few evenings with us, and replicas of the St. Paul "pow-wows" were held. He took the chair, and the Tribesmen were represented by my parents and sisters, who listened to his splendaciously mendacious stories with bated breath and wide-open eyes.

At last the day arrived when it was time to look for another ship. By that time Mac was one of the family, and we all went to the docks to see him off on a ship bound for Montreal.

Having supplied myself with a new outfit, I returned to the same owners, and towards the end of July, 1911, I proceeded to Liverpool to join their S.S. *Cynthiana* as Second Officer.

CHAPTER IX

ROYAL NAVAL RESERVE

" The trivial round, the common task."

THE above words are a brief but quite comprehensive résumé of the next year or two. Such incidents as being cast away on St. Paul Island, though interesting for me to look back upon and, I hope, for you to read, only happen at rare intervals in the lives of us ordinary men—fortunately for us. There are years between them when we merely go to and fro on a ship about our business, just as you do in your baby Austin. We have, of course, small annoyances—minor strandings, collisions, and the like; but they are to us only what flat tyres and dents in your wings are to you, and would not make interesting reading.

The work and routine on the *Cynthiana* during the following months were a repetition of those of the *Indiana*, and we were employed in the same trade: North Atlantic. She was slightly smaller, being of 2,045 tons, and when I arrived on board I found that she was a "two-Mate" ship. There was no Third Officer, which meant that the Chief and I would be watch and watch on the bridge at sea. Having paid my own fare to Liverpool, however, and requiring but a few months before being eligible to sit for my Master's certificate, I signed on.

Friends of mine ashore obviously think I am spinning them a "tall yarn" when I tell them that steamers of over 2,000 tons register sometimes carried only two officers. They find it hard to believe that, although parents had had to pay a premium for their son to be trained as

277

an officer and he had succeeded in obtaining his certificates
of competency as Mate and Master, he was expected to
spend eighty-four hours a week on the bridge, in charge
of and responsible for the safety of the ship and of 5,000
tons or more of merchandise in addition to his other duties.

That was by no means a rare thing in 1911. Now
apparently even worse conditions exist. I quote the
Daily Telegraph of August 14, 1936:

" Mr. Greenwood (Soc., Wakefield) brought up the
question of the Merchant Shipping Advisory Committee's
Report. . . .

" Complaining of undermanning, he instanced a vessel,
very little under the 2,750-ton mark, which sailed to the
Black Sea carrying a master (*i.e.*, captain) and one mate.
The Board of Trade permitted the vessel to sail when they
received a letter from the master to the effect that he
would take watch during the voyage.

" That meant that the master would be working 84
hours a week apart from his responsibilities as master.
But he had no option. His job was at stake. It was a
criminal offence for the Board of Trade to permit a ship
to sail under conditions of that kind.

" He asked for some specific and definite undertaking
from the President that he meant to take active steps to
get rid of the ' slums of the sea.' . . ."

That, I admit, is a digression, an old sailor's growl, and
I will hark back to the common tasks of the *Cynthiana*,
which, like those of the *Indiana*, consisted in running up
and down ladders to the holds in port, nursing her through
the Atlantic gales, and handling her drunken crews.

The worst example of the latter was a Saturday midnight sailing from Liverpool. Of the " deck crowd," only
the Captain, Chief Officer, and I were sober. During the

run down the Irish Sea and round the Tuskar the former kept watch on the bridge while we two steered the ship in turn. Fortunately the weather was fine. Eventually we managed to get some life into the men, and we heaved a sigh of relief to see the hatches properly secured and the decks squared up before any deep depressions west of Ireland moved east to meet us.

I left that ship in December, 1911, and returned home for my final examinations. After obtaining the compulsory Master's certificate I went back to the navigation school, and in a short time succeeded in passing the voluntary exam. for extra-Master.

As I had no intention of going back into cargo boats, I was then faced with the problem of deciding to which passenger-ship company I should give the opportunity of acquiring my services. Here I was fortunate. Before beginning the wearisome round of offices I happened to hear of a vacancy in the Atlantic Transport Line, and I joined that company as a junior officer in March, 1912.

The life in that rank on that class of ship was even less eventful and the common tasks were easier than those of the *Indiana* or *Cynthiana*. We were employed on a four-weekly service with passengers and freight between London and New York. There was little work to do, the same crew signed on voyage after voyage and were sober, and on those large comfortable bridges one forgot the significance of the words " Bad Weather."

Being a junior officer, I was merely a " dog's body " with no responsibility. The senior officer kept watch on the bridge and looked after the ship. I assisted him with the navigation, did the rounds, and generally made myself useful to him.

Promotion, of course, was slow. One joined that class of company with the intention of settling down and awaiting one's turn. As the older men retired we gradually moved step by step up the ladder to the coveted position of "command."

One reached the top much earlier in cargo boats, but personally I could see nothing up there that attracted me. There was little money, no comfort, and few opportunities to see one's home.

After a trip or two in that company I heard the senior men talking about the Royal Naval Reserve. I discovered that some of them were Lieutenants R.N.R., and that the management encouraged their officers to join, granting them leave for their annual drills. What they told me interested me, and eventually I informed the Marine Superintendent that I wished to send in an application. He raised no objection and I did so.

In due course I was accepted. The Superintendent not only gave me leave for the four weeks' probationary training as Sub-Lieutenant, but also for the gunnery and torpedo courses and for the twelve months' sea-service as Lieutenant on one of H.M. ships.

This brought about another uprooting, similar to the two previous ones: the first at the age of 15 when I left home to start life all over again among the "Iron Men," my Eton suit and mortar-board hat being thereby transformed into dungarees and sheath-knife; and the second, five and a half years later, when I had to begin once more as a babe in arms and learn the A B C of a People whose world relied for its proper functioning on steam engines and winches in place of the canvas and "pully-hauly" with which I was familiar. My foster-parents then were of the "Ganymede" type of seafarer.

In the spring of 1913 I departed that life and was born again on H.M.S. *London*, a pre-Dreadnought battleship, my original dungarees and sheath-knife having, in the course of evolution, developed into a frock-coat and sword.

My new nurses belonged to another strange race, whose habitat was *The*-Service. Their language was every bit as difficult to learn as that of the "Iron Men" and the "Ganymedes." For some time it seemed to be a jargon of such words as "eighteen-inch-R.G.F.-mark-six-star," or merely of scraps of the alphabet such as "A.C. 1st B.S." and "T.G.M." Instead of climbing into a hold to see that cargo was stowed "bung up and bilge free," I had to go down a ladder into a magazine and look at rows of twelve-inch "projs."

I cannot remember much about that probationary training on H.M.S. *London* beyond the difficulty of making my sword behave itself when I walked up the gangway and on to the quarterdeck to report myself.

From there I was sent to the gunnery school at Whale Island, Portsmouth, for eight weeks' strenuous training. I doubled up and down the drill ground during squad and company drill, learned how to handle and not climb round a rifle, and was taught how to wear and not trip over my sword. The mysteries of fire control and "spotting" were made clear to me, I fired real guns at targets, and eventually succeeded in stripping and reassembling a breech-block without having any bits of it left over.

Finally I was given a squad, and told to drill it and march it about. Drilling it was a simple matter, but there were pitfalls to be avoided when one had them on the march. For example: I formed them in fours and paraded them in front of me. Then I right-wheeled them and they began to march away from me. Unfortunately I over-estimated the carrying power of my voice and did not shout "About turn!" until they were out of earshot. The result was that they "foot-slogged it" to the opposite side of the ground, where they were brought up all standing by the drill shed.

The-Service Man who was putting me through it looked at me, and we both grinned.

"And that's that," he remarked as we walked after my army to collect and reorganise it.

Having obtained the gunnery certificate, I began a course of electricity and torpedo on H.M.S. *Vernon*. During the following eight weeks my brain buzzed with induction coils and Menotti test batteries, with warheads and low-power impulses. When I passed out from there my shore training was completed and I was appointed to another pre-Dreadnought battleship for the twelve months' service afloat.

I joined her in December, 1913, by which time I had become a citizen of that world, able to speak the language fluently and carry my sword correctly when I walked up her gangway and saluted the quarterdeck.

The next few months were interesting and enjoyable ones. There was so much to see and to learn, not only in connection with the profession, but also with the officers and men. Among the former were the various drills, exercises with the fleet, and the organisation of a warship.

The knowing and understanding the latter—the "seeing the other fellow's point of view"—required time, just as it did during the first few months in sail and in steam. I, a member of a service whose job is to feed and supply you, had an opportunity to see behind the scenes of the one who protects you. Each had heard of the other, but knew very little about him. After a while, when I was no longer a "stranger in a strange land," I was known in the ward-room as "Mister." Apparently there was a legend in the King's Navee to the effect that Merchant Service officers wore bowler hats and red carpet-slippers while on duty on the bridge, and that they called each other just plain "Mister."

It would be an exaggeration to say that that was the

naval idea of a Merchant Service officer, but to a certain extent it is indicative of what they knew about us. We, on the other hand, or those of us who had never met them, had equally fallacious notions about them.

One night early in 1914 another officer and I dined with the Captain. After dinner the conversation drifted round to wars, rumours of wars, and the probability of a war. He told us something of Germany's bid for sea-power, her preparations to invade France by way of Belgium, and the Navy's task of keeping the trade routes clear in order that there might be no let or hindrance to the work of the Merchant Service: the transport of men, munitions, food and supplies.

Whether intentional or not, that dinner was part of my Naval Reserve training. It brought home to me the fact that, no matter what they think of each other, the two services are the component parts of one immense world force, Britain's Sea-Power; that they are the right and left arm of Britannia, as necessary to each other as both are to the rest of her body—You-Who-Live-Ashore, who would lack the necessities of life without the one and never know a moment's feeling of security without the other.

It also developed a vague thought that had been in my mind for some time: that as the "Iron Men" had hammered me into a rough shape, and as the "Ganymedes" had followed on by filing off the ragged edges and giving to me a definite pattern, so The-Service was adding the final touches and polishing me; and that when their work on me was completed I should be the finished article, a Royal Naval Reserve officer, a link between the two services, able when "der Tag" dawned to understand the methods and languages of, and to play a useful part among, any of the Peoples of the Sea-World.

Probably all Merchant Service officers who have been

through the Royal Naval Reserve training will agree with me that it was an invaluable part of their education. It could do no harm if it were compulsory for all of us, officers and men. It would create a better understanding between the Royal Navy and the Merchant Service than existed in 1913, and make easy a close co-operation between them such as was necessary in 1914.

On June 28th of that year came the news of the murder of the Archduke Charles at Sarajevo. As the days passed and the international tension tautened the atmosphere in the ward-room changed. Jane's "Fighting Ships" was frequently referred to. In the after-dinner arguments golf and beagles were replaced by gun-power and blockades. Daily the Flag-Lieutenant assumed a more secretive and important mien when he strolled into the ward-room with a sheaf of signals under his arm. Time "wasted" on torpedo drills caused high blood pressure in the arteries of the gunnery officer—and vice versa. Snatches of the surgeons' conversations that I overheard almost made me hope there would be no war.

On July 17th and 18th we were among those present at Spithead when the King reviewed the whole fleet after the test mobilisation. That concentrated mass of matériel must have given a sense of security to the layman when he looked at it from the scare-headlines of his daily paper. Had he been able to see through 12 inches of armour and watch the personnel going calmly about their business of preparation while governments wrote notes and politicians talked, he would have felt even more reassured.

Only those who lived among the personnel could understand and appreciate the value of the third element, the essential one that was lacking in the youthful fleet on the other side of the North Sea: Tradition and Prestige, built up during centuries by a race of seafarers.

On the evening of August 4th the Flag-Lieutenant came into the ward-room, looking more portentous than ever. He had with him a signal which he read aloud to us:

" Admiralty to all ships. General message. The war telegram will be issued at midnight authorising you to commence hostilities against Germany, but in view of our ultimatum they may decide to open fire at any moment. You must be ready for this."

CHAPTER X

WAR-TIME—I

(August 4th, 1914, to February 27th, 1916.)

" Commence hostilities against Germany ! "

WHILE the occupants of the ward-room were still arguing as to when the German Fleet would come out and where we should meet them—there was unanimity as to the result—the war telegram, of which the above caption is the interpretation, came through.

At the same time it was flashed to all the harbours, ports, mud-holes and creeks on the Seven Seas and up the rivers off them. All over the world men serving under the White Ensign began a task for which drills, exercises, and evolutions had been preparing them since their boyhood.

Those who sailed under the "Red Duster," having seen the last sling of cargo on board, secured their hatches and proceeded to sea, carrying on "business as usual" under war conditions for which they had received no training or instruction. Instead of being taught in peacetime to co-operate with H.M. Navy, to keep station in convoy, to use guns, and to manœuvre their ships against submarines, they had to start at the beginning and learn by actual experience.

Meanwhile much bad temper and language were expended by both Services. Take, for example, such an essential thing as signalling between a warship and a tramp steamer. The former closed the latter with a string of flags flying. A number of trained and experienced

286

signalmen, ranging from an officer and a yeoman of
signals down to a boy, equipped with efficient telescopes
and glasses, stood by to haul down, read the reply, bend
on more flags and run them up.

There was a long wait before even an answering pennant was shown on the tramp; and a still longer one
before a reply was "close up." During that interval the
Captain, officers, and signalmen on the warship waxed
more and more sarcastic in their comments on the slack-
ness of the "damned old tramp."

What nobody seemed to understand then and probably
few realise even now is that the damned old tramp carried
a Master, two Mates, and eight or ten seamen of various
nationalities, the latter being the scourings of sailor-town,
who did not know or want to know the difference between
the code pennant and the flags A and Z.

The two Mates, or officers, were watch and watch—
eighty-four hours a week on the bridge under war conditions in addition to their other duties. The Master, or
Captain, hardly ever left the bridge and was more or less
dead-tired. If they were lucky, the ship possessed one
or two pairs of binoculars, though it is doubtful if they
could see much better with them than with the naked
eye.

When they were able to see that a signal was hoisted on
the warship the officer who was below and asleep had to
be called out to come up to the bridge and give a hand.
While the other continued to look out for submarines or
to keep the ship in station in the convoy he and the Captain read the message and bent on and mast-headed the
answering pennant. Then they had to look up their reply
in the signal-book, pick out the flags, bend them on and
run them up. If the signalling was by semaphore, the
Captain or one of the officers would have to climb on to
the rail of the bridge where he could be seen, balance him-

self there, and " gesticulate " the reply. Nobody else on the ship knew anything about it.

The " talky-talk " probably ended by the warship sending a final " snotty " message and growling about the slowness and incompetency of the Masters and Mates of the Merchant Service; and by the tramp continuing on her leisurely eight or nine knot gait, wishing she had a chance to tell the " bloody war-boat " what she thought about her.

While such ships as that instanced by Mr. Greenwood, carrying only a Master and *one* Mate, are let loose on the ocean, communication between the two Services will be even more difficult. We do our best, poor as that may be, judged by what they can do with their trained and disciplined crews.

Once more I quote the *Daily Telegraph*, this time of November 19th, 1936:

" A warning of the British Merchant Marine's shortage of ships and men was given last night by Mr. E. H. Watts, vice-chairman of the Shipping Federation. . . .

" ' In the event of war, our depleted Royal Navy will want to call on some thousands of men from the Merchant Service,' said Mr. Watts. ' I am going to state categorically . . . that there will be no men available from the Merchant Service.'

" The present cargo section of the British Mercantile Marine, quite apart from any calls that would be made upon it by the Navy, was utterly inadequate for the responsibilities it might be called upon to shoulder, Mr. Watts declared. . . .

" The final estimates made by Mr. Watts of the shortage in our cargo-carrying fleet was 700 ships, though he said many shipowners would put the figure as high as 1,500. He revealed that he had discussed the possibility of an agreement with Norwegian politicians and shipowners, whereby they would guarantee a certain tonnage of cargo vessels to be available in time of war.

" ' In each individual case I received the same reply,' added Mr. Watts. ' Their homes are so close to one or other of the probable combatants, and they are so utterly defenceless from air attack, that they cannot enter into any agreement to help us in the event of our being a belligerent.' "

If the Norwegians can be persuaded to change their minds in the next war, the King's Navee will have to exercise even more patience when they wish to communicate with " our " Merchant Marine; and if Britannia has to beg for foreign ships and men to rule the waves for her, let's hope that Drake will hear the Drums and leave the Port of Heaven to help us!

In the beginning of this book I set out to depict the life of the Merchant Service officer as lived by myself, it being typical of the ordinary man. During those years, 1914 to 1918, however, while I served on " big ships " of the Navy, my experiences in no way resembled theirs. Mine included an occasional hectic " moment "; but there were long intervals between them when I laid comfortably at anchor behind boom defences. At sea I was on a heavily armed and armoured ship, surrounded by a screen of destroyers.

The ordinary men of the Merchant Service, a big proportion of whom drifted about the ocean on unarmed, eight-knot tramp steamers, had even more hectic times, and no respite. My company, the Atlantic Transport Line, owned four passenger ships in the London-New York trade. At the end of the war none of them remained afloat. Some of the men with whom I had sailed on them were lost with the ships.

One evening after the war, when I was an officer in the Red Star Line, we were "swopping lies" about our experiences. Stopping a bullet with my thigh at the Gallipoli landing did not seem much "to write home about" after listening to a story by one of the other officers.

He was Second Mate of a small, unarmed cargo boat that was attacked by a German submarine. After a shell had exploded in the engine-room, while his ship was stopped and unmanageable, he and the rest of the crew stood on the bridge and on deck while the submarine slowly and methodically blew them to pieces. Fortunately a British destroyer appeared on the scene and took off the survivors just as the ship was going down.

In the Prologue I referred to an officer who had been obliged to take a job as quartermaster when the Red Star Line ships were sold to the Germans. During the war he was serving on a mine-sweeper. One morning while engaged in that work his boat was blown up by a mine. He was picked out of the water by another vessel, also a sweeper. Later in the day the same thing happened to her and he "went up" for the second time. He was landed that evening with fractured ribs and limbs.

Much has been written about the exploits of officers and men of individual ships of the Navy, of their heroism during an action or when working their disabled ships back to port, and of the way in which they upheld the prestige and tradition of their Service; but apart from a few isolated cases, one reads of the Merchant Service that on such-and-such a day so many ships were "sunk without trace," together with dry statistics of the number of troops and tons of munitions that were transported.

Books could be written about the way in which those officers and men upheld the traditions and prestige of their Service as they plodded year in and year out across the

Seven Seas. There was only a decimal point of an inch of plating between them and a torpedo, and no multitudinous watertight compartments to keep them afloat when they were hit. They also realised that if they managed to get away in the boats, the submarine would probably come up and push them under.

Like the Navy, none of those men want a "song and dance" written of what they did; but a little more of that sort of publicity would enable the country to understand more fully than it appears to do now the vital importance to Britain of a sufficiently large and efficiently trained Mercantile Marine. That in its turn might get something done to prevent us from being "caught short" in the next war.

I will end this peroration with a quotation from Mr. Winston Churchill's book, "The World Crisis":

"The foundation of all defence (*i.e.*, against submarine attack) lay in the fact that Merchant-seamen three or four times 'submarined' returned unfalteringly to the perilous seas, and even in the awful month when one ship out of every four that left the United Kingdom never came home, no voyage was delayed for lack of resolute civilian volunteers."*

This has been a very long and, I am afraid, wearisome digression. I will therefore recommence this chapter by answering the time-honoured question: "What did you do in the Great War?"

I did so little that the most suitable reply would be that of the old Frenchman who was asked what he did in the Revolution: "I survived!"

* Lest we forget : in April, 1917, 423 merchant ships aggregating 849,000 tons were sunk by German submarines (figures from "The World Crisis," by Churchill).

So much has been written about the war that I will skim over my share of it. At the beginning we were one of the Channel Fleet, patrolling the Channel while the Expeditionary Force crossed to France. From time to time transports, resembling floating hives swarming with khaki-coloured bees, passed and exchanged cheers with us.

Then for a while we laid at Sheerness and were aroused one morning by a violent explosion close to us: H.M.S. *Bulwark* was no longer with us and among us.

On the night of December 31st we were once more in the Channel. When the year 1915 was about two hours old a signal was passed from ship to ship, informing us that the *Formidable*, the last ship of the line, had been torpedoed.

In the spring of 1915 we were sent out to the Dardanelles to replace casualties suffered during the bombardment of March 18th. There on April 25th we took part in the first landing of the Australians. That has been described in so many books that I will not attempt it here. Later on, while at anchor off " Anzac " Beach, I was able to demonstrate the utility of Royal Naval Reserve officers as a link between the two Services. A ship of my own company, the Atlantic Transport Line, arrived with troops and munitions. In view of the fact that I knew her Captain and officers and that our cellars were becoming depleted, it was decided to send me on board her to negotiate for a supply of beer.

Eventually, when Italy " joined up," we were one of four British battleships that were sent to Taranto to augment her fleet. While there I was sent for a month or two to Brindisi. A number of British drift-net fishermen were based on that port and employed in fishing for submarines at the mouth of the Adriatic. I had to supervise their guns, ammunition, and explosives. Periodically I

went to sea on a small Italian steamer, to take them stores
and to see that they were " on the job."

During my first trip on her I had the responsibility of
upholding the prestige of both the British Navy and
Merchant Service. She was a small coasting vessel,
manned by Italian naval ratings and commanded by an
Italian Lieutenant. I was the only Britisher on board.
She was very cranky, the type of ship of which it is said:
" She'd roll in dry dock!"

We sailed early in the morning, and as soon as she
poked her nose outside the harbour she developed such a
combination roll, pitch and toss as I had never experienced in all my sea career. By 10 a.m. I felt queasy. At
noon, definitely seasick!

About one o'clock lunch was served. If there was one
thing on earth, or sea, that I did not want, it was food;
but I was a Britisher, alone among Italians; I belonged to
the two Services which were busy ruling the waves and I
could not let them down.

In an agony of suspense as to whether I could make
mind triumph over matter I descended to the saloon. It
was very small, very dirty, very stuffy, and very smelly.
The food was very Italian. I can conscientiously say that
I sat right through the meal and that I ate plate for plate
with the Italian Lieutenant, who was both accustomed to
the motion of the ship and hungry.

I admit that I refused a cigarette at the end of it, and,
as an excuse to get on deck, said I would go up and see
if any of the drifters were in sight. There I found a
secluded corner, and to this day no Italian knows what I
did during the next few minutes.

While at Brindisi I had an opportunity to see our drift-
net fishermen " doing their bit "—another branch of the
Merchant Service of whom books could be written, and
whose war records are far worthier of being chronicled

than my own. Here are some extracts from a letter I
wrote home concerning them. It was written during a
few days I spent at sea on one of the drifters:

"This submarine hunting is most interesting, and I'm
glad I've had a chance to see a bit of it. At present, for
a few days while this stunt is on, I'm actually on the job
myself and at sea in one of their boats, a thirty-ton fishing
boat.

"So behold me, living in an atmosphere that smells
strongly of cockroaches and galley-smoke, gloriously
filthy, and probably as odoriferous as the ship itself. It's
great fun, though. They are only small fishing boats with
engines, and there is no such thing as accommodation.
When I sleep I roll up in blankets and lie on bare boards.
The sanitary arrangement is a bit primitive: I merely
take my own bucket to the stern.

"They are splendid sea-boats and will stand any
weather, though they jump about like nothing on
earth. The men are a jolly good crowd, practically all
Scotchmen, and in peace-time all of them are fishermen.

"The cook has just brought along my dinner—a plate-
ful of most awfully scraggy-looking meat, potatoes, cab-
bage, and a basin of tea, with duff and jam to follow. I'll
get through it and finish this letter afterwards.

"*Later.* Have finished my repast. Oh, Lord! It was
solid, especially the duff! Recently this boat met a
German submarine while the cook was making a duff.
When they opened fire on the submarine he ran out of the
galley, shouting, 'If there's time to tie the —— cloth
round my duff, I'll heave it at the ——.'

"That is supposed to be a fact. If the duff was like
the one I had today, I'd be sorry for the submarine. I
have a black-handled knife and fork, and no spoon.

When I finish the meat course I lick the fork and use it for the duff.

" While the present stunt is going on a number of these boats are stationed a long way from the base. A few days ago I was going over to them in my Italian coaster, to take them stores and to act as depôt-ship for them. At the last moment she broke down and could not go. The stores had to be sent, though. We divided them between three Italian destroyers, and some men and I went with them.

" Didn't we have a time! I expect Phyl told you all about it. We sailed in a gale of wind, and you know what a destroyer is like in bad weather—under water most of the time.

" When we arrived there the drifters came alongside for their stores, and the deck was crowded with Scotch fishermen and Italian naval ratings, swopping cigarettes and each talking in his own language. The drifter skippers foregathered on the afterdeck of the destroyer, solemnly discussing the chances of netting a submarine, just as though they were at home, talking about herring. Some of them must be over 60 years old, and are out here on this kind of job. One of them came to me with a letter and asked me to post it when I had a chance, adding, ' Ye'll no ferget it, Lootenant, wull ye? My woman'll be lookin' fer it.'

" You bet I didn't forget it! We had to stay with them until we could get a ship to bring us back, but were only away thirty-six hours. We slept on a different destroyer each night, and spent the day on a third.

" In Brindisi the drifter crews are known as the ' Pirates.' The Italian admiral never asks for our Commander—always for the Pirate Chief. He is a great old boy. When they bagged their first submarine he wanted, I suppose, to do a very British thing to show his appreciation. He got somebody to make some ' Jolly Rogers ' (pirate flags: black, with skull and crossbones), and presented one to the boat that got the submarine. They always fly it, going in and out of port.

"One thing here is giving me grey hairs: the way the drifter men play about with their explosives. Of course, these shouldn't go off until a safety arrangement is removed; but I sometimes go on board them, to see that their guns, ammunition, and explosives are all right, and find the safety gadgets lying about on the deck. The other day one of the skippers came to me with something in his hand.

"'Wull ye be lookin' at this,' he said. 'Ah'm thinkin' it's oot o' one o' they bomb things.'

"Sure enough, it was the safety arrangement of one of his depth charges. I put it back in a hurry!

"A few days ago a drifter arrived from England. I could find no detonators on board, and the skipper didn't know what I meant when I asked for them. I described them to him.

"'Och! Them things!' he said. 'Ah'm thinkin' them'll be in the wheel-hoose.'

"I went with him to the wheel-house. He opened a locker containing, among other things, marline-spikes and a hammer. He pulled out a lot of gear, and then said, 'Aye! Yon's what ye'll be lookin' fer.'

"There, lying about in the bottom of the locker, were a number of fulminate of mercury detonators. He had come out from England across the bay to Italy, with them rolling about among marline-spikes and all sorts of junk.

"They have no idea of naval discipline. When naval ratings return from shore leave they are fallen in two deep on the quarterdeck, have to answer their names, and are inspected. The other day a lot of these drifter men went ashore. Most of them were drunk when they came back. A sergeant of marines who acts as our ship's police managed to get them fallen in, and began to call their names. Some answered and some didn't. All were talking at the top of their voices. He told them several times to stop talking. Finally he got angry and yelled: 'Stop talking, those men forud there!'

"At that, a little withered-up old Scotchman, very drunk and about 60 years old, solemnly took two paces forward from the front rank, saluted the sergeant, and stood to attention.

"'Sergeant,' he said. 'Ah'm tellin' ye, ah'll no stop talkin' fer ye!'

"Then, equally solemnly, he took two paces back, and began telling his pals about an 'Eye-talian gur-r-l' with whom he had whiled away the afternoon.

"The sergeant's face was a study. I went round the corner and howled with laughter."

Eventually I returned to my ship in Taranto. Early in 1916 we left the Italian Fleet and went to Gibraltar to dry-dock and refit, expecting to be there about three weeks.

20

CHAPTER XI

FEBRUARY 27TH, 1916

" Lo ! some we loved, the loveliest and the best
That Time and Fate of all their Vintage prest,
Have drunk their Cup a Round or two before,
And one by one crept silently to rest."

Rubáiyát.

THE letter in the preceding chapter contains a reference to
" Phyl." Phyllis was my wife; we were married in 1913.

When it was learned that we should remain about three
weeks in Gibraltar she and the wife of another officer
arranged to come out to us on the S.S. *Maloja*, P. and O.
Line.

Hardly had we found accommodation ashore when
news was received that the *Maloja* had been sunk by
mines or a torpedo off Folkestone.

Some time elapsed before we could get any further information, but eventually the other officer heard that his
wife was safe.

I no longer have the telegram that was sent me from
home, but I can remember it. It read: " *Maloja* sunk by
mines. Phyllis not saved."

" Then to the rolling Heav'n itself I cried,
Asking, ' What Lamp had Destiny to guide
Her little Children stumbling in the dark ?'
And—' A blind understanding !' Heav'n replied."

Rubáiyát.

CHAPTER XII

WAR-TIME—II

(February 27th, 1916, to March, 1919.)

" Rule, Britannia, Britannia rule the waves."

A FEW days later I was granted leave and came home on one of the smaller P. and O. boats that called at Gibraltar. At the expiration of my leave I was ordered to Whale Island, Portsmouth, to go through a requalifying course in gunnery while awaiting another ship.

In the beginning of May, 1916, I was appointed to one of the new 15-inch-gun ships that had just been completed and was being commissioned in Devonport. She proceeded to Scapa Flow to join the Grand Fleet and, having carried out satisfactorily our preliminary "shoots," we were able to be present at Jutland on May 31st.

I know little about that fight beyond what I have read in books. As the port 6-inch control officer, stationed in the foretop, I merely saw what took place inside one half of a circle: from right ahead round the port side to astern, the radius varying according to the thickness of the smoke and mist.

At some time during the afternoon "Action Stations" was sounded. We closed up and tested communications and fire-control instruments. From time to time scraps of information filtered up to us: light cruisers and destroyers in action with hostile light forces; enemy battle-cruisers sighted; Beatty and the battle-cruiser fleet heavily engaged; and finally the German High Sea Fleet sighted. The last item interested us—they were our meat.

Presently a faint rumble could be heard. It resembled the muttering of thunder.

"Hear it, Makes?" asked my "opposite number," a naval lieutenant who was starboard 6-inch control officer on the other side of the foretop. (I answered to the name of "Makes" in that ship.)

"Yes! Guns! The battle-cruisers, I suppose," I replied.

"Sounds like Drake's Drums," he remarked.

Whether or no I am constituted internally like other people, I cannot say; but situated in the centre of my midriff is something resembling a small magnetic field, capable of being excited by certain outside influences. While sitting in the dentist's chair, for example, his action of arranging the instruments of torture reacts on it, causing it to give a little squirm and thrill. During my younger and more romantic days straightening my tie preparatory to ringing the bell at the house of the current lady-love was a strong excitant.

On the afternoon of May 31st, 1916, I learned that dentistry and love are not the only external forces to which it is sensitive. At the first sound of the guns I experienced the identical squirm and thrill.

As their muttering slowly increased in intensity to a loud conversation one noticed that the visibility was deteriorating. Two of our older armoured cruisers could be seen some distance ahead of us. Presently one saw the flashes of their guns and the conversation degenerated into a brawl. With the visibility then obtaining it was impossible to see what they were firing at; but almost immediately it was obvious that they were engaging big ships. Large-calibre enemy shells fell into the water all round them, causing "splashes" that resembled huge geysers. Within a minute or so one of them was evidently heavily hit. There was an explosion and an eruption of flame from her hull; and when a dense cloud of smoke had drifted away she had disappeared.

Soon the Grand Fleet deployed into single line ahead. Seen from the foretop, it resembled a long line of insects, six miles of them, the turret guns, swinging round and extending some distance beyond the ship's side, their antennæ, sensing an enemy.

Six miles of ships with their attendant cruiser squadrons and destroyer flotillas, the visibility such that at times those in the rear of the line could not be seen from the van; owing to a lack of the necessary information, an uncertainty as to the exact locality of the enemy's battle-fleet; a possibility, perhaps a probability, of destroyer and submarine attacks developing behind the curtain of mist and smoke within effective range of their torpedoes before they could be seen and repelled; and the responsibility for manœuvring that fleet rested on the shoulders of one man on the *Iron Duke,* he himself no more sheltered from hostile gunfire and torpedoes than were any of us. In his mind would be the certain knowledge that a wrong manœuvre, due to an error of his own judgment or to faulty information supplied by others, might result in the total defeat of Britain and her allies.

Hardly was the deployment completed when enemy battleships were seen and our rear opened fire. As other hostile vessels showed up in the mist the din increased. The 13·5-inch guns of our " next ahead " put out tongues of fire at the enemy and spat 1,400-pound projectiles at him; and almost immediately our 15-inch guns gave an ear-splitting roar underneath me.

I have no idea how long it lasted without referring to books; and I am not attempting to write an authentic history of the fight, merely to describe the little I saw from the foretop while standing by to repel destroyer or submarine attacks with my 6-inch battery, guns crashing and roaring underneath and on all sides.

Before long, however, " Fritz " disappeared in the mist and the first round ended, giving a respite to our eardrums.

Later on he was seen again, and once more the guns of the Grand Fleet " did their stuff."

From time to time during the night there was a glare of searchlights astern, followed by gun-flashes and rumbles, indicating that the light forces were making a night of it.

The following day, after cruising about until noon like a terrier watching a hole into which it has driven a rat, the Fleet returned to Scapa Flow, and in a few hours it was ready for another " rough house."

Notwithstanding such comments as this, written by one gentleman in his periodical: " Someone has blundered! I am distressed and disturbed!" that is more than can be said of the " Luxus Flotte " on the other side of the North Sea.

Little of interest, so far as I at Scapa Flow was concerned, occurred during the remainder of the war. It was a long, monotonous period of drills and exercises, waiting for another " tag."

A good deal of my spare time was occupied with the ship's concert party. A fleet store-ship, the *Gourko*, had a stage fitted on one of her lower decks. During the long winter evenings she laid alongside ships while their " funny party" gave a show on board her.

As time went on the performances became more and more elaborate, and finally developed into revues. We painted our own scenery, designed and made our own costumes, trained our best-looking boys as chorus girls, practised for hours with lip-stick, grease-paint, and powder, and wrote and produced our own shows. After trying them on our own ship's company the *Gourko* took us alongside "chummy ships" and we performed for them. They did the same for us.

At the end of one of our "premières," when officers from other ships had been invited, there was a rumble of an explosion and the *Gourko* gave a shudder. It was the blowing up of H.M.S. *Vanguard*. A few of her officers, who were with us, and the picket boat's crew who had come to fetch them were, I believe, the sole survivors.

On November 11th, 1918, the Fleet was at Rosyth. After breakfast that morning we were landed for a route march, and on the way back heard bells and cheers welcoming home the Dove of Peace.

We of the Royal Naval Reserve then had to divert our thoughts from gunnery to what we should do after demobilisation. In my case, all the passenger ships of my company had been sunk, and there only remained a few old ships and cargo boats. I began to wonder if there would be a place for me, and, if not, where I should go. The majority of shipping companies were similarly situated, and all had their own officers returning from the Navy.

Our ship was among those which escorted the German Fleet into the Forth. The family kept the letter I wrote concerning it, and I add a few extracts from it:

"Am beginning to realise that the war is over. The censoring of our letters is stopped now, and we can say what we like. We are anchored in the Forth, with the German Fleet close to us.

"We have had a fairly strenuous but most interesting week. You will have read all about it in the papers, of course, how it began with the arrival of the German light cruiser *Königsberg*, bringing delegates to arrange about interning their ships.

"Some days later orders came out about meeting them

and escorting them in. Beatty had told them to be fifty miles east of May Island (just outside here) at 8 a.m. on Thursday, and that they would be met by a *sufficient* force. We weren't told who the sufficient force was until Wednesday, so you can imagine the ' buzzes ' as to who was going, and the groans if we heard that our squadron was not included.

" On Wednesday we were informed that the whole fleet would be there, and the King came up and inspected it. That evening the destroyer flotillas sailed, and we left about 2.30 a.m. on Thursday. At 7.30 a.m. we all closed up to ' action stations.' While the guns were not to be trained round, they had to be ready to open fire immediately if necessary.

" We met them about nine o'clock. It was rather an exciting moment. Even then it was hard to believe that a fleet like theirs would come across and tamely surrender. It seemed probable that they would trust to our not expecting anything and suddenly open fire on us, in the hope of damaging us as much as possible. They would be able to fire first, which would be a big advantage. At such a short range they could hardly help hitting us.

" However, they didn't, and our fleet picked them up and brought them into the anchorage. Since some of our people have been on board to search them one realises that there was no chance of it. I wasn't able to go myself. It was a gunnery and torpedo expert's job: seeing that they had no ammunition, bombs, or comic things like that stowed away. They found nothing, but they said that the ships were in a disgusting state of filth. . . . Their description of it sounded very much like that of a Paris mob on a small scale, without the guillotine: just a crowd of dirty men, hanging about in groups, taking orders from others, who wore red armlets. . . .

" One of their officers, decorated with an Iron Cross,

spoke sharply to one of the men, who jumped up, saluted, and clicked his heels. Then apparently he remembered that he was a free citizen, or comrade, or whatever they call themselves, for he put his pipe back in his mouth and slouched away. They said that the expression on the officer's face was quite funny. . . . They are like a flock of sheep: don't seem to know what to do, or to have any mind of their own, even about keeping things clean. . . . It's rather pitiful to think of men being in that state. Our officers said that it was the most depressing thing they had ever seen. However, they asked for 'Der Tag' and they got it. Their men wanted to talk, and were asking what they had come over for. They didn't seem to know anything about it.

"They are all going to Scapa Flow to be interned. Some go each day. We take our lot up on Monday, arriving on Tuesday. . . . We hear rumours that we shall be there three days, so hope to get the *Gourko* and give a show. It may liven things up a bit. At present everyone is down in the dumps. It's the sight of those darned ships. It is not natural for ships to be in that condition. Even the look of the outside of them gives one the hump.

"Nearly mail time, so will finish this letter. Hope to get rid of those darned German ships in a day or two."

I was demobilised early in March, 1919. I left the ship on Thursday night, arrived in London on Friday morning, and went straight to the Atlantic Transport Line's office to see the Marine Superintendent.

"Want a holiday now, I suppose," he said.

"I want a ship," I replied.

He fumbled among some papers, and picked up one on which were the names of the surviving ships. For a moment he looked at it.

"Damn few ships left for you fellows," he remarked

at last, adding after a pause, " Lot of the old men went with them, too."

There was another long pause, and then he asked suddenly, " When can you join?"

" This afternoon," I answered.

" Join the *Manitou* as First Officer in Tilbury on Monday morning," he said, picking up the telephone and nodding to me, to indicate that that was that.

At noon on Monday, after five and a half years' absence, I was back once more among my own people, trying to talk intelligently about cargo stowage and trimming-tanks.

CHAPTER XIII

COMMAND

" If you have built castles in the air, your work need not be lost ;
that is where they should be. Now put the foundations under
them."—THOREAU.

IN pre-war days the Red Star Line, though quite distinct
from the Atlantic Transport Line, was nevertheless closely
associated with it. The ships sailed under various flags:
British, American, and Belgian. The management was
German, and a considerable number of German officers
were employed afloat. The passenger traffic was chiefly
between Antwerp and New York.

During the war that trade, of course, vanished. Two
passenger ships remained under the American, and two
cargo boats under the Belgian flag. The remainder were
transferred to British registry and employed as necessary
with other British tonnage.

After the war the company was reorganised under a
manager who came from New York. Apart from the
American-flag ships, there were then, in 1919, only two
cargo boats running to Antwerp: the *Samland* and the
Gothland, both under the Belgian flag.

After I had served about five weeks on the *Manitou*,
carrying government stores between London and continental ports, the Red Star asked the Atlantic Transport
Line to supply two officers for the *Samland*, no Belgian
officers being available.

Another officer and I were therefore sent to Antwerp to
join her for a voyage or two: he as Second, I as First
Officer. We arrived about five o'clock one morning,

signed on Belgian articles, and sailed the same day. Besides us, there was a British Captain and a Belgian Chief and Third Officer.

On the return trips from the United States on that ship we carried over a thousand head of cattle " on the hoof." Those live cargoes added to my store of general knowledge. Not only were the decks down below full of them, but also practically the whole of the upper deck. To get to our rooms, we had to run the gauntlet between rows of horns. Apparently they never sleep. Only thin iron plates, the " walls " of our cabins, separated us from them. During the night they drummed on them with their hoofs, rattled their horns against them, and carried on loud conversations with friends in distant parts of the ship. We lived in such a farmyard atmosphere that even our food tasted and smelt of it.

In fog they were an added worry to the Captain and the officer of the watch. On the first voyage we spent a night crawling up Channel in dense fog, feeling our way past other ships' whistles. That only elicited growls from us, we were accustomed to it. What was new to us, and gave rise to more than growls, was the fact that our four-legged passengers apparently mistook our own whistle for the voice of a dear one left behind on the far-western prairies, for from time to time the thousand of them bellowed a reply. The noise was so great that we were unable to hear other ships, and had to stop altogether to let them find their way round us. At all events, we were safe. They could have experienced no difficulty in hearing our thousand bovine fog-horns. Even had they been deaf, their noses would have detected our presence in sufficient time to give us a wide berth.

At the end of the first voyage the Belgian Chief Officer left, and we all moved up one place, I taking his.

Time passed, and still there was no mention of our being

sent back to London. Then there were rumours that the
passenger service was going to include British-flag ships.
We therefore sat tight and said nothing about going home.

Early in 1920 the officer who went to Antwerp with me,
and I, were asked if we would transfer permanently to the
Red Star Line. We agreed, the Atlantic Transport Line
concurred, and we were appointed to the *Zeeland*: he as
Second, I as First Officer.

The reorganised passenger service consisted of two
American-flag ships, with which, of course, we were not
concerned, and two British: the *Lapland* and the *Zeeland*.
About three years later the *Belgenland* was added and I
was promoted to Chief Officer of the *Lapland*.

At the same time the officer who had transferred with
me was appointed First Officer of the *Belgenland*. After
serving a short time on her his eyes began to fail and soon
he was unable to pass the eyesight test. That meant, of
course, that his career at sea was finished, and he suddenly
found himself "stranded on the beach."

He could find no employment of any kind in England.
Having sufficient money of his own to pay a third-class
fare for his wife and himself to New Zealand, he went
there. The prospects were no better than at home, and
he was reduced to the necessity of taking any odd jobs.
He worked for a time as a dock labourer, loading and
discharging ships, and even as a "coalie," bunkering
them.

Eventually he and his wife made their way to Western
Canada, and finally he found employment as a tally-
clerk on the dock in one of the Puget Sound ports.

I may now be said to have reached the end of the life
and training of an ordinary man of the Merchant Service
in so far as it is of any interest to You-Who-Live-Ashore.
I had attained the position of Chief, or Executive, Officer

of a large passenger-ship. It was then only a question of a few more years of uneventful life on an Atlantic ferry boat. The castle I had been building in the air since leaving home at the age of 15 was clearly in sight.

I slowly climbed the hill that led to it. The American-flag ships were taken off the run and replaced by British tonnage, the *Pennland* being one of them.

In due course I was transferred to the *Belgenland*, as Chief Officer in the Atlantic trade during the summer, and as Staff-Captain on the winter cruises round the world.

While away on one of those "joy-rides" the Captain of one of the ships died. I was next in turn, but being on the other side of the world, a man junior to me was given command of the *Pennland* in the meantime. When we returned to Antwerp I immediately reminded the Marine Superintendent that that was my ship.

"It's being decided at the meeting this afternoon," he said. "Come and see me tomorrow morning."

As I walked into his office next day the magnetic field, mentioned in the previous chapter, was squirming and thrilling as it had never done before.

"Good morning, *Captain* Making!" he said, emphasising the third word with a grin. "The manager wants to see you at eleven o'clock."

"The *Pennland*?" I asked.

"Yes!" he replied. "Now remember: the company likes their ships to run to schedule and arrive on time; but, more important still, they want them to *arrive safely*. Don't take any fool chances to catch a tide. If you get in a day late, they'll probably ask you where the hell you've been. That doesn't mean a thing. Have an accident through cutting corners or going too fast in fog, and what they'll say will mean a lot—probably your job. Get your ship and passengers home safely!"

After the interview with the manager I invested some

money in uniforms, and a cap with oak-leaves on the peak. My steward, or "Tiger," as he was generally known to his mates in the "glory-holes," moved my dunnage up to the Captain's quarters. There, during the years that followed, as I was putting the foundations under my castle in the air, I was occasionally made to realise the truth in the words spoken to me by the Captain of the *Aristomene* when he promoted me to Third Mate: "When I was your age I didn't know much. *When you're mine you'll still be learning!*"

A few minutes before sailing time, my first voyage in command, I went up to the bridge with the pilot and looked over *my* ship. Six bells were struck. The gangway was lowered and the shore-gang stood by the lines on the dock.

"Let go aft!" said the pilot. "Tell the tug to pull her stern off!"

Suddenly I remembered that I had left my binoculars down in my cabin.

"Quartermaster!" I said. "Go down to my steward. Tell him to bring me my glasses."

As the after tug pulled the gap between the stern and the quay slowly widened. Two toots were blown on the whistle: a signal to the forward tug to pull the bow off.

"Slow astern port, slow ahead starboard!" said the pilot, and there followed a jangle of engine-room telegraph gongs.

There was still no sign of my steward or my glasses. I sent a quartermaster down again to hurry him up.

"He's just coming, sir," the man reported when he returned.

The stern was swinging back towards the stone quay and I walked to the wing of the bridge to look aft.

"Here's your steward, Cap'en," I heard the pilot say, "and the glasses, too!"

I turned round. The company's pilot whom we had known for years was grinning. The officers and men, stationed on the bridge, were gazing with horrified expressions on their faces at the "Tiger," who had just arrived at the top of the bridge ladder. He was a big, stout, solemn man, the type of butler one sees caricatured on the movies. Arrived there, he stood still a moment, looking round for me. Then, in full view not only of the pilot, officers, and men on the bridge, but also of the passengers who had gathered on deck, and of their friends, the manager, and company's officials on the dock, he walked across the bridge to me. He carried a tray, covered with an immaculate white doily. On it were glasses, two of them, together with two split sodas and a bottle of whisky.

Words failed me; I could only "shoo" him into the chart-room, out of sight, while the pilot shouted: "Stop port, half ahead both. Let go the after tug!"

Thus, with the help of my "Tiger," I began to put the foundations under my castle.

EPILOGUE

HAVING "shaken down" in command in the Red Star Line, I took it for granted that I should remain there until I reached the retiring age of three-score years. I assumed that, having lived among, and learned the languages and ways of, the different Peoples of the Sea-World, there were no more migrations in store for me.

I proposed. The depression disposed; for in February, 1935, when the company was taken over by the Bernstein Line, and the German flag had been run up in place of the "Blood-and-guts of old England," I had to fold up my tent once more and steal silently away.

It was a far more serious uprooting than any of the others. Although it required time to know and to be able to converse intelligently with the various Sea-Faring Peoples, there was one thing common to them all: the "salt drop in the blood." In fine weather and in the piping times of peace their ideas differed and they even quarrelled at times; but when they met in the presence of an Act of God or of a King's Enemy one realised that fundamentally there was a complete understanding of each other's thoughts and methods.

The setting of the Red Star catapulted me on to Dry-Land, where I found myself marooned among a strange race called You-Who-Live-Ashore. While they knew little about the "Great Waters" other than that one swam in them and was ill on them, my ideas of their world were equally vague: one went to theatres, cultivated roses, and had all sorts of holidays, including every Saturday afternoon and Sunday. For some time I gave a passable impersonation of a fish out of water and was probably a pest to all my "landward kin."

That boxful of old letters was a godsend. It gave me something to work for at a time when I was badly afflicted with an "inferiority complex. The men of my Sea-World were "up and doing." Outside Malta the White Ensign was causing Italian submarines to "pop up like corks"; in the Spanish ports it was caring for refugees. The Blue Ensign was winning back for Britain the Blue Riband of the Atlantic. All over the world the Red Ensign was busy on its Lawful Occasions, deviating at times from them to go to the assistance of "those in peril on the sea."

All those on shore, among whom I was living, had a useful part to play on the world's stage. Even a street-cleaner had to shoulder the responsibility of seeing that there was no orange peel or banana skin on which I might slip and hurt myself.

With nothing to do but watch the hands of the clock revolve, I felt so utterly useless and futile in the general Scheme of Things.

Could I, however, with no previous training or experience, write a book with the material supplied by those letters that would give you at home a fuller knowledge and understanding of the men who man your Merchant Service, I should be accomplishing something.

"To strive at all," wrote Charles Dickens, "involves a victory over sloth, inertia, and indifference."

I promptly made a start—in fact, many starts before I was able to steady myself on a definite course and proceed.

In the spring of 1936 I had a busman's holiday to New York, and met a man who had several books to his credit. I had with me the little I had already written, about 12,000 words.

After reading some of it he gave me a letter of introduction to my present publishers, and when I arrived home I forwarded it to them, together with my badly-typed 12,000 words. They replied to the effect that they were interested in it, but that there was not sufficient for them to make a decision. If, however, I were prepared to go ahead on that slight encouragement, they would be glad to consider it when I had more to show them.

That was a spur. It was all I wanted, and more than I had expected. I don't think I was ever sanguine enough to believe it would be published; but if they had the patience to read it, it was up to me to try to deliver the goods.

For months I wrestled with it. I wrote, tore up, and rewrote; typed, revised, and re-typed. Whole chapters which, when written, seemed to me to be the stuff of which Best Sellers are made, were obviously utter tosh when I read them a month later, after gaining a little more experience. I treated sentences as in days gone by I had done threefold rope-purchases: "turned them end for end," trying to make them say what I meant. I pored over all sorts and conditions of books, hoping to discover how real authors did it. After a few headaches and some fatherly advice from an oculist I respectfully "took off my hat" to such men as Frank T. Bullen and Joseph Conrad, who, with no letters or diary to help them, had so successfully accomplished what I was attempting.

Gradually, however—word by word, one might almost say—it grew, and finally attained its present quantity and quality, whatever the latter amounts to. As Bunyan wrote:

" And so I penned
It down, until at last it came to be
For length and breadth the bigness which you see."

INDEX

A

ACAPULCO, 40, 104-106, 126
Aden, map, 146; 151
Albany, map, 97; 274
Albatross, 101
Amsterdam Island, 174
Anjer Point, 34; map, 35
Antofagasta, map, 58; 90-92
Atlantic Transport Line, 279, 289, 307
Australian kindness, 274, 275

B

Banka Strait, map, 35; 36
Barnevelt Island (between Staten Island and Cape Horn), 41; map, 58
Batan Island, 37
Belaying-pin (description), 7
Bellingham, map, 87; 107-109
Bernay, Rev., missions to seamen, 121, 124
Black Hole, 170
Black-leg firemen, 159
Blubber, description, 31; cutting in whale's, 96; seal's, as food, 235; seal's, thickness of, 252
Blue paper, B.O.T. examination, 159
Boat-steerer, whaling, 95, 96
Boat-work, apprentices', 59-61, 62
Bombay, 152
Booby, 55
Boston, Mass., 156
Braces, 38; sketch, 39
Bridge, cargo boat, 161
Brindisi, 293, 295
Broach-to, 100, 127
Bunker Hill, 156
Buntlines, sketch, 39; 40
Burgoo and molasses, 24
Burial at sea, 28, 185; on St. Paul Island, 224

C

Calcutta, 170
Caleta Buena, map, 58; 59, 92-93
Cape Hens, 21

Cape Horn, 41; map, 58; 66, 100-101
Cape pigeons, catching, 21
Cape Stiff, sailors' name for Cape Horn
Cape Town, 33, 94-98, 122-124
Cattle on the hoof, 308
Caught aback, 49
Changy for changy, East Indies, 34-35
Chinese junk, 36
Chipping, 108, 109
Clewed up, 40
Clewlines, sketch, 39; 40
Clew of sail, 38
Cock-fighting, 106
Cocos Island, 54
Coon hunting, 83
Cork, Ireland, 79, 80, 103
Cremation, Hindoo, 152
Crossing the Line, 149-151
Curios, 85-86

D

Dardanelles, 292
"Davy," 68-80
Demobilised, 305-306
Doldrums, 101
Drift-net fishermen, war-time, 293-297
Drunks, 65, 67, 74-75, 80, 84-85, 104-105, 106; punishment, 113; 122, 157, 278-179

E

Electric storm, 40-41
Employment, seeking, 141-142
Esquimault, map, 87; 87-88, 106-107
Eyesight, 309

F

Fiddley, 165
Fife-rail, description, 7
Fire on shipboard, 155-156, 176
First aid at sea, 167-169

317